Indian from the Inside

Anishnawbe World View by Ahmoo Angeconeb.
Private collection of J. Douglas Rabb.

Indian from the Inside

Native American Philosophy and Cultural Renewal

SECOND EDITION

DENNIS H. MCPHERSON *and*
J. DOUGLAS RABB

Foreword by Jace Weaver

McFarland & Company, Inc., Publishers
Jefferson, North Carolina, and London

LIBRARY OF CONGRESS CATALOGUING-IN-PUBLICATION DATA

McPherson, Dennis H.
Indian from the inside : Native American philosophy and cultural renewal / Dennis H. McPherson and J. Douglas Rabb ; foreword by Jace Weaver.— 2nd ed.
p. cm.
Includes bibliographical references and index.

ISBN 978-0-7864-4348-2
softcover : 50# alkaline paper ∞

1. Indian philosophy — North America. 2. Indians of North America — Social life and customs. 3. Social values — North America. 4. Indians in popular culture. 5. Indians in motion pictures. I. Rabb, J. Douglas. II. Title.
E98.P5M47 2011
970.004'97 — dc22 2011015003

BRITISH LIBRARY CATALOGUING DATA ARE AVAILABLE

On the cover: detail of *Anishnawbe World View* by Ahmoo Angeconeb (Private collection of J.D. Rabb); title accents © 2011 Shutterstock

Manufactured in the United States of America

McFarland & Company, Inc., Publishers
Box 611, Jefferson, North Carolina 28640
www.mcfarlandpub.com

Acknowledgments

We thank the Centre for Northern Studies, Lakehead University, Thunder Bay, Canada, for publishing the first edition of this work in 1993, and for permitting the publication of this revised and expanded second edition, allowing us to go beyond our earlier northern focus, and discuss Native American philosophy in the broader context of the United States as well as Canada.

We thank the Rockefeller Foundation for two institutional grants to our Native Philosophy Project, which made Lakehead University the first Canadian site for the prestigious Rockefeller Foundation Visiting Humanities Fellowship Program. We thank all those who participated in the project. We dedicate this volume to two of our many visiting fellows:

The Late Dr. Deborah Doxtator
(Rotinonshyonni, Mohawk, Bay of Quinte Band,
Tyendinaga Reserve. d. 1998),
Rockefeller Foundation Visiting Humanities Research Fellow,
Native Philosophy Project 1994–1995.

The Late Dr. Viola Cordova
(Jicarilla Apache/Hispanic. d. 2002),
Rockefeller Foundation Visiting Humanities Research Fellow,
Native Philosophy Project 1996–1997.

We thank Lakehead University, under both the Rosehart and Gilbert Administrations, for the kind of support provided to the Native Philosophy Project in particular, and its Native students generally. We found in such support confirming evidence for the conclusions we present in our final chapter.

We are truly grateful to the publishers of *Intervox: Magazine of New Directions* for permission to use as we have in Chapter Three their interview with Douglas Cardinal published in *Intervox,* vol. 8, 1989/90.

We thank Canadian composer Brian Hubelit for permission to cite his composition *Ojibwe Landscapes* in our discussion of writing language back into the land. We also thank him and choir director Susan Marrier, who commissioned the piece, for reading early drafts of our discussion and making helpful suggestions.

We are also most grateful to Native artist Ahmoo Angeconeb, for permission to use as we have his drawing *Anishnawbe World View,* which we commissioned for the cover of the first edition.

We thank Jace Weaver for the kind words in his foreword, and for his long-time support of the Native Philosophy Project. We also wish to thank colleague Mike Richardson for proofreading the entire manuscript and offering helpful suggestions.

We are deeply indebted to all who have worked with us over the years. We should like to give honorable mention to each and every member of our first class in Native Philosophy which we taught in 1990: Ahmoo Allen Angeconeb, Madeline Beardy, Nancy Bouchard, Brian Brisard, Carol Ronald Delaney, Gilda Dokuchie, Philip Edwards, Sarah Faulkner, Jim Finlayson, Kimberley Gosnell, Gloria Hendrick, Dorothy McPherson, Jamie McPherson, Deborah Morrisseau, Paul Nadjiwon, Eleanor Pelletier, Judith Petch, Shelly Skye, Lorraine Sponchia (Mayer), Cherrilee Watts, Lori Watts, James White, Mervin Wilson, and Peter Vanderkam. Together we found that the gizzard of the ruffed grouse can indeed hang aloft.

Thank you, one and all.

Table of Contents

Foreword

by Jace Weaver

In October 1994, I went to a conference on Native Studies at Lakehead University in Thunder Bay, Ontario. As I always do when visiting an institution away from home, I went to the bookstore to see what was being used in courses on the subject there. I came across a slim volume that was wholly new to me, the recently published *Indian from the Inside: A Study in Ethnometaphysics.* I bought it and began to read it immediately. I was enthralled. Here was the first attempt to discuss Native philosophies from an internal perspective. I met the authors, Dennis McPherson and J. Douglas Rabb, at the conference and asked them to "scribble" in the front of my copy.

Upon my return to New York, I immediately ordered it to assign in my course the next semester at Union Theological Seminary (affiliated with Columbia University). I thus became, I believe, the first person to teach the book in the United States. After I moved to Yale in 1996, I brought along *Indian from the Inside,* teaching it in my Native American Studies methods course. It worked easily in such a course because, though the contexts in Canada and the United States are obviously different, the experiences of Natives on both sides of that imaginary border — which separates Anishinaabe from Anishinaabe, Haudenosaunee from Haudenosaunee, Blackfoot from Blackfoot — broadly parallel each other.

Methodology is, in fact, what attracted me to the book in the first instance. Dennis and Doug's attempt to provide a counterpoint to the "outside view predicate" instantly spoke to me as a Native person. But, as a trained lawyer, I was really captured by their discussion of how to treat early ethnographies. The authors argue(d) that in using notoriously unreliable accounts we do best when we know quite a lot about the persons writing them. We are then able to (as best we can) filter out their biases. They contend that therefore the best source we have for a given region is the *Jesuit Relations*: after all, the Jesuits recorded their encounters with indigenes voluminously, and we know where they stood on absolutely *every* issue. Filter out their biases, and whatever remains is likely to be accurate.

In the law, there is an exception to the hearsay rule known as an "admission against interest." It is a statement made by a party that is so contrary to his or her interests in a case that it may be admitted as evidence: why would he or she have said such a thing unless it were true? A classic example is the motorist involved in an accident who leaps from the car, crying, "I'm sorry, it was all my fault." When the Jesuits say something about Natives contrary to their Christian biases, it must be regarded as likely to be true.

I like that Dennis and Doug take worldview seriously. Their pioneering indigenous philosophy course was called "Native Canadian World Views." They write that some would argue that it is not in the end "very interesting that different peoples have radically different worldviews. Such differences may be of interest to the anthropologist who is studying different peoples, but these differences do not cast any light on the nature of ultimate reality." McPherson and Rabb know differently, and as a scholar of religious traditions, I agree with them. They also know that the first impulse of a people confronted by the new or novel is to attempt to understand it within their existing frames of reference, to incorporate it into their worldview.

Natives seeing horses for the first time called them things like "sky dogs" or "sky elks." Sky as in reaching the sky, big. It is said that when the first European ship arrived off the coast of Vietnam, the people were terrified. Courtiers ran to tell the emperor. The emperor, however, demonstrated no interest in going to see the strange sight. Instead he consulted his sacred texts and proclaimed the thing in the harbor a dragon. It was thus part of the natural order and nothing to be alarmed about. Worldview shapes how we see and apprehend reality. In the process it shapes reality itself.

So I admired *Indian from the Inside* and I taught it. Published by the Centre for Northern Studies at Lakehead, the book became increasingly hard to get. I eventually dropped it from my syllabus. Recently, however, in a piece analyzing the current state of Native American Studies in *American Indian Quarterly* (revised for my book *Notes from a Miner's Canary*), I discussed it as an underappreciated text in need of rediscovery. This new and revised edition is therefore both welcome and timely.

I must admit, though, that despite my admiration for that original volume, I considered *Indian from the Inside* a flawed work. It had a wonderful approach and contained some genuine jewels. Nonetheless, I felt it didn't quite cohere. It was somehow less than the sum of its parts. This problem has been completely solved by this new edition.

It reminds me of Vine Deloria's second edition of his classic *God Is Red*. Although the core remains intact, the text has been so thoroughly revised it is almost a completely new book. The new subtitle of the present volume suggests this. I was pleased to see the authors engage excellent, more recent scholarship in the field from scholars like Keith Basso, Lee Hester, Robert Miller, and the late Viola Cordova. I was even more pleased to see them deconstruct *Disrobing the Aboriginal Industry* by Frances Widdowson and Albert Howard. Subtitled *The Deception Behind Indigenous Cultural Preservation*, this evil and aggressively assimilationist text is potentially one of the most dangerous entries into discussion of indigenous policy in recent years, because it has been so avidly embraced by both anti–Indian forces and those ignorant of the issues involved (the latter group comprising most of Euro-Canadians and Euro-Americans). In a sort of post-modern out-of-body experience, I read Dennis and Doug writing about me writing about them.

In its sweep, this wholly new *Indian from the Inside* is like Rob Williams' *The American Indian in Western Legal Thought* or John Mohawk's *Utopian Legacies*. All three excel at setting the widest possible context for the events of encounter and conquest. Without sacrificing either a colloquial writing style or their indigenous lens, McPherson and Rabb discuss and draw in philosophers as varied in time and theme as Aristotle, Augustine, Aquinas, Locke, Kant, and Merleau-Ponty. I love their characterization of Socrates as a "city boy" within their discussion of Western alienation from land. And their "Red reading" of Plato alone is worth the price of the book.

In the e-mail inviting me to write this foreword, Dennis referred to it as a "forward." I immediately shot back a reply, teasing him for his typo. But the more I thought about it, that error was fortuitous because not I but McPherson and Rabb, with this new edition of an underappreciated classic, move our collective discussion in Native studies forward. And they would move forward the understanding of indigenous culture and issues among those Widdowson and Howard hope to bamboozle — if only they would pick it up and read it. I can hope, can't I?

Jace Weaver is Franklin Professor of Native American Studies and director of the Institute of Native America Studies at the University of Georgia in Athens.

Preface

Native American philosophy has enabled Native American cultures to survive more than five hundred years of attempted cultural assimilation. Further systematic research in Native American philosophy will ensure that Native American cultures will flourish in the 21st century and beyond.

We have been doing research in Native American philosophy for close to thirty years. We can honestly say that this book was nearly thirty years in the making. It was back in 1982 when Dennis McPherson first contacted Lakehead University in Thunder Bay, Ontario, Canada. At that time he was executive director of Weechi-it-te-win Child and Family Services, Inc., an Indian-run child welfare organization in Fort Frances, Ontario. He contacted the university because he wanted a professor of Social Work to speak to his organization about Social Work practice with special reference to Native families and Native communities. But he wanted something else as well. He approached the Department of Philosophy and asked why that department, in what professed to be a regional university, did not offer courses in Native American philosophy, more specifically in Ojibwa philosophy. He pointed out that his examination of the university catalogue (calendar) revealed that the department offered courses in ancient Greek philosophy, in German idealism, and in British empiricism. It even offered a course in Eastern philosophical systems, in the philosophies of India, China and Japan. Why not in Native American philosophies? To reply to this sort of question by saying that there is simply no such thing would be to reveal a kind of ethnocentric prejudice. When confronted with this question, Lakehead philosopher J. Douglas Rabb was forced to reply that no one in the department knew anything about the subject.

Dennis McPherson set out to rectify that situation. He registered as a student at Lakehead and has since graduated with a B.A. and an H.B.A. in Philosophy along with a degree in Social Work (H.B.S.W.). He has also earned degrees in Law at the undergraduate and graduate levels (LL.B. and LL.M.) from the University of Ottawa. Together we developed a philosophy course entitled Native Canadian World Views. This was truly a case of the student teaching the teacher. The course, team-taught by McPherson and Rabb (students called it the Dennis and Doug show), was first offered in the spring of 1990. It was the first course in Native American philosophy offered by a department of philosophy at a Canadian university. The calendar description read as follows: "Philosophy 2805 — Native Canadian World Views. This course is designed to introduce the student to the manner in which the world is viewed from the perspective of the Native peoples of Canada. Through a comparative analysis of the many interpretations placed upon the Indian perspective by mainstream society basic insights into the traditional Indian world view can be gained. The course discusses some of the distinctive aspects of Indian cultural perspectives. The significance of these aspects and their implications in contemporary issues concerning cultural, social, legal, political and economic matters is explored."

The first edition of this book was published in 1993. At that time it was in part a result of developing, preparing, and teaching Philosophy 2805 — Native Canadian World Views. Though we intended it to be used as a text for the course, and to facilitate the development of similar courses elsewhere, we also intended it as a genuine contribution to scholarship in this area. This revised edition expands upon our earlier work discussing Native American philosophy and culture in both Canada and the United States.

Although we do not speak for Native people, we do believe that the discipline of philosophy can teach us all how to listen to Native people. And we do mean "all," Native and non–Native alike. We argue that the discipline of philosophy can help Native people to listen to themselves, to acquire a deeper understanding of who they really are. After all, one of the first imperatives of philosophy is to "know thyself." We also argue that Native American philosophy will help non–Native people to see themselves in a new light.

If philosophy can help a first-year undergraduate to get inside the mind of an ancient Greek philosopher like a Socrates or an Aristotle, and to understand such thought, surely it can also help non–Native North Americans to better understand their Native neighbors. It should be noted in passing that when the majority of undergraduates of non–Native descent study ancient Greek philosophy, and hence the origins of Western civilization, they are gaining a better understanding of who they are, of their own background. This is not so for Native students. Native students have little opportunity for this kind of self-discovery, for this kind of typical university experience. Thus far universities have offered courses in "Native Studies." The perspective from which such courses are usually taught tends to externalize Native peoples, leaving them to be studied as objects — from the outside. But how does the Native American student view herself or himself and the world from the inside? It is partly to answer this question that we developed a course in Native Canadian worldviews. It is partly for this reason that we believe that the time has come for serious research into Native American philosophy.

We began our inquiry by simply asking: "Is there a Native philosophy?" Over the years this question changed to "Is the delineation of a Native American philosophy even possible?" and "Is it possible to discuss Native American cultures and traditions without discussing Native American philosophy?"

There is of course some difficulty in establishing just what an authentic Native American philosophy is. This is complicated, for example, by the fact that "McPherson" has become a post-contact traditional Ojibwa family name. But should we limit ourselves to discussing only post-contact views? If so, then where is the authenticity? If we turn to pre-contact views then there is the difficulty of establishing just exactly what these are. The European discovery of the Americas, usually recognized as occurring in 1492, represents what has been called a "documentary horizon" beyond which it is impossible to see, or at least to obtain any kind of written information regarding the Native peoples of the Americas (Callicott 1989, 203).

Professor J. Baird Callicott, one of the few Western-trained philosophers to discuss Native American philosophy, suggests that it is possible to glimpse beyond this documentary horizon using a combination of three methods, which mutually support and correct one another. The first involves using historical documents written as close to the time of first contact as possible. Such documents would include what is usually described as "explorer literature." Insofar as the discovery of philosophical views is concerned, one of the more important sets of documents is the *Jesuit Relations* (1610–1791), which consist of edited versions of annual reports sent to France from the various missionary districts in New France relating the most important events of that year, hence the title *Jesuit Relations*. As might be expected these are written with an obvious ethnocentric bias. However, the Jesuit philosophy is well understood and any trained philosopher should be able to make allowances for it. A good example of this approach is an article in *Laval Theologique et Philosophique* by Michael Pomedli, another Western-trained philosopher who takes Native views seriously. He concludes with the warning, "From reading the *Relations* alone, our procedure must be that of caution and our conclusions tentative" (Pomedli 1985, 64). However, he goes on to say, "I think it is possible to move across cultural spheres, distinct as the native oral and the European literal are. The credibility for such a crossing are the facts that the missionaries made great efforts to understand native lifestyles and language, that they noted teachings quite opposed to their own, that they confessed that even after conversion to Catholicism, natives lapsed into former patterns of life" (Pomedli 1985, 64).

Though Callicott does not mention the *Jesuit Relations*, he does note that historical documents of this kind "portray Indian material and cognitive culture at first contact or more or less soon thereafter, prior to generation upon generation of ever-increasing cultural influence from Europeans" (Callicott 1989, 213). Callicott sees the ever-increasing cultural influence of European technologies as a barrier to the discovery of pre-contact, pre-Columbian, worldviews. "To buy guns, motors, and mackinaw jackets is to buy, however unintentionally, a world view to boot" (Callicott 1989, 212). For this reason, Callicott argues, the relatively recent (mid–19th century to the present) accounts and testimonials by Native spokespersons must be treated with suspicion, and is also for this reason he suggests that the work of contemporary ethnographers must be checked against historical records. At the same time, as a second method, Callicott insists that these more contemporary accounts can be used to cut through the ethnocentric bias of historical documents. "The often casual and unsystematic and always ethnocentric and distorted quality of these early documents can ... be compared and cross-checked with the more systematic and objective, but always relatively recent, ethnographic accounts in such a way that ideally they mutually correct, supplement, enrich, and illuminate one another" (Callicott 1989, 213).

Callicott's more original contribution to this area of study is the development, with fellow philosopher Thomas W. Overholt, of a third method, a distinctively philosophical one, which can be used as yet another countercheck on the other two. In their book *Clothed-in-Fur and Other Tales: An Introduction to an Ojibwa Worldview*, a book which we have found extremely useful, Callicott and Overholt examine the Ojibwa narrative tradition, the "fund of myths, legends, and tales," using what amounts to a combination of philosophical analysis and literary criticism (Overholt and Callicott 1982).

They argue that "the narrative legacy of culture embodies in an especially charming way its most fundamental ideas of how the world is to be conceptually organized and integrated at the most general level, and that part of the special function of narratives within a culture is to school the young, remind the old, and reiterate to all members how things at large come together and what is the meaning of it all" (Overholt and Callicott 1982, 20). Many of the narratives appearing in *Clothed-in-Fur* are from Ojibwa communities in the vicinity of Lake Superior. They were collected and translated by Mesquakie anthropologist William Jones (Ph. D., Columbia, 1904). Having access to these narratives allows some of our students to study the philosophical origins of their own culture, through narratives indigenous to their own communities. As we will show, narratives can and do function as philosophical arguments. We hope that our study, and similar research, will hasten the day when this kind of culturally congruent educational experience will be the norm, will be something all Native American students can expect, can insist upon!

Unlike Callicott and Overholt, we do not discuss in detail specific Native narratives. Nor do we present a close textual analysis of *Jesuit Relations* and similar historical documents. Such work constitutes the preliminary research upon which our philosophical study is based. It also provides a kind of background against which our general conclusions can and should be assessed. We expect that most Native American readers will either agree or disagree with us on the basis of their own lived experience. This is as it should be.

We draw, though not uncritically, on the conclusions and methodology of Callicott and Overholt. To their method of philosophical analysis we add two others, one from the philosophical tradition of existential phenomenology, and the other from philosophical hermeneutics. We explain existential phenomenology in Chapter Three, "Dancing with Chaos: Phenomenology of the Vision Quest." In the same chapter, we also make much use of a first-person account of the vision quest by Blackfoot-Métis architect Douglas Cardinal. In Chapter Seven, our final chapter, we discuss philosophical hermeneutics and argue for its use in cultural interpretation grounded within community-based research. To date, that is where our study concludes, with community-based research and education. This really represents a new beginning, in fact a reawakening of the Indian from the inside!

We begin our book with a brief discussion of the European and British worldviews imposed upon the original inhabitants of the Americas from first contact to the present. Our portrayal of Western philosophy in chapters one and two is painted in broad brush strokes, producing more caricatures than detailed portraits of individual philosophers. It is Native American philosophy that interests us most in this study. Still, it is important that Native students have a good understanding of Western philosophy. It is the foundation of the laws and culture of the dominant society, which are largely responsible for the perception and description of Native American people through what we call outside view predicates. Rejecting this "outside view" of what it is to be Native American, we turn to the discussion of Native American philosophy in Chapter Three, beginning, as we said, with the phenomenology of the vision quest. In Chapter Four we discuss the Native concept of "person," including "other-than-human persons," drawing on modern science, including second-generation cognitive science, to support traditional Native conceptions of person and place usually presented through narrative and story. Chapter Five examines the Native concept of place in greater depth, exploring how to write language back into the land, and explaining why it is necessary to do so. Chapter Six looks to film and popular culture as natural extensions of narrative argument, using modern technology to support traditional values. Each of these chapters points toward the need for community-based research and education, which, as we noted above, is the topic of our final chapter.

ONE

Philosophical Foundations

Is Native American Philosophy, Philosophy?

This work is first and foremost a study in philosophy. We mean by philosophy the search for wisdom, for truth, as the origin, the etymology, of the word "philosophy" suggests. Although we also attempt to say something new about some of the aboriginal people of the Americas, Native American and Canadian Indians, it is important to note that this is not a study *of* aboriginal people. They have been studied enough; the expression "studied to death" is now widely used by aboriginal communities. We have no wish to treat aboriginal people as the object of yet another study. We undertake this work in the firm conviction that the discipline of philosophy can help people see themselves as people, as experiencing persons, not mere objects to be experienced, to be studied. Human beings experience the world and themselves in unique and special ways. Philosophy can help us to comprehend this experience as experience, and to understand the relation, if any, this experience has to the reality it is an experience of. The first point which we wish to establish in this work is, then, that the discipline of philosophy can help the aboriginal people of the Americas to understand themselves. A second and we believe more important point for which we shall argue is that aboriginal people have something to contribute to the discipline of philosophy. These two points are obviously so closely interrelated that establishing the one will inevitably provide evidence for the truth of the other as well. We shall argue that the aboriginal people of the Americas can fully understand themselves only in the context of a Native American philosophy, in the context of their own values and worldview.

Pan-Indianism and Ethno-Metaphysics

Is there such a thing as a philosophy, a worldview, unique to the aboriginal people of the Americas? Is there a Native American philosophy? We, of course, argue that there is. In doing so, however, we shall have to counter a number of possible objections and dispel more than a few perceived difficulties. One such difficulty is the current academic attitude toward "pan-Indianism." The internationally renowned expert on Native North American religions, Swedish professor Åke Hultkrantz, explains "pan-Indianism" as the false assumption "that Indian religious symbols basically cover the same concepts in all tribes since all Indians are really ethnically and culturally identical, and the movement to realize this idea" (Hultkrantz 1987, 140). In his book *Native Religions of North America*, Hultkrantz captures perfectly the current academic attitude toward pan-Indianism. Maintaining that pan-Indianism is "a late idea, formed under the pressure of white domination" (27), he argues that given the diversity of the "multitude of tribes and other social units" there is no such thing as "*the* Native American religion" (11, italics in original). Although he admits some tribes seem to share similar cultures and can be classified accordingly Hultkrantz insists that "each tribe has its own practices and customs, and we must remember that there are as many Native American religions as there are tribes" (11).

If this is true of Native American religions and if the same can be said of their philosophies, of their worldviews, then we shall have difficulty in establishing our thesis. We are consoled by the fact that when Hultkrantz does permit himself to generalize he is forced to admit that "four prominent features in North American Indian religions are a similar worldview, a shared notion of cosmic harmony, emphasis on experiencing directly powers and visions, and a common view of the cycle of life and death" (20). In the course of our study we shall attempt to explain philosophically — that is, give meaning and content to — each of these four concepts. While we do not wish to argue explicitly for pan-Indianism, we do suggest that a better understanding of the philosophical underpinnings of North American aboriginal culture in both Canada and the United States will make pan-Indianism seem a little more plausible than mainstream scholars such as Hultkrantz would allow.

Before discussing these philosophical underpinnings, the worldview of the aboriginal people of the Americas, we must meet a further possible objection to our thesis, an objection which might come from fellow philosophers. In discussing the philosophy of a particular people we are engaged in what has been called "ethno-metaphysics." The term was introduced by anthropologist A. I. Hallowell in a paper with the wonderful title "Ojibwa Ontology, Behaviour, and World View" in which he argues, "Human beings in whatever culture are provided with cognitive orientation in a cosmos; there is 'order' and 'reason' rather than chaos" (Hallowell 1960, 20). Even if they are not consciously articulated by the people themselves, this implies certain basic principles and premises, a philosophy or worldview. If we explore this philosophy deeply enough we are confronted with the "relatively unexplored territory" of "ethno-metaphysics" (Hallowell 1960, 20).

The Save-the-Savages Argument

The further philosophical question inevitably arises: "Is ethno-metaphysics possible?" Many philosophers would argue that it is not possible, that there is no such thing as ethno-metaphysics. They would say that metaphysics deals with the nature of reality, with ontology — literally the logic of being — the way the world is. Further, reality is as it is. We do not invent it. It is there for us to discover. There certainly are different metaphysical theories about the nature of reality but only one of these theories can be right, the one that actually corresponds to reality. The argument here would be that it is not philosophically very interesting that different peoples may have radically different worldviews. Such differences may be of interest to the anthropologist who is studying different peoples; but these differences do not cast any light on the nature of ultimate reality which is what the philosopher is interested in when doing metaphysics. The most vicious form of this kind of argument would include a claim that modern science (or Christianity) has given us the true picture of reality and hence the primitive beliefs of mere savages (or heathens) ought to be discarded, by the savages themselves if they wish to cease being savages. We shall refer to this sort of argument with deliberate disrespect as "the save-the-savages argument." How do we counter it? How do we justify ethno-metaphysics?

At this point our argument of necessity becomes a little complicated. We will proceed as follows. We begin by examining critically a classic justification of ethno-metaphysics. By identifying what we think is wrong with this particular justification we lay the groundwork for our own proposed justification of ethno-metaphysics and rejection of the save-the-savages argument. The classic justification was presented in 1982 by Thomas W. Overholt and J. Baird Callicott in their groundbreaking study, *Clothed-in-Fur and*

Other Tales: An Introduction to an Ojibwa World View. Although we are critical of some of their arguments we must acknowledge our great debt to their important pioneering study. Their study is the first book on North American Indian thought produced by professionally-trained philosophers. We find in them kindred spirits willing to take seriously the philosophy of the aboriginal people of North America. We rejoice in following the trail that they have marked. Our joy is tempered somewhat by the discovery that when Callicott wanders off by himself far from the moderating guidance of Tom Overholt he tends to lose the trail, as we show in some detail in Chapter Four. Still, our debt of gratitude is to both of them.

Overholt and Callicott begin their book with a definition of "ethno-metaphysics." After giving due credit to Hallowell they explain: "Ethnometaphysics may be understood as a subdiscipline of philosophy (related to metaphysics as ethnohistory is to history) concerned with the exploration and analysis of the conceptual structures of different cultures. One of its implicit assumptions is that all people do not cognitively organize human experience in the same way and thus that there exists a variety of 'world views,' perhaps as many as there are distinct cultures" (Overholt and Callicott 1982, xi). Their justification of ethno-metaphysics involves questioning a basic assumption implicit in what we have called the save-the-savages argument. That argument assumed that we do not invent reality, that it has a nature of its own independently of the way we think about it. On the basis of this assumption, the save-the-savages argument can go on to say that since modern science is slowly discovering the true nature of reality it follows that pre-scientific or primitive views are just wrong, mere superstition.

Ethno-Metaphysics and Cultural Relativism

Overholt and Callicott head off the save-the-savages type of argument by rejecting its basic assumption. They present what amounts to a relativistic account of the nature of reality. They point out that modern ethnology has shown that radically different cultures have different cognitive systems, different ways of conceptually organizing experience. The way we see the world, the way we conceive of reality, is then relative to the culture in which we have been raised. "The cognitive system for the interpretation of experience ... is mapped out in the semantic/syntactic morphology of a culture's language ..." (Overholt and Callicott 1982, 18). It is important to note that they are not saying merely that users of radically different languages have different labels for the same thing. Rather they are claiming that speakers of different languages do not have cognitive access to the same thing at all. There is a very real sense in which they live in different worlds, worlds created by their different languages. "The semantic categories and grammatical forms are learned in infancy as the infant acquires skill in its mother tongue and are then, as it were, projected onto the continuum of otherwise undivided and inchoate experience. The native speakers of whatever language then uncritically assume that experience is 'given' *as so structured,* and the 'world' as thus mediated by language is naively taken to be real" (Overholt and Callicott 1982, 13). Overholt and Callicott insist that we do not have access to reality-in-itself independent of the cognitive structures dictated by our native tongue. Since reality must be perceived from the perspective of our own language and culture we cannot have a non-perspectival view of reality. There is therefore no way of telling which cognitive structure, which culture's worldview, presents the more accurate, the "true" account of reality. Overholt and Callicott conclude that "no culture's world is privileged in respect to truth" (Overholt and Callicott 1982, 16). They suggest that we must therefore use something like pragmatic value or usefulness instead of truth as a criterion for deciding which worldview is preferable. "The neoWestern scientific world view has been so spectacularly successful in its essentially mechanical mastery of the natural environment that its advocates sometimes claim that it is therefore both a better and a *truer* representation of the real than any of the nonWestern alternatives. However, despite the appeal of our unsophisticated desire for fixed belief and unshakable truth, the only thing for which technological success is evidence is that acting *as if* the neoWestern world view were true, the doing of certain things (propelling projectiles, creating large explosions, arranging concrete and metal on a vast scale, sending signals rapidly, transplanting organs from one body to another, etc., etc.) is facilitated" (Overholt and Callicott 1982, 16–17, italics in original). In other words, pragmatic value is not a criterion of truth. Just because a certain way of looking at the world is useful does not imply that it is an accurate representation of the way world actually is. Overholt and Callicott, however, are not content to demonstrate merely that the scientific worldview is not any more accurate than an Ojibwa worldview. They also contend, on purely pragmatic grounds, that it is not any better, that it is not in actual fact preferable. They suggest that, in the long run, the ultimate pragmatic test of a worldview is how well it helps the holders of that view to survive. Despite its long list of impressive accomplishments (some of which are listed above), Overholt and Callicott express concern for the long-term viability of the scientific worldview. Noting in particular "the development of nuclear technology and the general environmental degradation consequent upon the successful mastery of nature," they state: "Today, doubts have been expressed about the sustained viability of neoWestern civilization which may, it is feared, prove to be self-destructive and therefore ... fail the ultimate challenge of the principle of natural selection" (Overholt and Callicott 1982, 17). Insofar as the environment is concerned, Overholt and Callicott suggest that the older Ojibwa worldview has much to teach neo-Western civilization. The worldview of the West recognizes only human beings as persons, as beings deserving moral and legal consideration. On the other hand "the Ojibwa acknowledge other-than-human persons, among them 'plants and animals' and even 'soils and waters'" (Overholt and Callicott 1982, 154–155). Further, these other-than-human persons (plants, animals and even minerals) "are not ... rightless resources, as is the case in Western economic assumptions" (154). This means among other things that humans are required to adopt appropriate attitudes such as respect and lack of arrogance "toward the non-human members of their polymorphous community" (155). Overholt and Callicott conclude that "the Ojibwa complex of attitudes and behavioral rules in relation to non-human beings deserves ... to be called an environmental *ethic*" (155). It would not be too much of an exaggeration to say that J. Baird Callicott, Jr., has since built his reputation as an internationally-recognized environmental philosopher by working out the implications of this claim about the influence of Ojibwa (and other Indigenous) worldviews on Western environmental ethics.

We will discuss the relation between Native American philosophy and an environmental ethic in more detail in our chapter on Native values, Chapter Four. At this point what is important is to examine Overholt and Callicott's arguments justifying the study of ethno-metaphysics. Their justification is roughly this: Not only does the save-the-savages argument rest on a rationally unjustifiable assumption, but those so-called savages may well possess an ancient wisdom which might just save neo-Western civilization from its own self-destructive tendencies. We approve of the way Overholt and Callicott turn the tables on the save-the-savages argument by making "neoWestern civilization" the culture which requires saving from itself. It is precisely this sort of claim we had in mind when we said that a principal aim of our study is to show that aboriginal people have something to contribute to the discipline of philosophy. One purpose of this book is to discover and tap that ancient wisdom, to make it accessible to everyone willing to approach it with the respect that it deserves. We must, however, emphasize the point that this is only an introductory study of Native American Indian philosophy. We are only too well aware of the fact that we are merely scratching the surface. Much work remains to be done in this area. Until further work is completed we must treat Overholt and Callicott's suggestions concerning the pragmatic value of that ancient wisdom as just that, intriguing suggestions rather than established facts. Still, as we said, of this aspect of their argument we approve. We would like it to be so, and we suspect that it is. However, we do have some difficulty with the other aspect of their justification of ethno-metaphysics.

Pragmatism and Metaphysics

We find it difficult to accept the radical kind of relativism which Overholt and Callicott seem to think is necessary to accept in order to justify ethno-metaphysics. Oddly enough, certain developments in American philosophy near the end of the 20th century seem to support their relativism. We shall argue, however, that these same developments in actual fact count against Overholt and Callicott's justification of ethno-metaphysics. What are these developments? In 1982, the year in which Overholt and Callicott published *Clothed-in-Fur and Other Tales,* another book appeared which was to have a dramatic impact on the philosophical world. That book, *The Consequences of Pragmatism* by American philosopher Richard Rorty, together with his previous book, *Philosophy and the Mirror of Nature* (1979), shook the philosophical community to its very foundations. Indeed, the books were intended to shake those very foundations themselves. While *Clothed-in-Fur* was largely ignored — after all, it was only about Indians — Rorty's *Consequences of Pragmatism* exploded on the philosophical scene like a bombshell destroying, or at least seriously shaking, much of what had for centuries been taken for granted. Not everyone agreed with Rorty's position, but if you did not agree you were expected to show why. Rorty's position could not be ignored. Yet it is remarkably similar to that outlined in *Clothed-in-Fur* as a justification of ethno-metaphysics.

Rorty, like Overholt and Callicott, rejects the traditional notion of philosophy as the pursuit of truth, and the traditional concept of metaphysics as the quest for the non-perspectival account of reality as it is in itself. Siding with the American pragmatist John Dewey (1859–1952), Rorty argues that the whole point of philosophy is "to perform the social function which

Dewey called 'breaking the crust of conversation,' preventing man from deluding himself with the notion that he knows himself, or anything else, except under optional descriptions" (Rorty 1979, 379). Rorty's notion of optional descriptions here sounds not unlike Overholt and Callicott's claim that "no culture's world is privileged in respect to truth" (16). Rorty opts for a kind of pragmatism which he calls "edifying philosophy." He defines "edification" as the "project of finding new, better, more interesting, more fruitful ways of speaking" (Rorty 1979, 360) and contends that "the point of edifying philosophy is to keep the conversation going rather than find objective truth" (377). Rorty sees the truth seekers as divided into two warring camps: the realists or scientific empiricists, or positivists, on the one hand, who see the world only in materialistic terms, and, on the other, the idealists from Plato to the transcendentalists who have a more spiritual conception of reality. "Within Philosophy, there has been a battle ... between the 'transcendental philosophy' and the 'empirical philosophy,' between the 'Platonists' and the 'positivists'" (Rorty 1982, xv). Rorty rejects both of these metaphysical accounts not because he has a better conception of reality but because we cannot know anything "except under optional descriptions." As one sympathetic interpreter of Rorty has put it: "We simply have never succeeded in 'grounding' our preferences and choices in anything beyond those preferences and choices.... We have never found the standard we have sought so long, and the pragmatist sees no need to assert its non-existence: only to point to the total lack of productivity of the search" (Prado 1983, 446).

On the basis of these kinds of considerations Rorty insists that pragmatists "do not invoke a theory about the nature of reality or knowledge or man which says that 'there is no such thing' as Truth or Goodness. Nor do they have a 'relativistic' or 'subjectivist' theory of Truth or Goodness. They would simply like to change the subject" (Rorty 1979, xiv). It is here that we detect a major difference between Rorty's position and Overholt and Callicott's. In their defense of ethno-metaphysics, Overholt and Callicott seem to accept a relativistic theory of truth. Rorty, as we have just seen, does not. Rorty sees that one of the major consequences of pragmatism is that metaphysics is impossible. Philosophy cannot be the pursuit of truth, as we all once thought; its role is merely "to keep the conversation going." It is important to note that Rorty reaches this radical conclusion using the same kind of evidence as Overholt and Callicott use in their defense of ethno-metaphysics. What Overholt and Callicott seem to have shown albeit inadvertently is not that ethno-metaphysics is possible, but rather that all metaphysics (including therefore ethno-metaphysics) is impossible. In other words, Overholt and Callicott have failed to show that ethno-metaphysics is related to metaphysics as ethnohistory is to history. After all, ethnohistory does not destroy history. Unfortunately, as Rorty's arguments clearly show, the relativism which Overholt and Callicott wish to use to justify ethno-metaphysics does in fact destroy metaphysics. Overholt and Callicott thus find themselves in the position of a surgeon who is able to say that the operation was a success but unfortunately the patient (ethno-metaphysics) died.

Still, even if ethno-metaphysics is not possible, it is conceivable that the position which Rorty spells out is all we really need in order to justify talking about Native American Indian philosophy. In other words, it is possible that Rorty can be used to counter the save-the-savages argument. That argument assumed that the modern scientific worldview is more accurate than, superior to, the so-called primitive views of mere savages. What Rorty claims to have done, and certainly the reason he is currently so popular at least outside the scientific community, is that he seems to have shown that the scientific worldview cannot justify its claim to superiority, in the sense of a more accurate account of reality. Rorty puts the scientific worldview "on a par with the various alternative descriptions offered by poets, novelists, depth psychologists, sculptors, anthropologists, and mystics" (Rorty 1979, 362). If this is the case then it is open to us to argue that Native narratives, for example, constitute conversations just as interesting and, if Overholt and Callicott's pragmatic argument is right, just as fruitful as any scientific description. After all, as Rorty says, "the point of edifying philosophy is to keep the conversation going rather than find objective truth" (Rorty 1979, 377).

Is it really necessary to change the role of philosophy so drastically in order to show that the aboriginal people of America have their own distinctive philosophy? We think not. As much as Rorty's account of philosophy might make our job easier, we cannot accept it. We see philosophy as the pursuit of truth, and it is in this more traditional sense of philosophy that we believe that the aboriginal people of North America have their own distinctive philosophy.

Ethno-Metaphysics and the Polycentric Perspective

It is possible to accept much of Overholt and Callicott's justification of ethno-metaphysics without accepting their relativism. We reject their relativism because it leads to Rorty's rejection of metaphysics thus making ethno-metaphysics impossible. "The point is that attempts to establish such things as objective standards of rationality, Truth, or the World as it must be for all, have failed" (Prado 1983, 446). Since, as Rorty has shown, a non-perspectival view of reality, "the World as it must be for all," is not possible, we propose adopting what has been called a polycentric perspective.

This perspective, this polycentrism, recognizes that we finite human beings can never obtain a God's-eye view, a non-perspectival view, of reality, of philosophical truth. Every view is a view from somewhere. Hence it follows that no one philosophical perspective can ever provide an entirely adequate metaphysical system. But this does not mean, as Rorty claims it does, that philosophical systems do not point toward truth, that they have nothing to say about truth. It merely follows that no one perspective can contain the whole truth. Although Overholt and Callicott are on the right track when they say that "no culture's world is privileged in respect to truth" (16), they are wrong to think that this fact leads to relativism. The fact that different cultures can have radically different worldviews reveals something very interesting not just about culture, not just about language, but about reality itself and the way in which we can come to know it. Though none is privileged, each culture's worldview, each different metaphysical system, contributes something to the total picture, a picture which is not yet and may never be wholly complete. Such is the polycentric perspective. Such is the human condition.

It may be helpful to note that the concept of the polycentric perspective was originally used to describe a technique employed by Thomas Carlyle in historical narrative to deal with the fact that whereas "all Narrative is, by its nature, of only one dimension; only travels forward towards one, or towards successive points" in actual history, as opposed to written history, "every single event is the offspring not of one, but of all other events, prior or contemporaneous, and will in its turn combine with all others to give rise to new." In short, history "is an ever-living, ever-working Chaos of Being" whereas narrative is merely and necessarily "linear" (Carlyle 1901, 88–89, cf. J. Rosenberg 1985, 44, and P Rosenberg, 1974, 12). The point which Carlyle is making here concerning history and narrative we are making about reality and metaphysical description or worldviews. Since, as Overholt and Callicott have argued, we may not have access to reality except through narrative, through language, in order to discover the true nature of reality it is necessary to examine as many different descriptions, as many different worldviews, as possible. Only by doing so and by attempting to accommodate and reconcile as many worldviews as possible can we hope to build up an accurate picture of reality, can we hope to do metaphysics.

Metaphysically speaking our position is not unlike that found in the classic story of the blind men and the elephant, to borrow a narrative from a very different Indian culture. The story itself is familiar enough. One blind man grasping the elephant's trunk declares an elephant to be like a snake. Another feeling one of its legs says an elephant is like a great tree. A third taking hold of the tail says it is really more like a rope, and so on. We finite human beings, unable to get a God's-eye view of reality as it is in itself, are very much like a single blind man groping his way about a great elephant. We never know what we will discover next and we can never be certain that we have finally put together a complete picture. It is therefore very helpful, we could even say essential, to compare what we have learned with the wisdom of others. This, of course, is exactly what the polycentric perspective requires us to do.

Though this notion of philosophy has been practiced by many thinkers, particularly it seems in Canada,[1] one philosopher who explicitly defended what he called this pluralistic, balanced or comparative philosophy was University of Manitoba professor Rupert C. Lodge (1886–1961). He argued that "for theoretical philosophers, a many-sided comparative study is of greater importance than adherence to a single view; and we have a feeling that inner convictions as to the essential rightness of any single view may well be regarded with suspicion" (Lodge 1937, 419).

Lodge was primarily concerned with realism, idealism and pragmatism. He spent much of his time attempting to show that all philosophical theories could be reduced to one of these three. What is important, however, is that he believed that the contradictions and inconsistencies between these theories could be resolved, or at least balanced through practical activity, through what he called applied philosophy. "What we *apply* is ... not the three academic theories in their 'pure' form, but a *balanced philosophy*: a sophisticated reflection which retains the divergent characteristics of all three philosophic attitudes, but holds them in balance against one another" (Lodge 1951, 19, italics in original). Lodge provides his own metaphor or analogy to explain how his balanced philosophy can still constitute a search for truth while at the same time accepting what is essentially Overholt and Callicott's point that "no culture's world is privileged in respect to truth" (Overholt and Callicott 1982, 16). Lodge thinks of experience as huge gold mine being worked by rival companies using different methods of ore extraction. From a Native perspective we note with amusement the linking of the search for truth with the search for gold. This is certainly a Western philosopher's metaphor. Still, we think that the point he is making applies to worldviews generally and therefore constitutes a justification of ethno-metaphysics. As Lodge himself puts it: "My point is that, if all ... companies work over the entire area, more gold will be extracted than if the mine were handed over to a single company ... on the whole, all ... companies will continue to be successful in practice ..." (Lodge 1940, 433).

One need not resort to Overholt and Callicott's relativism in order to justify ethno-metaphysics. Ethno-metaphysics is a genuine search for truth and is therefore a very real contribution to metaphysics. Indeed if the polycentric perspective is correct it may well be the only way of doing metaphysics.[2] Rorty and like-minded pragmatists reject metaphysics because they claim that in all the years of metaphysical speculation no one has ever discovered "the World as it must be for all." Rorty and many others have given up on metaphysics because they have failed to piece the puzzle together, to come up with "the World as it must be for all." They do not realize that, like someone working with an incomplete jigsaw puzzle, they do not yet have all the pieces. It is to the examination of some of these missing pieces that we now turn in our ethno-metaphysical study of Native American philosophy.

Two

Outside View Predicates

Do Indians Really Know Who They Are?

Of course Indians know who they are. Like everyone else, they are, after all conscious, self-aware beings. We contend, however, that one thing standing in the way of a full understanding of "self" for the Indians of North America is that they continue to live in the nations which originally colonized them, and under governments guilty of racism toward them not only in the past but also continuing to this very day. In the United States, the Indian Reorganization Act of 1934 confirmed tribal self government under federal jurisdiction, under Congress. Though this is a very limited form of sovereignty it is at least clear that Native American Indians are citizens of both their own tribal nation and the United States of America. Similarly, in Canada, some Native North Americans, those who are status Indians, are members of their particular Indian Act Bands while at the same time they are considered citizens under the Citizenship Act. Whether or not the descendants of Native North Americans now live in the United States or Canada they continue to be perceived and described by the dominant society through what we call "outside view predicates."

The Outside View Predicate

The concept of an outside view predicate is a product of two of the philosophical traditions we are using in this study, the British analytic tradition of conceptual analysis, and the tradition of existential phenomenology usually associated with continental Europe. The term "outside view predicate" was first introduced by American analytic philosopher Phyllis Sutton Morris in her book *Sartre's Concept of a Person: An Analytic Approach.* She uses it to explain the thought of the French existentialist Jean-Paul Sartre (1905–1980). Such predicates are "those which when applied to ourselves imply an 'outside view' in either a literal or figurative sense" (Morris, 1976, 136). However, to apply an outside view predicate to yourself is much more than merely seeing yourself as others see you, though it is that as well. It is allowing others to tell you who you are. It is in a sense giving up your freedom, your self-determination, to others: becoming what they want you to become rather than becoming what you have it within yourself to become. To accept an outside view predicate such as "ugly" or "ashamed," to use two of Sartre's favorite examples, is to fit into the plans and projects of others, to make it easy for them to manipulate you for their own ends, for their own purposes. It is, in a very real and frightening sense, to lose yourself, to become alienated, to become a stranger, an alien to yourself. Throughout this chapter it is helpful and very revealing to keep in mind these implications of outside view predicates. We begin with some first-person descriptions of growing up Indian offered by Dennis McPherson. Notice how quickly first-person descriptions—("I remember ...") become second and third-person descriptions—("You just won't pay attention.... They just can't learn ..."). Notice particularly how easy it is for alienation to set in.

Growing Up Indian

In the days of my grandparents, which ended very early in my childhood, I would spend hours listening to their stories of how they viewed the world. I vividly remember that buried in their tales was a prescription for dealing with the world as a place in which all beings were allowed the time and space to be themselves.

At the age of six I attended a Catholic primary school along with a nephew of the same age. In present-day terminology my nephew would probably fall into the category of a slow learner. But whatever his learning ability was at the time, it is irrelevant now: it was his presence which was of significance in providing me with my first concrete experience of different worldviews.

Throughout the first grade we had been grilled in the doctrines of Catholicism. We had to learn the Ten Commandments, how to make the stations of the cross, how to recite the appropriate prayers, and we were told to believe that the Trinity, God the Father, God the Son and God the Holy Ghost, all resided in the tabernacle resting on the altar. I could never understand the trinity concept as a child: how could three great big guys fit into such a small space?

Our teachers at the time were Roman Catholic nuns, women who were somewhat skilled in educational instruction and who had studied religion because of a personal calling to their God. In our case, their role in serving God was to educate us Indians. I remember as if it were yesterday the difficulty my nephew encountered as a seven-year-old because he could not recite the multiplication tables. As if by clockwork, the sister would ask him to provide an answer for a mathematical problem. "What is 2 times 6?" she would ask. "Thirteen!" he would answer. Out would come a large leather strap. "You Indians are all the same!" she would scream as she whipped him. "I'll teach you to say the right answer, you little savage!" I was to meet this kind of racism many times again in future years. It is part of being an Indian.

Besides these personal experiences there was the actual content of what I was being taught. For example, while studying Canadian history I learned that the Jesuits were given a hard time by the Iroquois. Apparently, these early missionaries carried the word of God to the Iroquois and the Iroquois in turn planted the missionaries' heads on poles. For this, the missionaries are depicted as martyrs, the Iroquois as savages.

As a child, I spent a lot of time looking at my grandparents' house conjuring strange images of the people who lived within those walls. I continually analyzed the behavior of my grandparents, my parents and my brothers and sisters, trying to make a connection between what I was taught in school, i.e., that Indians were savages, and what I knew was true at home, i.e., that these were my ancestors and my relatives. Their beliefs were my beliefs. If they were savages, then I must be a savage too. Funny, they didn't look like savages to me, and I didn't feel like a savage — at least not at that time.

What I did learn through these experiences was that there are at least two ways of viewing the world. The morally right way stemming from the European school of thought and what is, unfortunately, still believed by some of aboriginal descent to be "the Indian way." I still remember the words of my grandmother when she would say, "Don't act like an Indian." It seemed a rather strange and simplistic statement to me at the time, but now I am beginning to understand what it was that she meant by her phrase, act like an Indian. Indians have not always been around. They gained their first real prominence at contact!

What Is an Indian?

Whether or not the use of the predicate "Indian" to describe the aboriginal peoples of the Americas was due to Christopher Columbus' thinking that he had reached India in 1492 when he had in fact reached islands off the coast of what is now called the Americas, there can be no doubt that the term "Indian" was at the time of Columbus, and sometimes still is, an outside view predicate. It is certainly a description brought to the Americas from the outside. According to the *Oxford English Dictionary* (OED), the first recorded English use of the word "Indian" to mean American aboriginal occurred in 1553 with the publication of a *Treatise of the New India*. The OED indicates that America was frequently called "New India," and that by 1613 the name "India" was applied indiscriminately to "all far-distant countries." "Indian" not only denoted the aboriginal inhabitants of America (1553) but also of the Philippines (1697) and Australia and New Zealand (1769). In fact, with the discovery of the New World, the term "Indian" became a very general one designating those in far away lands, those other than Europeans, those other than Christian, those other than civilized.

Unfortunately, the popular Columbus discovery story, that he was looking for a new route to India, is not consistent with the fact that almost half a century after Columbus landed, the original people of the "New World" were not treated as the Europeans had been treating the people of India. The people of India were sought out for trade, whereas the Indians of the New World were not even considered to be persons (men). The ongoing slaughter and extermination of the Indians by Christians raised concern about eternal damnation. The slaughter was justified by reading the Requerimiento to the impending victims. The Requerimiento administered in either Latin or Spanish demanded the Indians acknowledge the sovereignty of the king and accept the Christian faith. Refusal to comply with this demand, issued in a language the Indians did not understand, resulted in their death. Acknowledged in the Requerimiento was the fact that the fault for their own deaths lay in their failure to comply (Berger 1991, 3). Hence the souls of those administering the Requerimiento were not at risk.

The Catholic Church, of course, faced a dilemma. If the Indians of America were not humans, were mere animals, then it made no sense to convert them to Christianity. On the other hand, to recognize them as humans is to admit they have certain human rights and cannot be indiscriminately exploited. It was not until 1535 that a papal bull was issued recognizing the original people of the Americas as men: "Indians and all other people who may later be discovered by Christians, are by no means to be deprived of their liberty or the possession of their property, even though they may be outside the faith of Jesus Christ" (cited in Morse 1985, 44). Bartolomé de Las Casa in 1542 argued that the Spanish king "must undo the wrongs committed by the conquistadores in his name, and restore to the Indians their lands, the wealth taken from them, and their own rulers" (cited in Berger 1991, 17).

Over the next two centuries European expansion in North America, led mainly by France and Britain, and mainly driven by the economics of the fur trade, furthered the exploitation of the Indians started by Spain. Competition between France and Britain for trade with the Indians eventually led to war in the mid–1700s and was resolved by the Treaty of Paris in 1763. All French holdings in the New World were relinquished to Great Britain except for the islands of St. Pierre and Miquelon. In October of 1763 King George III issued the famous royal proclamation extending British governance to the newly acquired territories formerly held by France, while at the same time recognizing the notions put forth by La Casa over 200 years before, that Indians do have some right in law.

The Royal Proclamation

Following the resolution of war between the French and the English in Europe, which culminated in the Treaty of Paris of 1763, vast territories in the Americas formerly controlled by the French were turned over to British rule. These areas extended from present-day Florida in the south to points as far north as Cape Breton Island. On October 7, 1763, King George III of Britain, by His Royal Prerogative, issued the Royal Proclamation with respect to the governing of what was then British North America.

The Royal Proclamation of 1763 has two main features. In the first place the proclamation sets out four new British colonies with their own governmental and judicial systems. These are the Government of Quebec, the Government of East Florida, the Government of West Florida and the Government of Grenada. Secondly, the Royal Proclamation recognizes what has become known as "aboriginal title" to a large portion of North America. It says,

> We do therefore, with the Advice of our Privy Council, declare it to be our Royal Will and Pleasure, that no Governor or Commander in Chief in any of our Colonies of Quebec, East Florida, or West Florida, do presume, upon any

> Pretense whatever, to grant Warrants of Survey, or pass any Patents for Lands beyond the bonds of their respective Governments, as described in their Commissions; as also that no Colonies or Plantations in America do presume for the present, and until our further Pleasure be known, to grant Warrants of Survey, or pass Patents for any Lands beyond the Heads or Sources of any of the Rivers which fall into the Atlantic Ocean from the West and North West, or upon any Lands whatever, which, not having been ceded to or purchased by Us as aforesaid, are reserved to the said Indians, or any of them.

Concerning Indians, the Royal Proclamation has three distinct functions.

• Even to the present time, it is a foundation document in the debate over many Indian legal issues in Canada. This is so because the Royal Proclamation seems to say that at least some of the land west of Quebec, except for Rupert's Land, belonged to the Indians. Indians held aboriginal title to these lands through their use and occupation. In this respect the Royal Proclamation says,

> And, whereas it is just and reasonable, and essential to our Interest, and the Security of our Colonies, that the several Nations or Tribes of Indians with whom We are connected, and who live under our Protection, should not be molested or disturbed in the Possession of such Parts of Our Dominions and Territories as, not having been ceded to or purchased by Us, are reserved to them, or any of them, as their Hunting Grounds.

• The Royal Proclamation is also the basis of the reserve system. It says quite distinctly that the colonial governments of the time were not to posses or use land outside of their own territories. Lands outside the territories of colonial charters were held in "reserve" for the use and occupation of Indians.

> And, we do further declare it to be Our Royal Will and Pleasure for the present as aforesaid, to reserve under our Sovereignty, Protection, and Dominion, for the use of the said Indians, all the Lands and Territories not included within the limits of Our said Three new governments, or within the Limits of the Territory granted to the Hudson's Bay Company, as also all the Lands and Territories lying to the Westward of the Sources of the Rivers which fall in the Sea from the West and North West as aforesaid.

• The Royal Proclamation set out a procedure for ceding land and extinguishing aboriginal title through the treaty process. In this process, the proclamation forbade any private sale of land from Indians to non–Indians. This meant that Indians could only sell land to the Crown at a public meeting called for that purpose. Indians must consent to the sale. Apparently it was not an expectation of the time for Indians to sell land to other Indians. Monies for land transfer were held then, and still are, by the Crown in trust for the use and benefit of the Indians. Because of this procedure of transfer of Aboriginal Title of land to the Crown, a special fiduciary relationship was established between Indians and the Crown. A fiduciary relationship between Indians and the Crown flows from their historic relationship in which Indians were viewed as "wards of the state" whose welfare and care are a political trust of "the highest obligation." In this respect the Royal Proclamation says:

> And, whereas great Frauds and Abuses have been committed in purchasing Lands of the Indians, to the great Prejudice of our Interests, and to the great Dissatisfaction of the said Indians; In order, therefore, to prevent such Irregularities for the future, and to the end that the Indians may be convinced of our Justice and determined Resolution to remove all reasonable Cause of Discontent, We do, with the Advice of our Privy Council strictly enjoin and require, that no private Person do presume to make any purchase from the said Indians of any Lands reserved to the said Indians, within those parts of our Colonies where, We have thought proper to allow Settlement; but that, if at any Time any of the Said Indians should be inclined to dispose of the said Lands, the same shall be Purchased only by Us, in our Name, at some public Meeting or Assembly of the said Indians, to be held for that Purpose by the Governor or Commander in Chief of our Colony respectively within which they shall lie; and in case they shall lie within the limits of any Proprietary Government, they shall be purchased only for the Use and in the name of such Proprietaries, confirmable to such Directions and Instructions as We or they shall think proper to give for that Purpose.

Summary of the Royal Proclamation

First of all, the Royal Proclamation followed from the Treaty of Paris as a result of the transfer of control of the French colonies in America to British authority. In this vein, four new colonial governments were established by the British and given authority to make their own laws based on the British model of government and judiciary system. Through the proclamation, the British concept of real property was applied in the colonies, and the colonial governments in America were given the power to collect tax on these properties. As a means to encourage settlement of these new lands, the proclamation outlines a scheme for rewarding persons who had participated in the recent war between England and France. Parcels of land were provided upon application to persons who had served in the British army or navy, and these parcels were to be owned tax-free for the first ten years. As far as Indians are concerned, under the Royal Proclamation they were given an equitable right in the unceded territories allowing them possession and use of these territories as their hunting grounds. Dominion over these unceded territories was held by the Crown while the territory was held in reserve for the use of the Indians. No private subject was allowed to buy these lands from the Indians. Indians could only sell to the Crown. In the event that anyone had purchased land from the Indians in the past, the proclamation voided any such purchase. Any future purchases of land by the Crown could only be done in public. Finally, all British subjects were encouraged to trade with the Indians upon obtaining a license to do so. A license to trade with the Indians was obtained free of charge but the license could be revoked should the person holding the license refuse to obey set regulations. Lastly, the Royal Proclamation directed that all "outlaws" residing in Indian territory be apprehended.

Philosophical Underpinnings and Implications of the Royal Proclamation

Though there are many creation stories, both Native North American and others throughout the world, the empirical evidence suggests that *homo sapiens* originated in, and began their journey from, Africa. If this is in fact the case, the one thing we can be certain of is that, at one time, we were all one family, we were all in this state of Nature equally susceptible to natural forces. Though the journey progressed throughout the world, Euro-Western philosophy evolved from those who settled around the Mediterranean basin. In their search for truth, early Greek philosophers began questioning the world around them, eventually producing what are often called naturalistic explanations, moving from mythology toward more scientific approaches. These explanations did not really diverge all that much from Native American narratives, myths, and ceremonies. Thales (c. 624–546 B.C.) argued all things are water, or come from water. Since this included living things, Thales probably believed that water itself was alive. Others like Anaximander (c. 610–546 B.C.), Anaximenes (c. 585–528) and Heraclitus (c. 535–475 B.C.) opted for air, fire or an indefiniteness or boundlessness as the primary substance. Pythagoras (c. 525–500 B.C.) opted for number and form, arguing, for example, that health is harmony and balance.

From a Native American perspective it is with Socrates (470–399 B.C.), Plato (c. 428–347 B.C.) and especially Aristotle (384–322 B.C.) that things start to go horribly wrong. Socrates is considered the father of Western philosophy. He was probably the first to call himself a philosopher. The term itself is from the Greek and means friend or lover (*philos*) of wisdom (*sophos*).

He taught that true wisdom was knowing that one does not know, and in genuine philosophical humility he distinguished himself from those in Athens who called themselves wise men (sophists) by referring to himself as a seeker or supporter of wisdom, a philosopher. In a similar way today we use the root word "philos" when we speak of for example a "philharmonic orchestra" or a "philharmonic society" meaning one which supports music or harmony (*harmonos* being a Greek term for music). It is easy to see how Western civilization has its foundations in ancient Greece. Every philosophy department in every university in the Western world teaches courses on or including Socrates, but very few teach anything about Native American philosophy, though a great many include East Indian, Chinese and Japanese philosophy in the curriculum. To skeptics of Native American philosophy who argue that at least philosophers from these other non–Western countries wrote books, we like to point out that Socrates, the founder of Western philosophy, wrote nothing, not a book, not a paper, not a thing. What we know of Socrates comes from his student Plato and a few other writers of his time who talk about his teachings. Some of the things Plato says about him make Socrates sound not unlike a Native American elder of today. For example, Socrates is portrayed as believing that knowledge is a communal affair. He did philosophy by talking to other people, not necessarily specialists or wise men (sophists), but also folks in the streets and marketplace of Athens, the city in which he lived. He was against disputation, or arguing just for the sake of arguing, and thought he could gain truth in genuine dialogue with others. Unlike Thales, Anaximander and company (who have come to be known as the Pre–Socratics), Socrates was more interested in people and society than in more esoteric questions like the metaphysical nature of reality in itself. Unlike most Native elders, Socrates was a city boy. Plato in his Dialogue, *The Phaedrus,* reports that Socrates said he could learn nothing from trees and rocks, he preferred people and books. As we show in Chapter Four, "Values, Land, and the Integrity of Person," this may well represent the beginning of the alienation from the land, which was to permeate Western thought and civilization to the present day. Plato contributes further to this Western alienation, extending it from Nature (forests, trees and, so forth) to all objects we can perceive by our senses (sight, smell, taste, hearing and touch). These he argued were like mere shadows on the back wall of a cave in which all of us are prisoners chained so we can see only the shadows, which we mistakenly take for reality. This is Plato's famous analogy of the Cave. Philosophical enlightenment, he maintained, was breaking free of our chains so we could turn around and discover the source of the shadows, thus discovering that the shadows were indeed nothing but shadows and then finding the entrance to the cave and escaping to the clear light of day which would at first be somewhat blinding. We find it interesting that this analogy for employing intellect or reason rather than our five senses to discover reality actually uses visual imagery (shadows, chains and the cave) as well metaphorical or analogical thinking in order to represent rigorous rational or philosophical thought. As we will explain in more detail in Chapter Four current findings in cognitive science suggest that our thinking is actually governed more by image schemas, metaphor and narrative than by abstract logical reasoning. This privileges Native storytelling as a respectable form of philosophical thought and makes Plato's manner of presentation, at least, less foreign to Native students.

When we discuss Plato's Cave with our Native students one thing they have often found speaks to them is Plato's admission that when the philosopher returns to the cave and tries to tell the prisoners there that they are in fact imprisoned in a cave perceiving only unreal shadows the poor philosopher is laughed at and dismissed as crazy. Many of our students have told us that when they return to their reserves and share with the folks back home some of the things they have learned in university about, for example, colonial involvement in setting up the reserve structure they too are resented, not believed, and often laughed at. It is probably not a good idea to tell the chief and band councilors that they do not represent the people who elected them; that they are really civil servants and work for the colonial government, which set up their positions in the first place. As we will see in the following chapters, not all is as it seems on the rez, much is unreality, mere shadows. According to Plato, true reality is discovered by the intellect and consists in what have come to be called Platonic forms. These are in fact universals, which are supposed to contain what all particular instances of them have in common, their very essence, or essential characteristics. Since we are looking at Plato from a Native American perspective we will use the beaver as an example. The Platonic Form of beaver would be the true reality and all the particular beavers would be beavers because they participated in the form of beaverness, what they all have in common, that which makes them all beavers. Each beaver is then an instance of the Platonic form of beaver. Some writers have even maintained that this closely parallels a Native American, or at least an Ojibwa, view of reality, suggesting that the physical world is but a reflection of the real spirit world (Skelton 2007, 78). The Ojibwa believe that returning the bones of a beaver to the lake or stream in which it was snared ensures that it will be reclothed in flesh and fur. Not to do so would show lack of respect and encourage the "beaver boss" to change the luck of the trapper (Overholt and Callicott 1982, 154–155). Whether or not we would want to say that the Ojibwa "beaver boss" is really the Platonic form of beaver, the point of Joan Skelton's comparison is to complain that while the Ojibwa philosophy is often dismissed as primitive, in universities something quite similar is taught as the philosophy of Plato (Skelton 2007, 78 and Magnus Theatre). We will discuss this in more detail in Chapter Four when we address native values. Here we are more concerned with the philosophical underpinnings making sense of the Royal Proclamation. Plato's claim that Reason must be used to control our appetites and desires as well as to reveal the forms is relevant. The whole notion that reason governs our passions and emotions plays a large role in Western philosophy from Plato to the present day.

Though Plato's famous student Aristotle rejected Platonic forms, arguing rightly the form could hardly exist on its own without matter (something to be informed or shaped), he nevertheless maintained the superiority of Reason over passion, or the mind over the body. "Wherever there is the same wide discrepancy between two sets of human beings as there is between mind and body or between man and beast, then the inferior of the two sets, those whose condition is such that their function is the use of their bodies and nothing better can be expected of them, those I say, are slaves by nature" (Aristotle 1962, 33–34). On the basis of this Aristotle famously concluded: "Between male and female the former is by nature superior and ruler, the latter inferior and subject" (Aristotle 1962, 33). It is perhaps a little unfair to judge Aristotle by today's standards. He did after all argue in support of democracy (as opposed to Plato's philosopher king). In Aristotle's democracy all citizens were considered equal. Of course the concept of citizen did not extend to women or slaves. The Native American notion of a kinship with all animals would certainly be foreign to him. Aristotle seemed to think that the other animals were created solely for our use. "Plants exist for the sake of animals.... All other animals exist for the sake man, tame animals for the use he can make of them as well as for the food they provide; and as for wild animals, most though not all of these can be used for food and are useful in other ways; clothing and instruments can be made out of them. If then we are right in believing that nature makes nothing without some end in view, nothing to no purpose, it must be that nature has made all these things specifically for the sake of man" (Aristotle 1962, 40). Unfortunately Aristotle's misogyny and anthropocentrism persists through Western civilization and especially through Christianity right up to the present day.

St. Augustine (354–430) argued that a complete philosophy was not possible without Christian revelation, and philosophy really was nothing more than Christian theology. Boethius (480–524) in *Consolation of Philosophy* argued that philosophy, the love of wisdom, is the love of reality, the love of the ultimate cause of everything, hence, philosophy is in actual fact the love of God. With the Christianization, and ultimately the fall, of the Roman Empire in A.D. 476 the development of philosophy, and learning in general, came to a halt for the next several centuries. This we now call the Dark Ages. St. Thomas Aquinas (1225–1274) reconciled Aristotle with the Christian faith, not by conflating philosophy and theology, but by distinguishing natural philosophy based on Reason alone, from dogmatic philosophy, which has its foundation in, and reasons from, divine and Biblical revelation (dogma). From Aristotle St. Thomas Aquinas gets natural reason, natural law and virtue, which facilitates the choice of the good, but since, according to Revelation our ultimate end or goal is God, Aquinas argues we need something more than natural law, we need also divine law. The state is supposedly autonomous, independent from the Church, in that it administers human law or positive law based on natural law, keeping the common good. Because we are also spiritual beings; the state may not enact laws that would interfere with our spiritual nature. For Aquinas, our ultimate end is God and that is the domain of the Church. Given our ultimate end, natural law is one aspect of eternal law, and in the state, the sovereign actually has authority from God to ensure the common good of society, subordinate only to the laws of the Church.

Under Canon law, the Roman Catholic Church could and did grant various sovereigns, kings and princes permission to conquer non–Christian lands, those occupied by infidels, as occurred in the medieval Crusades to Jerusalem, c. 1096–1271, "liberating" the Holy Land. Lumbee legal philosopher Robert Williams, in his book *The American Indian in Western Legal Thought: The Discourses of Conquest,* discusses in some detail the extensive legal discourse on colonization used to justify such wars and links this discourse to the colonization of "normatively divergent non–Christian peoples" in the Americas, those Aristotle would have called slaves by nature. Williams identifies the foundation of colonization as the "suprajurisdictional papal authority over infidels ... where it was clearly necessary for the pope to intervene in order to protect the infidels' spiritual well-being" (Williams 1990, 14; see also our discussion of Thomas Aquinas above). In his article on laws of Indian communities to Frederic Hoxie's *Encyclopedia of North American Indians,* Williams observes that "most Americans would likely be surprised to learn that the basic rights of Indian governments in this country are circumscribed by a legal doctrine that evolved out of European Christian justifications for the crusades of the Middle Ages" (Hoxie 1996, 335).

King George III through his *Royal Proclamation* of 1763 asserted "dominion" over all the listed lands, by virtue of divine right and, in the case of Indian territory, by appeal to the right of discovery as well. Unlike the earlier conquistadores and crusaders, the British king by asserting dominion in the 1760s actually extended the British model of government and legal system to the new lands, as we explained above. Ironically, inherent in the British legal system of common law are the notions of fair play and justice. How could the Crown, in all good conscience, base the taking of land that had not been conquered in war, on the right of discovery and divine right, and still feel justified in doing so when it was a well known fact that the lands in question were inhabited by other peoples? Apparently in order to avoid any feelings of injustice, from a British perspective, as the Royal Proclamation makes clear, the "Laws, Statutes, and Ordinances for the Public Peace, Welfare, and good Government of our said Colonies, and the People and Inhabitants thereof, [must be] as near as may be agreeable to the Laws of England, and under such Regulations and Restrictions as are used in other Colonies." It seems, as long as the laws were the same as those of England in order for the settlement to enjoy continued expansion "if at any Time any of the Said Indians should be inclined to dispose of the said Lands, the same shall be Purchased only by Us, in our Name," then everything would accord with the British sense of justice and fair play. After all, the argument could be made that it was the Indians who decided to sell their land. In response, the British simply bought it.

In order to reconcile the founding principles of right of discovery and divine right with the notions of fair play and justice the legal and philosophical concepts of "property," "purchase" and "cede" become paramount. To purchase lands really means to purchase property (not a thing of any kind, but a legal right, an aspect of ownership). To cede lands means to give up all the rights of ownership of the lands. *Black's Law Dictionary* defines "cede" as follows: "To yield up; to grant; to surrender; to withdraw." "'Cede' is a legal term generally used to designate the transfer of territory from one sovereign government to another" (Black 1979, 202). The Royal Proclamation assumes that the would-be purchasers (the British) and the ceders (the Indians) share the same concept of land-as-commodity. The Indians' so-called right of ownership has come to be called "aboriginal title," though this term has never been clearly defined. Jack Woodward in his book *Native*

Law offers the following attempt: "Aboriginal title is the all-embracing right of an Indian society to exclusive possession of the land" (139). But aboriginal title is really what we have called an outside view predicate. This sense of "title"—defining both the land and the people—is a predicate alien to the worldview of the people upon whom it is imposed.

The British regarded "aboriginal title" as a right that must be extinguished in some manner. And, of course, the easiest method of extinguishing such title is for the Indians to cede it, to give it all away. In order to understand the concept of "land-as-property" in the English system it is necessary to look briefly at the legal, philosophical and historical roots of this concept. In the days of the feudal system in England all land was held by the Crown (again through divine right). In other words, the Crown had seisin (see below) and granted all land "in fee simple." This means that the Crown possessed all the "rights," but the notion of the Crown holding all the "rights" to all the land is of limited utility by itself. After all, what good is ownership unless there is some benefit to be accrued from it? In this system, which is a system of "estates," the king gained benefit by granting certain land "rights" to his lords and knights for services rendered. In turn, the new land owners would grant certain "rights" to persons of lesser rank, allowing them to use the land. In this manner a system of rents or fees developed whereby those lower in the system paid the nobility for the privilege of using the land. This is no different than entering into a rental agreement for the use of an apartment today, and is in fact the legal origin for such agreements.

In feudal times nobility received a "right" for an indefinite period of time which granted them possession of all the "rights" to the land. This made them "freeholders" or holders in "fee simple." A freeholder, who also had a "right" to possession, had "seisin" (from the middle English to seize, grasp or hold). To have "seisin" means that freeholders held all the "rights" to the land and could do whatever they wished with these "rights." For example, a freeholder could lease a "right" of possession to a serf for farming purposes. The serf would then hold an "equitable right" to or estate in the land providing he met the conditions of the lease and farmed the land. Should he discontinue farming, thus no longer meeting the prescribed conditions set out in the lease, the right to or estate in the land would revert back to the freeholder. In other words, even though the land was leased, the freeholder retained a "right of reversion" should the tenant, in this case the serf, fail to meet the conditions of the lease.

It is within this estate system of land ownership that the interests of the new settlers of North America and its original inhabitants are brought together. Although the British king through the Royal Proclamation claimed dominion over all of America within British control, he recognized that some of the territory remained outside his jurisdiction. Some of the territory was in the hands of the original inhabitants, the Indians. These Indians, from the standpoint of the estate system, were regarded as holding an estate, a right to, or in, the land. This outside view predicate came to be called aboriginal title. It is important to realize that this concept of aboriginal title was equally alien to the Indians and to the estate system, which was attempting to accommodate the reality of the New World. "Aboriginal title" is an outside view predicate to both. Though aboriginal and treaty rights are "recognized and affirmed" in the constitution of Canada (1982) "aboriginal title" is still, to this day, not clearly defined.

The Crown's dominion through the Royal Proclamation is further complicated by the fact that by the 1700s the feudal system in England was in deep decline. Enlightenment philosophies with their social contract theories were rejecting the whole system of nobility and privilege in favor of equality. This is perhaps best illustrated by the famous British empiricist John Locke (1632–1704). In 1690 he published two influential books, *An Essay Concerning Human Understanding* and *Two Treatises on Government*. Both, in their own way, reject authority. In the *Essay* Locke argues against *a priori* or innate knowledge, suggesting that prior to perception the mind is a blank slate. We each must use perception and reason to discover knowledge for ourselves, and we certainly cannot rely on the authority of others. What others tell us to be true we each must confirm for ourselves. This is very different from the Christian philosophers of the Middle Ages, for example. As we noted above, St. Augustine and Boethius appealed to the authority of the Bible, and St. Thomas Aquinas appealed to Aristotle as well as to the Bible, the most authoritative source, the word of God. Many ancient texts were, at this time, actually considered almost as authoritative. In fact, Aquinas referred to Aristotle as "the philosopher" and would cite him by writing simply "The philosopher says ..." Locke's rejection of authority comes out most clearly in his *Treatises on Government*, which he published anonymously, likely to protect himself from those very authorities. After all, he questioned the absolute authority of the monarch and argued that the people had a right to rebel against a government if said monarchs failed to protect the property rights of the people. In section 229 of the *Second Treatise* he asserts that "the end of government is the good of mankind," and he then poses the rhetorical question: "[W]hich is *best for mankind*, that the people should be always exposed to the boundless will of tyranny, or that the rulers should be sometimes liable to be opposed, when they grow exorbitant in the use of their power, and employ it for the destruction, and not the preservation of the properties of their people?" To understand why Locke might be somewhat nervous, it is important to remember that his *Treatise* was being published shortly after (two years after) the Glorious Revolution of 1688 in which the Catholic King James II was replaced, at the invitation of the English parliament representing the people, by the Protestant rule of William and Mary. The revolution is called "Glorious" because it is said that it was accomplished without firing a shot. This is not entirely accurate, but it was certainly much less violent than the two subsequent revolutions it (and Locke) inspired, the American War of Independence and the French Revolution. There is, incidentally, considerable evidence that Locke himself was anything but an innocent bystander during the Glorious Revolution (Ashcraft 1986 & Rabb 1988, 487–489).

Broadly considered, Locke's social contract theory presupposed a mythical state of nature in which all are equal and use the land in common, the origin of our notion of "the commons." Those who work the land, tilling it and making it more productive through their labor, create private property. Eventually, people will contract together to be governed to protect private property. The main role of government Locke conceived is to provide just such protection. Though the myth of the state of nature was really just a metaphorical way of suggesting that the people have a right to choose and to oppose who rules them, Locke's description of the state of nature sounds not unlike the way people were supposed to live in Africa at the very origin of our species, as we discussed above at the start of this section on the philosophy surrounding the Royal Proclamation. Locke was, of course, writing before the theory of evolution and he thought that the Americas were very close to his conception of the state of nature. Though there was some agriculture in the Americas prior to contact (e.g., corn, beans and squash) it was very different from that practiced in Europe with its comparative monoculture, clearing of forest and the widespread plowing of fields. More importantly, vast areas of the Americas were seen by the colonists as completely undeveloped, the Indians' hunting grounds. From a Lockean perspective, these forested lands were unproductive, wasted and certainly could not be the property of the Indians who hunt in them, any more than fishing the oceans makes the oceans the property of fishermen (the fish they catch, yes, but not the oceans they catch them in). It does not take too much imagination to see that North American colonists with a Lockean mindset would not be very sympathetic to Indian land claims.

One of the most famous Americans to be influenced, even inspired, by Locke was Thomas Jefferson (1743–1826), the author of *The Declaration of Independence*, third president of the United States, and founder of the University of Virginia (Honderich 1995, 428). Jefferson read Locke under the supervision of one Dr. William Small at the College of William and Mary in Williamsburg.[1] He would no doubt have also discussed the Glorious Revolution, which put in place the British monarchs in whose honor the College was named. Jefferson was most certainly inspired by enlightenment thinkers such as Locke. He described Locke along with Francis Bacon and Isaac Newton as his "trinity of the three greatest men the world ... ever produced."[2] The University of Virginia which Jefferson founded at Charlottesville in 1819 has maintained a history of Locke scholarship to the present. In fact one of us spent a sabbatical year at the University of Virginia writing a book on Locke (Rabb 1985). The reason for the year at the University of Virginia, as acknowledged in the preface of the book, was the opportunity to work with their distinguished Locke and legal scholar of the time, a famous Oxford philosopher they had attracted in 1966: "Special thanks are due to Professor A. D. Woozley who read and patiently discussed with me this entire manuscript chapter by chapter as it was being written" (Rabb 1985, vii). Although Anthony D. Woozley (1912–2008) came to Virginia via St. Andrews, he is best known as an Oxford philosopher because during his time teaching at Oxford he was an active member of a very influential group of philosophers, known as the "brethren" (Ignatieff 1998, 84–85). They were the very beginning of the influential Oxford ordinary language school of philosophy. Throughout the late 1930s they met after dinner Thursday evenings at All Souls College to discuss philosophy. Included in this "magic circle" were such notables as J. L. Austin, A. J. Ayer, Isaiah Berlin (in whose rooms they met), Stuart Hampshire, Donald MacKinnon, Donald MacNabb, and of course A. D. Woozley himself (Ignatieff 1998, 85). Woozley is also remembered for his studies of Locke including his edited edition of Locke's *Essay Concerning Human Understanding* (Locke 1976).

There can be no doubt that Locke had an enduring influence on America. Although it has been argued that Locke's influence on Jefferson was "decisive," Jefferson drew on both enlightenment and ancient ideals, as the classical architecture he designed for his University of Virginia clearly suggests, particularly the Greek columns that flank both sides of "Mr. Jefferson's Lawn" (Clapp 1967, 502).[3] From our perspective what is most interesting are the philosophical roots of Jefferson's attitude toward American Indians. It is not difficult to find quotations in Jefferson's own words indicating that he believed that if the "savages" would only abandon their nomadic ways (of hunting and gathering) and settle down and adopt European farming practices they would in time become "civilized."[4] Such views are obviously related to Locke's notions of labor and private property as explained above. Based on this it could certainly be argued that Jefferson was, indeed, a man of the enlightenment. However, his justification of westward expansion, into Indian country, seems to have been based on the much more ancient doctrine of discovery, the same doctrine which, we have argued, lay at the root of the Royal Proclamation. Robert J. Miller (Shawnee), in his book *Native America, Discovered and Conquered: Thomas Jefferson, Lewis & Clark, and Manifest Destiny,* makes the case showing how, using the doctrine of discovery, Jefferson conceived of the Lewis and Clark expedition as a way of making legal claims to the Pacific Northwest for the United States. Miller also argues that the later distinctly American notion of manifest destiny has its roots in the doctrine of discovery, and shows how this "discovery doctrine" still lies behind U.S. Indian policy today (Miller 2008). This, perhaps, helps to explain why, although the American colonies rebelled against the Royal Proclamation, their most hated provision of the proclamation reappears practically unchanged in the United States Constitution. Just as the Indians were permitted by *The Proclamation* to sell lands only to the Crown and not to individuals, so it turns out only Congress has the power "to regulate Commerce with foreign Nations, and among the several States, and with the Indian Tribes" (*http://www.usconstitution.net*).

Consequences of the Royal Proclamation

Two of the most startling consequences of the Royal Proclamation are the two nation states on the North American continent: Canada and the United States. Robert Williams, in *The American Indian in Western Legal Thought: The Discourses of Conquest,* certainly argues that the Declaration of Independence was, at least in part, a result of the provisions of the Royal Proclamation. The thirteen colonies felt hemmed in along the Atlantic seacoast. Much of the rest of the continent to the west had in essence been declared Indian territory. Not only could individuals not purchase land directly from the Indians, but those who had were directed by the proclamation to return it. Such sales were null and void. Some rather influential individuals had purchased land directly from the Indians and wanted to continue to do so, George Washington among them. "Americans such as

Wharton, Dunmore, Franklin, and Washington were more than ready by the early 1770s, the eve of their Revolution, to pursue their self-interest directly with the Indians without the troubling mediatory prerogative of an alien-born king" (Williams 1990, 279). Washington himself "directed his surveyor to violate the proclamation," dismissing it in his own words as "a temporary expedient to quiet the minds of the Indians," and candidly admitted he wanted "some 'good rich land' on the western frontier" (Williams 1990, 230). No "proclamation" by an English king was going to stand in the way of the American colonists' desire to expand their property holdings. After all, it was John Locke himself who had argued that the principal role of government is to *protect* private property. As Williams has argued, "The tyranny of a government devoted to destroying individual property, rather than rightfully preserving it, demanded the fiercest resistance" (Williams 1990, 228). Of course, other causes of the War of Independence include, for example, taxation without representation, but it must be remembered that the newly imposed taxes were required at least in part to support a British garrison needed to impose the provisions of the Royal Proclamation.

Williams, in *The American Indian in Western Legal Thought*, provides much more detailed arguments demonstrating the principal role of the Royal Proclamation in the alienation of the American colonies from the British Crown. We do not regard this conclusion as particularly controversial, and would refer anyone who does to William's book. We wish to turn now to the rather more controversial claim concerning the role of the Royal Proclamation in the founding of Canada. This claim can be found in John Ralston Saul's *A Fair Country: Telling Truths About Canada*. At least there he argues, "The Royal Proclamation and the Quebec Act represent the formal foundation of Canadian civilization" (Saul 2008, 118). He also describes the Royal Proclamation of 1763 along with the Quebec Act of 1774 as "the legal basis for Canadian civilization" (Saul 2008, 117–118). As we have shown in some detail above, the Royal Proclamation certainly acknowledges the precontact presence of Indians in North America and suggests ways of dealing with them. But Saul wants to argue much more than this. He claims the Royal Proclamation as one of the forgotten foundation documents of "Canadian civilization." We are, he argues, just now at the beginning of the 21st century, rediscovering that this proclamation together with the Quebec Act provided an otherwise British Canada with "a triangular foundation of Aboriginals, francophones and anglophones" (Saul 2008, 119). With pointed reference to the subtitle of his book, *Telling Truths About Canada*, Saul proclaims: "This foundation, the fundamental truth of Canada, formalized in the 1760s and 1770s, has now reasserted itself" (Saul 2008, 119). He claims to be revealing a deeply buried secret about Canada to the effect that aboriginal values have influenced policy to such an extent that, whether Canadians know it or not, Canada is in effect really a Métis country insofar as basic values and original mythologies are concerned.

Now, we are happy to argue in favor of Native American values such as the acceptance and indeed celebration of diversity, though not everyone agrees with us (Callicott 2000; 302). Saul wants to argue the even more controversial position, that the local officials of the time, both anglophone and francophone, responsible for the North American contribution to the wording of both the Royal Proclamation and the Quebec Act were influenced by such Native American values. We discuss this claim in the context of Native values in Chapter Four. Here we will illustrate just how controversial it is using the Quebec Act as an example. The act certainly seems to applaud diversity and respect for difference. Following its war with Britain, in the Treaty of Paris, France had ceded its North American holdings to Britain, out of which, by means of the Royal Proclamation, the British created the province of Quebec. The Quebec Act permits the French inhabitants of Quebec to maintain the French language, the Catholic faith and even French civil law. This was certainly unusual for that time and very different from the way Catholics were being treated in England, as we have illustrated above with the Glorious Revolution replacing the Catholic James II with William and Mary as Protestant monarchs. Saul admits that the provisions of the Quebec Act may have been a merely pragmatic decision rather than going to the expense of maintaining several garrisons to enforce British ways on a large francophone population so far from the mother land. But he still implies that the Native American respect for difference may have played a role. He states, "But these choices were not made anywhere else. And they weren't made in the twenty-first century. In the context of eighteenth-century statecraft and international politics, this was a revolutionary departure, far more revolutionary as a concept than that of setting up, a few years later, a European-style nation-state in the American colonies" (Saul 2008; 119).

As much as we want to argue that both Canada and the United States were influenced by Native American philosophy, we don't think that Saul sufficiently makes his case. Saul simply ignores a prominent Native voice on the Quebec Act. Robert Williams, the Lumbee legal philosopher we cited above, in his *The American Indian in Western Legal Thought,* observes that the Quebec Act expands the francophone Catholic Quebec with its French civil law into much of Indian territory once again hemming in the American colonies, this time between the newly expanded Quebec and the Eastern seacoast. Catholic Quebec with its French civil law now included much of the Indian territory between the Mississippi River and the thirteen colonies as far south as the Ohio River. This made a huge province of Quebec. It included that part of what is now Minnesota east of the Mississippi, and most of what is now Wisconsin, Ohio, Michigan, Indiana, Illinois and Ontario. Williams argues that the British ministry response to American colonists' continued violation of the Royal Proclamation was to put an even greater obstacle in their way. As Williams himself puts it, referring to the Indian territory in question as the "Northwest wilderness," "Resigned to the impossibility of enforcing the policy of a closed western frontier, the Ministry reluctantly decided to turn over control of the Northwest wilderness to the Canadians of Quebec ... recognizing that no Englishman would desire ever to come under the Catholic and alien-inspired government of a Canadian-controlled Northwest" (Williams 1990; 266). We see this observation by a Native American scholar as a more plausible explanation for the toleration shown by the Quebec Act of the French language and civil code as well as the Catholic religion than John Ralston Saul's hypothesis that the writers of the Royal Proclamation and the Quebec Act had somehow learned respect for difference from the American Indians. There is no doubt the Indians were seen as a problem. As Williams also observes, the Royal Proclamation was not intended to protect Indian rights. The provision that only the Crown in British colonies, and later only Congress in the U.S., could purchase Indian land was needed to resolve legal disputes between colonists themselves who had (often privately) purchased the same piece of land from the Indians (cf. Williams 1990: 308–17).

That the Indians were seen as a problem also comes out in the Canadian constitution, and in this sense we would agree with Saul that Canada is a result of both the Royal Proclamation and the Quebec Act. We should note at the outset that the constitution of Canada, like that of Britain, is not a single written document. The Royal Proclamation and the Quebec Act are both considered constitutional acts pertaining to Canada (*The Canadian Encyclopedia* 1, 406). Incidentally, this fact alone is all we really need to conclude, as we do above, that Canada is, at least in part, a consequence of the Royal Proclamation. Canada's primary constitutional document actually deals with the union or federation of the provinces of British North America. It is the British North America Act of 1867 passed by the House of Lords in England. It was renamed the Constitution Act, 1867, with the patriation of Canada's constitution in 1982 and is now officially subsumed, along with other statutes, by the Constitution Act, 1982. The preamble of the Constitution Act, 1867, makes it clear that the new dominion of Canada would be governed in a form similar to that of Great Britain. The parts of the province of Canada, which formerly constituted the provinces of Upper Canada and Lower Canada, were severed to form two separate provinces. Upper Canada became the province of Ontario and Lower Canada became the province of Quebec (a considerably smaller Quebec than that set out in the Quebec Act of 1774, though still maintaining similar rights for its majority francophone population[5]). The provinces of Nova Scotia and New Brunswick retained their former boundaries. The new provinces were divided into electoral districts, each sending representatives to serve in the House of Commons (MPs) and also in provincial assemblies (MPPs). Where the Constitution Act, 1867, is most notably like a single written constitution is in its detailed delineation of federal and provincial responsibilities. The powers or responsibilities of the federal government are spelled out in section ninety-one (s.91) of the Constitution Act, 1867, while provincial responsibilities are enumerated in s.92. Responsibility for the provision of education is delegated to the provinces under s.93. The federal government takes responsibility for "Indians and Land Reserved for Indians" under section 91, subsection 24. This, it should be noted, is very different from the American constitution in which, as we have seen above, Congress has the power "to regulate Commerce with foreign Nations, and among the several States, and with the Indian Tribes." To regulate commerce with the Indian tribes means in essence to purchase Indian land, though we would be the first to admit that subsequent acts of Congress and legal decisions of the courts permitted much more regulation of the lives of Indians by both Congress and even state and local governments. But this is not in the American constitution itself. The Canadian constitution, on the other hand, includes both Indian land ("Land Reserved for Indians") and the Indians themselves as federal responsibilities. Can we conclude from this that the framers of the Canadian constitution, "The Fathers of Confederation," also regarded Indians as problematic? Unfortunately, it is difficult to determine why Indians or anything else were specifically included in the constitution, or for that matter left out of it.

Peter W. Hogg in his book *Constitutional Law of Canada* raises the important question as to why an amending clause was omitted from the British North America Act of 1867. This is, after all, an act of the British parliament. If it is to function as the constitution of Canada, surely the Fathers of Confederation would have wanted to have the power to amend their own constitution rather than having to go back and ask the British parliament for amendments each and every time they thought one was required. Yet an amending formula was not included until 1982 with the patriation of the constitution. ("Patriation" is itself an odd word, distinctively Canadian, but the constitution could not be said to be "repatriated" as it was, and is, an act of the British, not the Canadian parliament). Did the Fathers of Confederation think that including an amending formula would sound to the British too much like a declaration of independence? We can never know. As Peter Hogg observes: "We do not have definitive information as to the reason for this omission, because on this point (as on many others) there is *no record* of any discussion at the conferences in Charlottetown, Quebec and London which preceeded the passage of the Act" (Hogg 1985, 3, emphasis added).

If our question about why Indians were made a federal responsibility in the Canadian constitution cannot be answered because there is "no record" of certain discussions in Charlottetown, Quebec and London, perhaps an answer can be found by looking at section 91, itself. Section 91 delineates the priorities of the new Dominion of Canada as seen by the "Fathers of Confederation." It appears that, to them, there were two major areas of responsibility which they felt must be retained in the hands of the federal government: economic enrichment and national concerns, threats or problems. First they made their plans for economic enrichment, which included borrowing money on the public credit; looking after their property and the public debt; raising money through taxation; regulating trade and commerce; operating a postal service and a militia; setting up military and naval defense; paying civil servants; installing beacons, buoys and lighthouses for navigation and shipping; maintaining maritime hospitals; regulating fisheries and ferries; issuing copyrights; and providing currency and coinage for the banking system (s. 91, subsections 2 through 23). They then looked towards their national concerns or potential problems. Heading the list of national concerns at section 91 (24) we find "Indians and Lands reserved for Indians." Since Indians and their lands lead the list of what can be characterized as the problematic issues which the newly formed government would have to deal with in order to protect its economic interests, we conclude that Indians and lands reserved for Indians seem to have been their primary national concern. This list of potential problems also includes "aliens" assumed to represent the illegal entry of persons into the country (s. 91 [25]), „marriage and divorce," (s. 91 [26]), and those identified as "criminals" as well as the long term housing of such persons in "penitentiaries" (s. 91 [27] & [28]).

We find it most interesting though somewhat disturbing that Indians and lands reserved for Indians heads this list.

Indian Treaties

One way in which the governments of Britain, Canada and the United States dealt with the "Indian problem" was through the treaty making process. John Ralston Saul, it seems, would have the treaty-making process as a further consequence of the Royal Proclamation, since he speaks of the Royal Proclamation of 1763 as "laying out the treaty rights of the First Nations" (Saul 2008, 116). Even though it is true that after 1763 Indian land could only be purchased by the government through a treaty set out or negotiated for that specific purpose, Saul's statement, as it stands, is misleading. Indians were well aware of a form of treaty making processes well before contact with Europeans, indeed as far back as c.1090–1142, according to some sources (cf. Johansen 1995, 62–63, Widdowson and Howard 2008, 124).

It is also necessary to point out the fact that the first treaties made between Indians and Europeans were not treaties dealing with land in particular. Instead they were treaties made to ensure enduring relationships over time and therefore resembled and were commonly referred to as treaties of friendship. An example of such a treaty is the Treaty of 1779 between the Mickmack Indians and Michael Franklin, the superintendent of Indian affairs in Nova Scotia.[6] It was designed to restore "Peace and Good Order in that Neighbourhood." As recorded in the treaty, in the months of May and July prior to its signing, a number of Indians, operating at the instigation of British deviants, attacked the stores of a John Cort and several other residents at "Mirimichy." In reprisal for this attack, Captain Augustus Hervey, commander of the British sloop *Niper*, captured sixteen Indians on the "Mirimichy River." One of the Indians was killed, three of them were released and twelve were transported to Quebec for trial.

In its wording, this treaty can be interpreted as something more than just an agreement between friends or an assurance of friendship. In some respects it was formulated on the basis of a binding contract. There is, for example, specific performance expected from the Indians by the British. In the context of English common law, in order for a contract to be valid it must contain the following elements: there must be an intention of both parties to enter into a contract which is either expressed or capable of being implied; there must be mutual agreement between the parties on the subject-matter of the contract; there must be some form of consideration given; there must be genuine consent by the parties; there must be a capacity for the parties to enter into the contract; and there must be legality of the object of the contract (cf. Waddams 1984).

In the Treaty of 1779 between the Mickmack Indians and the British Crown, six specific expectations were laid out by the British. First the British expected the Indians to "behave Quietly and Peaceably towards all his Majesty King George's good Subjects treating them upon every occasion in an honest friendly and Brotherly manner." Secondly, the British expected the Indians "at the Hazard of [their] Lives [to] defend and Protect to the utmost of [their] power, the Traders and Inhabitants and their Merchandize and Effects who are or may be settled on the Rivers Bays and Sea Coasts within the forementioned Districts against all the Enemys of his Majesty King George whether French, Rebells or Indians." Thirdly, the Indians were expected "whenever it shall be required [to] apprehend and deliver into the Hands of the said Mr. Franklin, to be dealt with according to his Deserts, any Indian or other person who shall attempt to Disturb the Peace and Tranquillity of the said District." The British, through this Treaty, then restricted the Indians from speaking to "John Allen, or any other Rebell or Enemy to King George." They also required the Indians to convince other Mickmack tribes in the province to enter into similar treaties and to "Renew, Ratify and Confirm all former Treatys, entered into by [the Indians]... with the late Governor Lawrence, and others His Majesty King George's Governors, who have succeeded him in the Command of this Province."

In exchange for meeting the six requirements of the treaty (which actually uses the legal contract language "In Consideration of..."), the Indians were allowed to remain in the districts mentioned in the treaty (where they were at the time) "Quiet and Free from molestation of any of His Majesty's Troops or other his good Subjects in their Hunting and Fishing." Secondly, immediate measures were to be taken by the British "to cause Traders to supply them [the Indians] with Ammunition, clothing and other necessary stores in exchange for their Furrs and other Commoditys."

The real beneficiaries of the Treaty of 1779 are obvious. Clearly, the specific performance requirements placed on the Indians were all to the benefit of the British. It was in the best interests of the British that the Indians behave; protect settlers; search out and deliver anyone, "Indian Rebell" or otherwise, who would disturb the peace, thus in effect siding with the British in the American war of Independence; talk other Indians into similar treaties; and renew and ratify former treaties. It was also in the best interests of the British that the Indians remain where they were. The Indians provided furs for the British to sell in the European market. In exchange the British did the Indians little favor by providing them the opportunity to purchase or trade for "ammunition, clothing and other necessary stores." Do East Coast states Indians today have a treaty right to engage in a commercial fishery, for example? Many non-native commercial fishermen do not think so and still literally run down the boats of their Native neighbors (cf. Rabb 2002). Yet this treaty, and others like it, does not restrict the Indians to subsistence hunting and fishing. In fact, it actively encourages them to exchange "their Furrs and other Commoditys" with British and other "Traders."

By the mid-1800s the purpose of treaties had begun to change. They needed to deal with the expansion of settlements and the ceding of Indian land in conformity with the Royal Proclamation. Treaties no longer merely reacted to disruptions, which might "Disturb the Peace and Tranquility of the said District." Treaties were no longer needed to keep the Indians on side in wars with other countries or, in the case of the British, with rebellious colonies, and so forth. The Robinson Superior Treaty is a good example of the renewed interest in settlement by the colonial government.

On September 7, 1850, at Sault Ste. Marie, Ontario, the Robinson Superior Treaty was signed between William Benjamin Robinson, on behalf of Her Majesty the Queen, and "the Ojibwa Indians inhabiting the Northern Shore of Lake Superior, in the said Province of Canada, from Batchewananng Bay to Pigeon River, at the western extremity of said lake, and inland throughout the extent to the height of land which separates the territory covered by the charter of the Honourable the Hudson's Bay Company from the said tract, and also the islands in the said lake within the boundaries of the British possessions therein."

Again the treaty provided for consideration to be given to the Indians. However, unlike the consideration given to the Mickmack in the Treaty of 1779, which allowed the Mickmack to remain where they had always been, do what they had always done, and provided them with "ammunition, clothing and other necessary stores," the Robinson Superior Treaty gave the Ojibwa "the sum of two thousand pounds of good and lawful money of Upper Canada, to them in hand paid, and for the further perpetual annuity of five hundred pounds, the same to be paid and delivered to the said Chiefs and their tribe at a convenient season of each summer, and not later than the first day of August at the Honourable the Hudson's Bay Company's Posts of Michipicoton and Fort William."

At first glance, it might appear that the Ojibwa were party to a good bargain. They received the sum of two thousand pounds and a perpetual annuity of five hundred pounds, now commonly referred to as "treaty money." However, the question must be asked: "What did they give up in exchange for this treaty money?" As spelled out in the treaty, the Ojibwa "freely, fully and voluntarily surrender, cede, grant and convey unto Her Majesty, Her heirs and successors forever, all their right, title and interest in the whole of the territory" mentioned in the treaty. In other words, the Ojibwa extinguished their aboriginal title and relieved the Crown of any encumbrance on fee simple legal title to the land. In particular, the Ojibwa exchanged "the Northern Shore of Lake Superior, in the said Province of Canada, from Batchewananng Bay to Pigeon River, at the western extremity of said lake, and inland throughout the exent to the height of land which separates the territory covered by the charter of the Honourable the Hudson's Bay Company from the said tract, and also the islands in the said lake within the boundaries of the British possessions therein," an area of over six hundred kilometers in length, stretching approximately from present-day Sault Ste. Marie, Ontario, in the east, past Thunder Bay, Ontario, in the west. They gave up all aboriginal rights to this land, except for the rights to hunt and fish on unoccupied Crown land, for a one-time-only payment of two thousand pounds and an annual payment of five hundred pounds per year to be shared equally on a per capita basis by all the Indians covered by the treaty area.

The areas of land the Ojibwa did not cede in the treaty were the reserved lands, which were, under the treaty, held in common "for the purposes of residence and cultivation." The treaty closely followed the wording of the Royal Proclamation of 1763 in stating that "should the said Chiefs and their respective tribes at any time desire to dispose of any mineral or other valuable productions upon the said reservations, the same will be at their request sold by order of the Superintendent-General of the Indian Department for the time being, for their sole use and benefit, and to the best advantage."

Again, similar to the Treaty of 1779, the Robinson Superior Treaty sets out specific requirements. But in this case, rather than expecting the Indians to "behave Quietly and Peaceably towards all his Majesty King George's good Subjects treating them upon every occasion in an honest friendly and Brotherly manner;" "to defend and Protect ... the Traders and Inhabitants and their Merchandize and Effects;" "to apprehend and deliver ... any Indian who shall attempt to Disturb the Peace; to not speak to "any ... Rebell or

Enemy" to the king; to solicit other Indians to sign a treaty; and to renew and ratify former treaties, the Robinson Superior Treaty promises, first, that Her Majesty and the government of the province of Canada will make the payments of two thousand pounds, and five hundred pounds annually; secondly, that the Ojibwa will have the privilege of hunting and fishing over the land except in areas that are leased or sold to individuals or companies; thirdly, that the Ojibwa will not sell any portion of their reservations without the consent of and through the superintendent-general of Indian Affairs; fourthly, that the Indians would not hinder or prevent persons from exploring for minerals in any part of the ceded territory; and lastly, that if the government had previously sold any mining locations or other property on areas designated to be reservations, then the money from the sale would be paid to the Indians.

The Robinson Superior Treaty also includes a clause which allows for an increase in the annuity should the ceded territory produce an amount of wealth which will allow the government to do so. But the annuity cannot be increased to more than one pound of provincial currency in any one year unless Her Majesty agrees to more. The annuity can also be decreased in proportion to the number of Indians alive at a given time who are entitled to receive the benefits of the Treaty. In Canada today aboriginal and treaty rights are now entrenched in the Constitution. Section 35, subsection one of the Constitution Act, 1982, reads: "The existing aboriginal and treaty rights of the aboriginal peoples of Canada are hereby recognized and affirmed." However, as we argued above these rights are generally undefined.

With the passing by the British parliament of the British North America Act (the Constitution Act), 1867, the treaty making process in Canada was given new momentum and a new significance. No longer were the treaties made just for peace and friendship as many of the earlier treaties had been. Following the intent of the pre–Confederation Robinson treaties, the post–Confederation numbered treaties became more specific in their demands upon the Indians. Treaty No. 9 is a good example of the post–Confederation treaties.

Treaty Nine was signed in 1905–1906 by Duncan Campbell Scott, Samuel Stewart and Daniel George MacMartin, commissioners of the government of Canada, on behalf of "His Most Gracious Majesty the King of Great Britain, Ireland and Canada," with the Ojibwa, Cree and other Indians inhabiting "that portion or tract of land lying and being in the Province of Ontario, bounded on the south by the height of land and northern boundaries of the territory ceded by the Robinson-Superior Treaty of 1850, and the Robinson-Huron Treaty of 1850, and bounded on the east and north by the boundaries of the said Province of Ontario as defined by law, and on the west by part of the eastern boundary of the territory ceded by Northwest Angle Treaty No. 3; the said land containing an area of ninety thousand square miles, more or less."

It is interesting to compare the wording of Treaty No. 9 with the wording of the Royal Proclamation. The Royal Proclamation declared: "*If at any time any of the said Indians should be inclined to dispose of the said Lands,* the same shall be Purchased only by Us, in our Name, at some public Meeting or Assembly of the said Indians, to be held for that Purpose by the Governor or Commander in Chief of our Colony respectively within which they shall lie" (emphasis added). Treaty No. 9, on the other hand, states: "Whereas, the said Indians have been notified and informed by His Majesty's said commission that *it is His desire* to open for settlement, immigration, trade, travel, mining, lumbering, and such other purposes as to His Majesty may seem meet, a tract of country, bounded and described hereinafter mentioned, and to obtain the consent thereto of His Indian subjects inhabiting the said tract, and to make a treaty and arrange with them, so that there may be peace and good-will between them and His Majesty's other subjects, and that His Indian people may know and be assured of what allowances they are to count upon and receive from His Majesty's bounty and benevolence" (emphasis added). From the wording of the treaty it would be safe to say that the agreement was entered into on the insistence of His Majesty, not in response to the wishes of the Indian people as stipulated in the Royal Proclamation.

A second factor is equally important in the indication that the "Ojibway, Cree and other Indians" inhabiting the said tract of land did not initiate the treaty. According to the treaty, the Indians were "requested by His Majesty's commissioners to name certain chiefs and headmen who should be authorized on their behalf to conduct such negotiations and sign any treaty to be found thereon, and to become responsible to His Majesty for the faithful performance by their respective bands of such obligations as shall be assumed by them." In other words His Majesty not only initiated the treaty process, whether the Indians were inclined to dispose of the said lands or not, but he also dictated to the Indians that they should appoint persons as chiefs and headmen to negotiate and sign the treaty on their behalf.

And what did the Indians get for signing the treaty? First, they each received "a present of eight dollars in cash" from His Majesty, through his commissioners, in exchange for extinguishing all of their past claims. Secondly, each Indian and his or her descendants received an annuity of four dollars per year in perpetuity treaty money. Coincidentally, the commissioners would not want the Indians with whom they were negotiating Treaty No. 9 to talk to the Indians who had agreed to the Northwest Angle Treaty, Treaty No. 3, because those Indians were receiving five dollars per year. The government was not prepared to pay this amount to the Indians in the Treaty No. 9 Area. Thirdly, each chief received a Canadian flag and a copy of the treaty. Lastly, His Majesty agreed to pay the salaries of teachers who would provide instruction for the Indian children. This was standard policy for Indian education based on the recommendations of an 1874 report following the ideas of Edgerton Ryerson. "The general recommendations of the report were that Indians remain under the control of the Crown rather than the provincial authority, that efforts to Christianize the Indians and settle them in communities be continued, and finally that schools, preferably manual labour ones, be established under the guidance of missionaries" (Haig-Brown 1988, 25). Again, as if as a carry over from the treaties of friendship of days long past, in Treaty No.9 the "Ojibway, Cree and other Indians" were required to swear allegiance to the king. In addition, they had to promise to obey the law, protect persons and property against "molestation," and assist officers of His Majesty in catching lawbreakers.

And what were the "Ojibway, Cree and other Indians" required to give up in order to receive the benefits promised in the treaty? In particular, as in the pre–Confederation Robinson treaties, the Indians were required to "cede, release, surrender and yield up to the Government of the Dominion of Canada, for His Majesty the King and His successors for ever all their rights, titles and privileges whatsoever, to the lands" covered by the treaty, an area of approximately ninety thousand square miles. In addition, the "Ojibway, Cree and other Indians" of the Treaty No. 9 Area were required to give up their rights, titles and privileges to all other lands wherever they might be located in the Dominion of Canada. The Indians were allowed to retain their right to continue their traditional practices of hunting, fishing and trapping for food in the ceded territory, subject only to whatever regulations may be made by the government and providing they did not practice these vocations on any lands which were being used for settlement, mining, lumbering, trading or any other purposes. One would wonder if anyone negotiating on behalf of the Crown ever explained to the Indians the expectations of how much land would be required for "settlement, mining, lumbering, trading or any other purposes" or what the regulations might be?

The Indians were also allowed to reserve land for themselves and their families to the extent of one square mile per family of five. Again, these lands, held in reserve for the Indians, are in fact held in trust by the Crown "for the benefit of the Indians free of all claims, liens or trusts by Ontario." This is one of very few treaties to include the Ontario government as a third party in the negotiations. As such, it is known as a tripartite agreement. We are tempted to ask if the provision in the treaty "for the benefit of the Indians free of all claims, liens or trusts by Ontario" was actually meant to be a *benefit* to the Indians? In actual fact it is not. It is really a benefit for the federal government, the Crown. If Ontario or anyone else were to place a claim, lien or trust against the lands held in reserve for the Indians, such claim, lien or trust would have to be placed against the federal government, not the Indians, because it is the federal government who claims to hold title to the lands held in reserve in trust.

His Majesty also reserved several rights unto himself. These include, first, the right to deal with trespassers on the lands reserved for Indians; second, the right to sell or dispose of the reserved land, with the consent of the Indians for their benefit; and third, the right to expropriate any of the reserved lands that may be required for public works, building railways or roads or whatsoever nature. Under the treaty, the Crown also forbade any attempt by the Indians to sell or otherwise alienate reserved land in any manner. "[T]he aforesaid reserves of land, or any interest therein, may be sold or otherwise disposed of by His Majesty's government for the use and benefit of the said Indians entitled thereto, with their consent first had and obtained; but in no wise shall the said Indians, or any of them, be entitled to sell or otherwise alienate any of the lands allotted to them as reserves."

In summation, under Treaty No. 9, the James Bay Treaty, "the Ojibway, Cree and other Indians" gave up or extinguished their aboriginal title to land extending from the Ontario/Quebec boundary in the east to the boundary of Treaty No. 3 in the west, and from the height of land in the south to Hudson Bay in the north, in all some ninety thousand square miles in northern Ontario. In exchange, they received a present of eight dollars each in cash and four dollars per year forever as well as reserved land of one square mile of land per family of five. They also retained the right to hunt, fish, and trap on lands not being used for other purposes or otherwise regulated. They gained schools, and Christian schoolteachers to teach their children, and each chief was given a Canadian flag and a copy of the treaty. This in the twentieth century, in 1906! It is interesting, indeed sobering, to note by way of comparison that in Tahiti of the early 1800s, almost 100 years before, local chieftains "would be baptized, crowned king, presented with a portrait of Queen Victoria, introduced to the bottle, and left to the work of conversion" (Lewis 1988, 13).

It is possible to gain a further insight into the real intent of the treaty making process by looking at the account published by one of the principal negotiators for the Crown, one Alexander Morris, in his 1880 book *The Treaties of Canada with the Indians of Manitoba and the North West Territories Including the Negotiations on Which They Were Based.* In comparing the policy of Indian reserves in Canada with that in the United States, Morris quite candidly states, "I regard the Canadian system of allotting reserves to one or more bands together, in the [widely scattered] localities in which they have had the habit of living, as far preferable to the American system of placing whole tribes in large reserves ... the breaking up of which, has so often led to Indian wars" (Morris 2000, 288). There can be no doubt that the Indians were feared. Even their "wandering mode of life" was seen as "a difficulty which the assignment of reserves was calculated to obviate" (Morris 2000, 288). In Canada, at least, the reserves were set up to diminish the strength of the Indians in the "remote contingency" of Indian uprisings. Morris actually says that: "The Canadian system of band reserves has a tendency to diminish the offensive strength of the Indian tribes, should they ever become restless" (Morris 2000, 288). When we first read this statement we could hardly believe that someone would actually use an expression so close to "the natives are restless" stereotype. According to Morris, the Indian reserves together with their chiefs and band councils were set up explicitly to control the Indians. Insofar as Indian Chiefs are concerned, Morris describes "how much advantage it is to the Crown to possess so large a number of Indian officials, duly recognized as such, and who can be inspired with a proper sense of their responsibility to the Government" (Morris 2000, 287). For Morris, both Indian chiefs and band councilors "are officers of the Crown, and ... it is their duty to see that the Indians of their tribes obey the provisions of the treaties" (Morris 2000, 286). He explains that that is why they are paid by the government. They become in effect government employees through "payment of an annual salary of twenty-five dollars to each Chief, and of fifteen dollars to each Councillor, or head man, of a Chief (thus making them, in a sense, officers of the Crown)" (Morris 2000, 286). Morris records explaining to the chiefs why they receive "suits of official clothing" under the provisions of the treaty: "I wear a uniform because I am an officer of the Queen, the officers of the police wear uniforms as servants of the Queen. So we give to the Chiefs and Councillors good and suitable uniforms indicating their office, to wear on these and other great days" (207). In other words they too become servants of the Crown. "The Chiefs ought to be respected, they ought to be looked up to by their people.... The Chiefs and head men are not to be lightly put aside. When a treaty is made they become servants of the Queen; they are to try to keep order amongst their people" (Morris 2000, 206).

The purpose of Indian treaties and the reserve system, besides dealing with the encumbrance of aboriginal title, was not only to control the Indians, but to get the Indians to control themselves. This kind of self-control was far from anything like self-government. In his book *Tortured People: The Politics of Colonization,* Métis philosopher and historian Howard Adams calls it "neocolonialism." He argues that it "involves giving some benefits of the dominant society to a small privileged minority of Aboriginals in return for their help in pacifying the majority" (Adams 1999, 54). In fact he defines "neocolonialism" as "the use of Natives to control their own people" (Adams 1999, 56). He makes it quite clear that "neocolonialism involves the use of Métis and Indian elite to control other Aboriginal Peoples" (Adams 1999, 54).

One of the most honest statements of both Canadian and American Native policy can be found in the Reverend George M. Grant's account of the Sanford Fleming expedition across Canada in 1872. Entitled *Ocean to Ocean*, it was first published in 1873. In it Grant speculates that there are three possible ways of dealing with the Indians. The first is "to hunt and shoot down all the Indians" (Grant 2000, 94). This he rejects as unchristian. "With regard to this policy of 'no nonsense,' thorough-going as selfishness itself, it is enough to say that no Christian nation would now tolerate it for an instant" (94). We draw attention to the word "now," no Christian nation would *now* tolerate it. The second way of dealing with the Indians according to Grant is to ignore them and "leave the struggle between the two races entirely to the principle of natural selection, and let the weaker go the wall. This course [he says] has been practically followed in many parts of America" (94). This he rejects because of the frightful atrocities to which it has led, some of which he details: "The Indians had no newspapers to tell how miners tried their rifles on an unoffending Indian at a distance, for the pleasure of seeing the poor wretch jump when the bullet struck him; or how, if a band had fine horses, a charge was trumped up against them, that the band might be broken up and the horses stolen; or how the innocent were indiscriminately slaughtered with the guilty; or how they were poisoned by traders with bad rum, and cheated till left without gun, horse or blanket"

(95). In fact he argues that "this policy of giving to the simple children of the forest and prairie, the blessings of unlimited free-trade, and bidding them look after their own interests, has not been a success. The frightful cruelties connected with it and the expense it has entailed, have forced many to question whether the 'fire and sword' plan would not have been 'cheaper and, perhaps, more humane'" (95). The third policy is that of paternalism. In Grant's words: "The third way ... the paternal, is to go down to the Indian level when dealing with them; go at least half-way down; explain that, whether they wish it or not, immigrants will come into the country, and that the Government is bound to seek the good of all races under its sway, and do justly by the white as well as by the red man; offer to make a treaty with them on the principles of allotting to them reserves of land that no one can invade, and that they themselves cannot alienate, giving them an annual sum per family ... establishing schools among them and encouraging missionary effort, and prohibiting the sale of intoxicating liquors to them" (95). This procedure, including the attempt to civilize the Indian through "missionary effort" and schooling, Grant notes, "has been the policy of the old Canadas and of the Dominion, and it is now universally adopted in America." He does admit that "the agents of the United States Government have often defeated its attempt to do justice and show mercy, by wholesale frauds; and the Indians, believing themselves deceived, have risen with bursts of fury to take vengeance" (95). He describes Canadian policy as really in effect attempting to civilize the Indian off the land, and though the Indian in the United States has experienced more violence, in the use of fire and sword, there is not, in actual fact, much to choose between the policies of the two nations. "In the United States they have, as a rule, dealt with him more summarily than in British America, but it comes to pretty much the same in the end, whether he is 'improved off,' or shot down at once as a nuisance" (34).

The Indian Act

The Indian Act was introduced into the House of Commons, on March 2, 1876, "to consolidate the several laws relating to Indians now on the statute books of the Dominion and the old Provinces of Upper and Lower Canada" (*Debates of the House of Commons* 1876, 342). One such piece of colonial legislation was entitled "An Act to encourage the gradual Civilization of the Indian Tribes in this Province, and to amend the Laws respecting

Indians" (1857). The object of this legislation was "to encourage the progress of Civilization among the Indian tribes ... and the gradual removal of all legal distinctions between them and Her Majesty's other Canadian Subjects, and to facilitate the acquisition of property and the rights accompanying it, by such Individual Members of the said tribes as shall be found to desire such encouragement and to have deserved it" (Issac 1993, 52). According to this act, only male Indians were deemed capable of being civilized. Males became civilized when the missionary to a tribe convinced the governor in writing that a particular male Indian over the age of twenty-one years was able to speak, read and write English or French, had received elementary education, was of good moral character and was free of debt (Issac 1993, 52–53). With the approval of the governor, the male Indian would be enfranchised. Upon enfranchisement he was to receive the civil liberties and legal rights enjoyed by other Canadian subjects of Her Majesty, the right to allotment of a parcel of land, for instance. The parcel of land allocated was carved out of the land previously reserved for the Indians. Enfranchisement was also applicable to female Indians except they did not receive the same benefit of civil liberties and legal rights as males would upon their enfranchisement. This difference was not because they were Indians, but because they were women. By law, civil liberties and legal rights are benefits only enjoyable by persons, and it must be kept in mind that women in Canada were excluded from the class of persons until well into the twentieth century (1929).

In 1868 the government of Canada created the Department of the Secretary of State. The same piece of legislation also created the superintendent general of Indian Affairs who was given responsibility for the control and management of the lands and property of the Indians in Canada (Venne 1981, 1). Section 15 of the Indian Act delineated who were to be considered as Indians entitled to "hold, use, or enjoy the lands and other immovable property belonging to or appropriated to the use of the various tribes, band or bodies of Indians in Canada" (Venne 1981, 3). With some minor modification of the criteria specified in colonial times the Indian Act continued to define who would be a status Indian:

> *Firstly.* All persons of Indian blood reputed to belong to the particular tribe, band or body of Indians interested in such lands or immovable property and their descendants;
>
> *Secondly.* All persons residing among such Indians, whose parents were or are, either of them was or is, descended on either side from Indians or an Indian reputed to belong to the particular tribe, band or body of Indians interested in

> such lands or immovable property, and the descendants of all such persons; And
>
> *Thirdly*. All women lawfully married to any of the persons included in the general case hereinbefore designated; the children issue of such marriages and their descendants (Venne 1981, 3).

In introducing his bill in the House of Commons in 1876, the Honorable Mr. Laird stated that the goal to be achieved through application of the enfranchisement section of the Indian Act was that "in every respect an Indian would cease to be an Indian according the acceptation of the laws of Canada relating to Indians" (*Debates of the House of Commons* 1876, 343). He felt that this new act would give the Indians "some motive to be industrious and sober, and educate their children" (*Debates of the House of Commons* 1876, 751). Other members of the House felt that the act could only be applied to the most advanced Indians. Therefore, as the Honorable Mr. Fleming recognized, the House needed to make a choice in the policy to be followed in dealing with Indians; either the Indians could be preserved as earlier legislation had attempted to do, or Indians could be absorbed and amalgamated into mainstream society (*Debates of the House of Commons* 1876, 753). But both of these policies presented difficult choices if they were to be applied to Indians who were semi-civilized (*Debates of the House of Commons* 1876, 932). In the final analysis, Indians must either be treated as minors (wards of the state) or as white men. If they should be found intelligent enough to exercise the rights of white men they could become enfranchised (*Debates of the House of Commons* 1876, 933).

The Indian Act resulting from discussions in the House of Commons in 1876 has remained fairly consistent in most respects since that time, but some major revisions have been made. For example, in 1951 the government introduced what became known as the double mother clause, a section of the act which was meant to hasten the enfranchisement process. In effect this clause changed the line of Indian descent from bloodline to male parent. Consequently, it became mandatory for children whose mother and grandmother had gained status through marriage to be enfranchised when they reached twenty-one years of age.

The latest major revisions to the Indian Act occurred in 1985. At that time the enfranchisement process was repealed from the act. Former Indians who had previously been enfranchised were allowed to be reinstated. As of April 17, 1985, persons can become Indians under the Indian Act if they are entitled to be registered. Access to registration is prescribed under section 6 of the act. Basic requirements are that "at least one of the biological parents of a person to be registered, are or were registered or entitled to be registered, or that person is a member of a body of persons that has been declared by the Governor in Council on or after April 17, 1985, to be a band for the purposes of this *Act*." Unfortunately, once a person becomes an Indian they no longer have the same civil liberties or legal rights as ordinary citizens. For example, although a status Indian can make a will, it has to be in writing and is of no legal force or effect until it is either approved by the minister of Indian and Northern Affairs Canada or is probated in a court of law.

Ironically, the wording used in the Indian Act in 1985 is inversely comparable in its meaning and substantive content to the wording used in the House of Commons in 1876. At that time "they had the power to make an Indian a white man, [but] they had no power to make him an Indian again" (*Debates of the House of Commons* 1876, 750). Today, the reverse is true. As a result of changes to the Indian Act in 1985, the minister of Indian and Northern Affairs Canada has the power to make enfranchised Indians into Indians again, but the minister no longer has the power under the act to enfranchise Indians — that is, to turn the Indians into "white men."

Implicit in the language used to describe Indians and their relation to the land in the Royal Proclamation, the various treaties discussed, and the Indian Act are outside view predicates in the sense defined at the beginning of this chapter. Such outside view predicates prevented the British and the Americans from seeing Native American Indians for who they really were, and ultimately caused the Indians, themselves, to lose sight of who they really were. In the following chapters, we attempt to go beyond these outside view predicates and ask what is it to be a Native American Indian, to be a person truly indigenous to the Americas.

THREE

Dancing with Chaos

Phenomenology of the Vision Quest

In this chapter we present a phenomenological analysis of the vision quest. Phenomenological analysis is a product of two of the philosophical traditions we are using in this study, the British tradition of conceptual analysis, and the tradition of existential phenomenology. Phenomenological analysis consists of phenomenological description and conceptual analysis (cf. Cowley 1968, ix, and Rabb 1985, 26).

It is important to understand at the outset the important notion of phenomenological description. In phenomenological description all preconceptions must be set aside so that our conscious experience can be apprehended with an open mind and described as such, rather than interpreted according to commonly accepted scientific (sociological or psychological) dogmas. We can and do become reflexively aware of such common experiences, such phenomena, as seeing, hearing, tasting, smelling, dreaming and hallucinating. Phenomenological description permits us to describe this experience in a neutral way, without interpreting it as, say, an hallucination. In phenomenological description we don't ask, "Is this a case of really seeing and hearing something or is it simply a dream or hallucination?" In the case of the vision quest, phenomenological description allows us to discuss it without dismissing such experience as mere dream or hallucination, as many non–Natives might be tempted to do. At the same time we are not required to admit that such experience is actually a glimpse into the spirit world, whatever that would mean. Note that many Native Americans believe that dreaming itself is a glimpse into the spirit world.

This is why it is so important not to classify experience according to preconceived categories. Everyone will agree that we learn much from experience. However, different people have different preconceived ideas about which kinds of experience are of importance. Generally speaking, Native people have a much broader concept of experience than that prescribed by Western scientific thinking. Hence, while scientific thought might dismiss some experience as "merely a dream," Native American Indian thought might see in that same experience something of great significance. The phenomenological method allows us, to some extent, to sidestep this debate and try to get at the experience itself.

We are fortunate to have a first-person description of the vision quest given by architect Douglas Cardinal, a contemporary Blackfoot Métis who is equally at home in the world of twenty-first century scientific technology and the world of traditional Native American ways. He is well known as an architect for, among many other things, his design of the National Museum of the American Indian for the Smithsonian Institution, Washington, D.C., and for the Canadian Museum of Civilization in Gatineau, Quebec, overlooking the Ottawa River and the Canadian Parliament Buildings in Ottawa, Ontario. Cardinal's description of the vision quest is contained in a long interview he gave to the magazine *Intervox* in 1989. We include the entire interview at the end of this chapter. In order to facilitate discussion we have numbered the questions and responses in the interview (Q1 refers to question one, R1 refers to response one and so forth). In the first three responses Cardinal is describing the experience of the sweatlodge.

Since the particular vision quest Cardinal describes begins with "a sweat" it is important to understand what is involved. It should be noted, however, that the sweatlodge is not an essential part of the vision quest. We have interviewed elders who describe the vision quest as involving several days of fasting in solitude but do not begin and end in the sweatlodge. "Fasting is where you go through four rounds [of the sweatlodge]" (R8). "You don't have anything to drink, you're just as dry as a bone when you walk out of there. You feel like you can spit dust. Then you go out into nature in a smaller lodge so you can just sit out there facing west, the setting sun. You stay out there for four days and four nights without water or food. On the fifth morning, after the second round, you get your first sip of water" (R9). It is during these four days and four nights that the vision quest is completed. Now, of course, the skeptic is bound to say that four days and four nights without food and water after completely dehydrating yourself in the sweatlodge is more than likely to produce hallucinations. We insist, however, that the experience Cardinal describes is far too significant to be dismissed on the basis of such narrow preconceived categories. Cardinal himself does describe part of his experience as hallucinatory. "The nights were rough. All the sounds at night made you hallucinate. You had all these demons you had to deal with that were just part of your imagination. You couldn't deviate for one second from holding the sacred pipe and always asking for strength. If you let yourself go and let your mind go, you'd be confronted with some nightmare monster in your head. Every second you'd have to hold on to your spirit to carry you through" (R8). It is important to realize that he is distinguishing these hallucinations, these nightmare monsters of his own imagination, not from the more mundane waking reality of everyday life, but rather from what he calls more "magical experiences" within the vision quest itself. "When I was out there I had these moccasins with butterflies made from beadwork on them. I remember seeing butterflies and saying to them, 'I'm lonely, why don't you come over here?' And they did. They came over and lit on my moccasins. I asked them to light on my hand, and they did; they lit on my hand. I was amazed, I was shocked. I looked up and said, 'Nothing will hurt you if you're with me, I'll protect you.' So each night before the elder closed my lodge and tied me in, these butterflies would come in and sit right above my head upside down in the lodge. All those magical experiences that don't make any sense" (R8). One could ask if there really were butterflies on the ceiling of Cardinal's lodge each night. Did they really light on his moccasins? on his hand? Or was he simply hallucinating while staring at the beadwork on his moccasins?

To ask these kinds of questions, however, is to miss the point. In one sense it really doesn't matter whether or not he was, in a technical sense, hallucinating. What is important is what you learn from such an experience, what you take away with you. "On the second day, like the elders say, you have to 'come in power.' If you set yourself in power with every living thing, then you can see — really *see* and communicate with every living thing. So then you start having these magical experiences" (R8). It is this insight, of feeling at one with everything, which is important. It comes up again and again in Cardinal's account. "The third day was like losing consciousness. The elders say, 'You ask all the living beings for strength because they are at one with their creator and you are part of creation'" (R8). At the end of the fourth day: "It seemed like I was a part of everything, and I felt very, very powerful. I just wasn't there" (R8). This holistic insight should be compared, or rather contrasted, with his experience after only one day and night of fasting: "After 24 hours you get bored of listening to yourself complain.

So you start looking outside yourself and you start seeing a whole myriad of life around you. The animals, insects, grass, the trees, the wind and the sky, sun, the stars. There's lots of stuff around you. It's a whole different universe. You feel that you've probably separated yourself from it. You feel almost like an alien being sitting on this earth. You have to then come to terms because you're sitting there and these creatures are really bothering you" (R8). At this earlier time, he is just beginning to recognize the enormous gap he has allowed to develop between himself and the rest of the universe. The whole of the vision quest is the progressive closing of this gap. In the end there is no distinction between himself and the universe. That is the significance of his mysterious claim cited above: "I just wasn't there."

Western Analogies

Because we have found that many non–Natives tend to dismiss the sort of experience Cardinal describes as nothing but unimportant dreams or hallucinations, in the course of our discussion we compare Cardinal's vision quest to two other kinds of experience more familiar to Western philosophy, the concept of cosmic consciousness and the near death experience. We make these comparisons not to subsume the vision quest under these preconceived categories. That would be equally misleading. It is important to keep the phenomenological method in mind. We do not wish to categorize the experience in any way at all at this time. Rather, we make these comparisons with Western concepts as a way to help the unsympathetic or skeptical reader conceive of the vision quest as something other than mere hallucination, as something to be taken seriously, as an experience from which knowledge can be derived. It is the experience itself on which we wish to focus. In other words we are attempting to help the skeptical reader follow the phenomenological method. Phenomenological description is really what we are after here.

Though some have found this kind of comparison to Western experience helpful, others, usually with Native backgrounds, argue that it is misleading. For example, University of New Mexico philosopher Fred Sturm, one of the very few Western-trained philosophers to have gained some real understandings of Native American philosophy, has taken us to task for our treatment of Cardinal's experience: "Before we read the experience's description it is suggested that it will be more meaningful if we bear in mind two concepts which have arisen in Western philosophy and scientific thought, viz, 'cosmic consciousness' and 'near death' or 'out-of-body' experience. We are warned 'not to subsume the vision quest under these preconceived categories.' However, the first part of the chapter is devoted to writings by Henry David Thoreau, John Muir, G. W. F. Hegel, Richard Bucke, Walt Whitman, and Raymond Moody. Like it or not, our reading of Cardinal's description begins with two Western concepts in mind as tools for interpretation!" (Sturm 1996, 139–140). As we have admitted elsewhere, "We certainly respect Sturm's criticism and in fact largely agree with him" (McPherson and Rabb 2003). We do, however, suggest that in cross-cultural studies of this sort, tools of interpretation are hard to come by. As we argue in Chapter Seven, a great deal more community-based research needs to be done before such cross-cultural studies are really feasible. We offer the following then, not so much as tools of interpretation, but as helpful assistants for skeptics who would not only interpret the phenomenological description of the vision quest, but interpret it negatively and dismiss the whole thing out of hand as some kind of illusory experience. Readers who, like Sturm, find that our attempts to be helpful here just get in the way should skip to the next section, the interview with Douglas Cardinal, which we take as a phenomenological description of the vision quest.

Insofar as Western interpretations of the vision quest are concerned we have found helpful Catherine L. Albanese's book *Nature Religion in America: From the Algonkian Indians to the New Age.* The feeling of being at one with the universe, which as we have seen above Cardinal alludes to, is not unlike a recurring concept in Western philosophy which has been called "cosmic consciousness." Albanese cites the American nature poet Henry David Thoreau who tries to capture it in expressing the ecstatic desire: "I to be nature looking into nature" (Albanese 1999, 99). John Muir, the wilderness preservationist, in his own fit of ecstasy, uses the following words in an attempt to capture this heightened state of consciousness: "I'm in the woods, woods, woods, & they are in me-ee-ee" (Albanese 1999, 99). In *The Phenomenology of Mind,* the nineteenth-century idealist G. W. F. Hegel takes a much more rational approach to this experience, tracing in detail the development of consciousness from simple sense perception through self-consciousness to consciousness of what he calls "The Absolute."

Less well known, perhaps, the early Canadian philosopher Richard Maurice Bucke (1837–1902) in his book *Cosmic Consciousness: A Study in the Evolution of the Human Mind* gives a detailed account of cosmic consciousness which strikes us as rather more similar to Cardinal's description of the vision quest. Bucke describes this cosmic consciousness as "a consciousness of the cosmos, that is of the life and order of the universe" (Bucke 1977, 2). Bucke claims that it is a higher form of consciousness which only a relatively few gifted individuals have achieved. He lists Buddha, Jesus, St. Paul, Plotinus, Dante, Blake, Balzac and the American poet Walt Whitman, among others. Bucke argues that this unique type of consciousness is "a third form which is as far above Self Consciousness as is that above Simple Consciousness" (Bucke 1977, 2). By simple consciousness he means the consciousness of objects in our environment and of our own limbs, and so on, the kind of consciousness possessed by most animals including humans. Self consciousness, on the other hand, is said to be possessed only by humans. It consists of a kind of consciousness of being conscious. It is because we are self conscious that we can become aware of and describe our own mental or conscious states. It is therefore that which makes possible the very kind of phenomenological description we are doing in this study. It is also because we have self consciousness, consciousness of *self,* that we create the gap between ourselves as humans and the rest of the universe, the gap which Cardinal sees and overcomes in his vision quest. As Bucke puts it: "By virtue of this faculty [self consciousness] man is not only conscious of trees, rocks, waters, his own limbs and body, but he becomes conscious of himself as a distinct entity apart from all the rest of the universe" (Bucke 1977, 1). It is important to note that at this level of consciousness, although we are aware of objects in our environment as *distinct* from us, the same is not true of our consciousness of self. When we become aware of our own consciousness this consciousness is not grasped as a distinct object. The consciousness and its object (consciousness) are one and the same thing. That is why it is called self consciousness. Consciousness reflects, literally turns back, upon itself. As the French phenomenologist Jean-Paul Sartre puts this important, often overlooked, point: "It is agreed then that reflection must be united to that which is reflected on by a bond of being, that is the reflective consciousness must be the consciousness reflected-on" (Sartre 1971, 213). It is essential to understand this point because at the level of cosmic consciousness the same kind of unity occurs, but between consciousness and the rest of the universe, the cosmos. As Bucke puts it, trying to describe, in the third person, the intellectual illumination of a cosmic consciousness: "Like a flash there is presented to his consciousness a clear conception (a vision) in outline of the meaning and drift of the universe. ... Especially does he obtain such a conception of THE WHOLE, or at least of an immense WHOLE, as dwarfs all conception, imagination or speculation, springing from and belonging to ordinary self consciousness, such a conception as makes the old attempts to mentally grasp the universe and its meaning petty and even ridiculous" (Bucke 1977, 61).

We suggest that there is more than a superficial resemblance between Bucke's description of cosmic consciousness and Cardinal's description of the vision quest. We are fortunate to have Bucke's detailed description of cosmic consciousness. He was a medical doctor, head of the psychiatric hospital in London, Ontario, in fact.[1] He used his medical training to give what amounts to a detailed "diagnosis" of cosmic consciousness. Insofar as the phenomenon itself is concerned, it is possible to find exact parallels between Bucke's account of cosmic consciousness and Cardinal's description of the vision quest. Bucke even allowed for cultural differences in the description of the experience. For example he says that Gautama (the Buddha) or one of his followers "called it 'Nirvana' because of the 'extinction' of certain lower mental faculties (such as the sense of sin, fear of death, desire of wealth, etc., etc.) which is directly incident upon its birth" (Bucke 1977, 51). Walt Whitman on the other hand "called cosmic consciousness 'My Soul,' but spoke of it as if it were another person" (Bucke 1977, 52).

Of course we would not expect Cardinal to use such terms as "Nirvana." However, his experience does have a profound effect on his life. Certainly the fear of death is gone. In response to the question "And what kind of difference does having an experience like that make in your life?" (Q10, below), Cardinal replies, "Well, you sort of look at things, like they say, from the other side. You know what you're going to have to face when you die. It's a question of whether you're going to be stupid in running your life. You have to think of things from the other side" (R10). At the conclusion of Cardinal's vision quest, the elder who guided him through it asks, "Are you afraid of death?" Cardinal replies, "No. I'm just afraid I ain't gonna live right." At this point the elder declares, "Then you're a fearless warrior" (R9).

Though Cardinal does not use Whitman's notion of a soul or the person within, it is interesting to note in passing that this notion does appear in other descriptions of the vision quest. For example, in *Lame Deer, Seeker of Visions,* Lame Deer, in recalling his first vision quest, says: "We Sioux believe that there is something within us that controls us, something like a second person almost. We call it *nagi,* what other people might call soul, spirit or essence. One can't see it feel it or taste it, but that time on the hill — and only that once — I knew it was there inside me. Then I felt the power surge through like a flood" (Lame Deer and Erdoes 1972, 6). Certainly Cardinal's description of the vision quest contains the loss of the fear of death, the sense of immortality, the moral elevation, and perhaps also the loss of the sense of sin if he ever had it. These are four "marks of the comic sense" as Bucke calls them. We have not yet mentioned the first of these marks or criteria. According to Bucke: "The person suddenly, without warning, has a sense of being immersed in a flame, or rose-colored cloud, or perhaps rather a sense that the mind is itself filled with such a cloud or haze" (Bucke 1977, 60). There is certainly a close parallel to this experience in Cardinal: "All of a sudden there was a light around me and I just started pulling out of my body. I looked back and could see myself sitting there like a shell. I was terrified. Terrified because I thought, 'I'm just thinking this, but no I'm not. I'm not thinking this. This hallucination is real. Here I am and here my body is, being surrounded by light.' It was painful" (R8). Of course it is important to read Cardinal's account of his vision quest within the context of the full interview. We have not even attempted to prove that the vision quest is a quest for cosmic consciousness. To do that we would have to compare many other accounts of the vision quest both with Cardinal's and with Bucke's notion of cosmic consciousness. Such a project lies far beyond the scope of this study. We think that the suggestion is an interesting and intriguing one. To test its plausibility we would also have to examine the full set of criteria Bucke uses to establish a case of cosmic consciousness. These are, in the order in which he gave them: "(A) The subjective light; (B) The moral elevation; (C) The intellectual illumination; (D) The sense of immortality; (E) The loss of fear of death; (F) The loss of the sense of sin; (G) The sudden instantaneousness of the awakening; (H) The previous character of the man — intellectual, moral and physical; (I) The age of illumination; (J) The added charm to the personality, so that men and women are always [?] strongly attracted to the person; (K) The transfiguration of the subject of the change as seen by others when the cosmic is actually present" (Bucke 1977, 61–62).

We have not dealt with criteria "H" through "K" since these do not really say anything about the conscious experience itself, the phenomenon. Bucke thinks, for example, that the usual subject is mature, between 35 and 45 years of age (criterion "I"). This does not fit with the Native experience of vision quests. They often occur at a much younger age. Lame Deer was sixteen when he had his first visions, Black Elk only nine years of age (cf. Lame Deer and Erdoes 1972, 1; Neihardt 1979, 20). Discrepancies of this sort, we submit, do not count against our hypothesis. On the contrary, we think they support it. As we noted above, Bucke believed that at the present stage in the evolution of the human race only a very few exceptional individuals could be expected to achieve cosmic consciousness. However, he also argued that "just as, long ago, self consciousness appeared in the best specimens of our ancestral race in the prime of life, and gradually became more and more universal and appeared in the individual at an earlier age ... so will Cosmic Consciousness become more and more universal and appear earlier in the individual life until the race at large will possess this faculty" (317–318). There can be no doubt that Bucke thought that cosmic consciousness was the next step in human evolution, and that we will be transformed by it. He concludes that "a Cosmic Consciousness race will not be the race which exists today, any more than the present race ... is the same race which existed prior to the evolution of self consciousness.... This new race is in the act of being born from us, and in the near future it will occupy and possess the earth" (318). In the Cardinal interview there is recalled the following conversation which Cardinal had with the Elder who guided him through the fast. "I told him of the experiences and asked him what he experienced on his first fast. He said, 'Oh, I experienced the same thing.' I said, 'Why didn't you tell me?' 'Then you wouldn't have done it. By telling you, I would have robbed you of the opportunity of learning that experience for yourself. It's yours,' he said." Cardinal concludes: "So, that's part of their culture, it's probably been done for thousands of years" (R9). Cardinal also notes, with some considerable anger, that "Imperialists that feared the Indian way of thinking did everything possible to destroy it" (R24). He goes on to remark, "Indian people are the spiritual people," and most revealing, "The Indian nations didn't know why a lesser being was destroying them" (R25). Yes, we are suggesting that it is just possible that here in the Americas, with centuries of isolation from the rest of the world, the "Indian nations" may well have taken a different path and in some respects developed far beyond Europeans. As Bucke might well put it, cosmic consciousness is as far beyond self consciousness as self consciousness is beyond the simple consciousness, of what are often called the "lower" animals.

We said above that we would compare the vision quest to *two* concepts more familiar to Western philosophy: cosmic consciousness *and* the near death experience. The concept of the near death experience first became widely known in the mid-1970s with the publication of two books by philosopher/psychiatrist Raymond A. Moody, *Life After Life* (1976) and *Reflections on Life After Life* (1978).

What Moody has shown first of all is that near death experiences are far more common than anyone ever thought they were. However what is even more astounding is that the majority of the reports are in actual fact strikingly similar. As Moody himself puts it, "What has amazed me ... are the great similarities in the reports, despite the fact that they come from people of highly varied religious, social and educational backgrounds" (Moody 1976, 15). In fact, the various reports are so similar, and contain so many common elements, that Moody has been able to construct what he calls a "theoretically 'ideal' or 'complete' experience." It must be remembered that no actual near death experience contains all the elements found in Moody's ideal model. Yet the majority of the reports he has collected mention many of them.

This model has become so widely accepted by those doing research in the area that it is now referred to simply as NDE (near death experience) or OBE (out of body experience, not Order of the British Empire). It consists of the following: A person is dying and in fact hears his doctor pronounce him dead. At the time he also begins to hear an uncomfortable ringing or buzzing noise and see a long dark tunnel through which he suddenly feels himself moving at great speed. He then has the odd experience of being, as it were, outside his own physical body, looking down on it and on those attempting to resuscitate it. As the emotional upheaval caused by this experience begins to subside he begins to realize that he still has a strange kind of body. He can reach out and try to touch those attempting to revive him, though they take no notice. He can move about the room, as if floating, and look at it from different points of view, usually from above. After a short time his attention is diverted from the room. Predeceased friends and relatives seem to come to meet him. They guide him wordlessly to "a being of light," a spiritual entity of a kind he has never before experienced. This being seems to cause him to see his entire life flash through his mind and to request him to evaluate this life. He encounters a point of no return, a border beyond which he is by now most anxious to go. Yet something calls him back and he finds himself reunited with his physical body (cf. Moody 1976, 21–23 and 1978, 5–6).

Comparing this ideal description of the NDE with Cardinal's account of the vision quest there can be no doubt that on the fourth night of his "fast" Cardinal experienced something very like a near death experience. All the characteristics of the NDE which Moody describes are present in Cardinal's account: the OBE, the light and a being that forces him to review and evaluate his life, the reluctance to return to "life," and the transformation when he is finally "brought back." We conclude from this that the vision quest at least may include a near death experience. The experience of the vision quest is, of course, much more besides. It is partly for this reason that we include the complete text of the Cardinal interview as the conclusion of this chapter.

Interview with Douglas Cardinal: A Phenomenological Description

The following interview first appeared in the magazine *Intervox,* vol. 8, 1989/90, pp. 27–31, 44–47. We are grateful to the publishers of *Intervox* for permission to use the interview here. As we have noted, to facilitate the above discussion we have numbered the questions and responses in the interview as follows: Q1 refers to question one, R1 refers to response one and so forth.

Intervox Q1: *Can you relate some of the experiences you've had in your native tradition?*

Cardinal R1: One of the things we do is the sweatlodge. That's where you go and you sit around and there are red hot rocks and it's incredibly hot. Then you pour water on the rocks. You make a commitment to go through it. It seems hotter than you can physically take, in fact if you even clench your fists your knuckles will burn. Your hair starts burning. There's no way out. It's like being trapped in a burning car. If you were trapped in that burning car you would have to release your spirit. You would have to surrender your physical being.

Your whole body is screaming and yelling and you want to get out but you just reach out and pray and sing spiritual songs. There is no way out because of your commitment. The person that runs the lodge brings it as hot as you can stand it and then past that point. You have a choice of burning or praying. When you reach out beyond yourself, all of a sudden you have some tremendous strength and your body suddenly becomes one with the earth, air, fire and water. You don't feel any pain — you're sort of above it. You're pushed to a point where you sense you're a spiritual being, you see the life force in yourself and other people. There's no way out.

You have to be real quiet. If you thrash around he just pours more water. You have to be real still and just sing songs. At a point where you feel almost like you're going to separate from your body, he opens the door.

If it's a doctoring lodge, say for example you have ulcers, it seems like that part of the body is out of balance. The body is trying to protect itself, it's trying to maintain a sense of balance but it can't. You would feel as though your whole midsection was on fire. It would seem as if all the pain was concentrated in the weakest part of your physical being. You would feel as if there was a hole in your life force. You would feel a tremendous pain there.

If the Elder is there doctoring you, he will touch all over your body with an eagle's wing. That part of your body like the chakras and nodes that they use in acupuncture, that's the part of your body that is most vulnerable. Like your Achilles' heel, he touches that and it feels like a spear is driving through you. As soon as he touches that, you can't help but cry out and when you do, he just takes the eagle's wing and keeps hitting you on that one spot. What flashes in your mind are all the things that have created that imbalance. Ulcers are not created by someone kicking you in the stomach. They are created by a perception in your mind that is in disharmony with your body. The mind has to let go of that perception. The mind thinks it's going to die and it wants to survive. So before you come to that instant you have to let go of it. You have to let go of whatever imbalance you have. You go through a real trauma psychologically. But there's no way out, it's too hot. The body's just chucking everything saying, "I gotta survive, I gotta survive. Chuck it, chuck it, chuck it!" When you come to terms with it, it's gone.

Intervox Q2: *You're healed?*

Cardinal R2: Yeah. That's how they cured illnesses. They believed all illness is psychosomatic. And they are.

They studied the mind and the body. They didn't spend their time with technology. Trying to survive on these plains, which is a pretty harsh environment, they developed all these rituals and ceremonies to know how they operated.

So you go through one of those four times, each time you go through the same experience, I have them every Friday.

Intervox Q3: *That intense of an experience each time?*

Cardinal R3: That's a doctoring lodge. Nobody wants to get doctored unless they *really* need it! It's pretty traumatic to go through but it just wipes out everything. It takes about two to wipe out a bad case of the flu. It's wiped out MS., cancer, and a lot of imbalance and modern illnesses.

Intervox Q4: *Beyond healing those illnesses, does it give you some self awareness you didn't have before?*

Cardinal R4: It gives you tremendous insights — how stupid you are, where you screw up and where your possibilities are. You just come right to terms with it. It's all personal. You *know*! You know when you're screwing up, especially when you go into the lodge. I learned all this from the elders and the elders all died off.

Intervox Q5: *So there aren't that many people who know about this any more?*

Cardinal R5: More and more, not too many. Quite a few more than there used to be, because the church had abolished it.

Intervox Q6: *So it's OK to practice these things again?*

Cardinal R6: Well, we *made* it OK. I did it on my land. I own my own land. When I went to the reserves, the priests and everybody fought it and excommunicated everybody who did it. After a while everybody went to the sweat and nobody went to the church. Now the priests and nuns go to the sweats. They say it's a good place to pray in.

Intervox Q7: *What are some of the other ceremonies you use?*

Cardinal R7: There's fasting. Fasting is where you go through four rounds [of the sweatlodge] and after each round the door is open. You sort of lay there after a round catching your marbles and then you go back in and go through another one.

Intervox Q8: *How long does one take?*

Cardinal R8: Maybe an hour or two. But when you go on a fast you go first of all through the sweatlodge but the door is not open. You have to be real together to go through that. Then you go out of there without talking to anybody. You don't have anything to drink, you're just as dry as a bone when you walk out of there. You feel like you can spit dust. Then you go out into nature in a smaller lodge so you can just sit out there facing west, the setting sun. You stay out there for four days and four nights without water or food. On the fifth morning, after the second round, you get your first sip of water.

The first day is when you're really complaining. You're being bitten by mosquitoes and slapping and killing everything around you, trying to survive. You're aching all over and thirsty as hell. But you have to sit there with this pipe in your hand and continually pray to be positive because you've made a commitment. Once you make a commitment you have to go through it because if you give up, you're giving up on yourself.

After 24 hours you get bored of listening to yourself complain. So you start looking outside yourself and you start seeing a whole myriad of life around you. The animals, insects, grass, the trees, the wind and the sky, sun, the stars. There's lots of stuff around you. It's a whole different universe. You feel that you've probably separated yourself from it. You feel almost like an alien being sitting on this earth. You have to then come to terms because you're sitting there and these creatures are really bothering you. On the second day, like the elders say, you have to "come in power." If you set yourself in power with every living thing, then you can see — really *see* and communicate with every living thing. So then you start having these magical experiences.

When I was out there I had these moccasins with butterflies made from beadwork on them. I remember seeing butterflies and saying to them, "I'm lonely, why don't you come over here?" And they did. They came over and lit on my moccasins. I asked them to light on my hand, and they did; they lit on my hand. I was amazed, I was shocked. I looked up and said, "Nothing will hurt you if you're with me, I'll protect you." So each night before the elder closed my lodge and tied me in, these butterflies would come in and sit right above my head upside down in the lodge. All those magical experiences that don't make any sense.

Same with the ants. I was sitting by an ant hill and they came biting me all the time. This one ant was biting me, so I reached out to kill him and I thought, "No that's not what I'm here for, I'm supposed to respect his life." So I pretended like I was going to squash him between my two fingers. He then raised up and threatened me with his pincers. I threatened him with my fingers. He threatened me with his pincers. I said to him, "I'm not going to kill you but just back off! I'm just going to sit here and be very quiet so just back off." All of a sudden I thought, "There's a very brave creature. I'm this big giant and he's willing to take me on to defend his own species." I thought, "I respect you." He turned around, walked away, and I wasn't bitten by ants anymore. Stuff like that, I learned a lot that day.

The nights were rough. All the sounds at night made you hallucinate. You had all these demons you had to deal with that were just part of your imagination. You couldn't deviate for one second from holding the sacred pipe and always asking for strength. If you let yourself go and let your mind go, you'd be confronted with some nightmare monster in your head. Every second you'd have to hold on to your spirit to carry you through.

The third day was like losing consciousness. The elders say, "You ask all the living beings for strength because they are at one with their creator and you are part of creation so just ask them for strength." I remember grabbing onto a tree and asking it for its strength so that I could live for just a second longer. So I got strength from the tree. Then the grass gave me strength, the clouds quenched my thirst, the sun gave me strength, the earth gave me strength.

As I kept asking and reaching and reaching out for life around me to give me strength and sustain me, I got stronger and stronger and stronger. I felt powerful. I felt I could walk through a wall. The elders say, "You gotta watch because now the forces will turn on you. The bad forces will start sweet-talking you." So then I heard all these things like "you don't have to do this anymore, look how powerful you are. You don't need anything you can just walk out of here and do anything." They were trying to sweet-talk me out of my commitment. I just held on, kept that pipe. I just kept sitting there not listening to it, seeing all the tricks that my human being would make to get me off and protect itself.

The fourth night was the hardest. The fourth day was strong but then I could sense the sun going down. The sun was going down and I could feel the strength going from me. The grass pulling the strength from me and the trees pulling the strength from me, the clouds dimming and life dimming around me. I didn't even have the strength to blink my eyes. All of a sudden there was a light around me and I just started pulling out of my body. I looked back and could see myself sitting there like a shell. I was terrified. Terrified because I thought, "I'm just thinking this, but no I'm not. I'm not thinking this. This hallucination is real. Here I am and here my body is, being surrounded by light." It was painful.

I could feel a being there. This being said, "You know, you don't have any control over your life or death, you arrogant creature."

I said, "Yes, but I want to live another second longer!" I cried and I bargained. And I said, "No, I want one more second, just one more second longer." There was no way. I was being more and more pulled out of my body. I just didn't want to go.

All of a sudden my life started rolling back and I could see things I had done. My wife, my children, my parents and my friends. I couldn't go back to say I was sorry. I couldn't go back to say I was stupid. I'd thought I was going to live forever and I had all these loose ends.

I said to this person around me, "I screwed up here and I screwed up there." All of a sudden I felt all of my life. And it was more and more painful because it seemed as if this being that I was being pulled towards was a very positive being and I happened to be a very, very negative being.

I went through all the things I did that were sort of stupid and angry and nuts and crazy. I was in terrible pain. Finally this being said, "You know, you're judging yourself," and "You have to come to terms with yourself. You're too arrogant, you're just a human being. Can you see that you're just a human being and that you're stupid? If you were real smart you wouldn't have made all these mistakes. Now let's walk through your life."

So I went through it and he said, "If you had known better like you know now, would you have done that?" And I said, "No." "Would you have done that?" "No." So he said, "Well you have to come to terms with the fact that you're just a human being. From all of these things that you've done in your life you can see that you're just a stupid human being, and don't be so arrogant." I said, "I'm just a human being." And I could see that. He said, "Yes." Then I said, "But I come to you with the knowledge of my life." "Yes," he said, "you have that — that whole knowledge of almost what not to do. You come with that knowledge."

So I said, "I'm ready to go. I feel at peace with myself." He said, "It doesn't matter whether you're ready or not, you're coming anyway. You're still arrogant, you know." "Yeah, I know, I'm a human being," I said. So I finally went. It seemed like I was a part of everything, and I felt very, very powerful. I just wasn't there.

The elder came out in the morning and he untied the lodge. He tried to help me come back with sweetgrass and whatever. I could hear him in the distance, "Come back." He was pulling me back. I thought, "I don't want to go back. There's no way I'm coming back. Why would I want to go back? I'm already on the other side and if I come back as a human being, I'm going to have to go through death again. Why should I come back? Then I'd be confined and limited and I would screw up and do all the stupid human being things. I'd be out-of-tune with myself and I'd have to go through all this pain again and all this remorse and suffering. I'm already over here and why do I have to do all that again. Besides, I'm free." The elder said, "You have to come back, just to see this day. You've never seen a day like today. There's dew on the grass, and sun shining on the dew and this golden hue is all over everything. The clouds are all red. The sun is brilliant and the sky is blue. It's the most beautiful day. You have to come back and see this beautiful day. It's wonderful to be alive and walk on this earth.

I thought, "It is wonderful to experience life." I said to that being, whatever it was, "Can I go back for a minute and see that day?" He said, "Well, you're a free spirit, you make your choice." I said, "I'll just check in for a minute and come right back." I came back in my body and opened my eyes and saw that day. It was a beautiful, fantastic day. I never had seen a day like that. I'd never really looked. The elder said, "See what a beautiful day it is and how wonderful it is to be alive?" I said, "Yes, it's just beautiful."

He said, "Are you afraid of death?" I said, "No. I'm just afraid I ain't gonna live right." He said, "Then you're a fearless warrior."

Intervox Q9: *Why is it we have to go through something like that to see those things?*

Cardinal R9: That's what I asked him. I said, "Why did you tell me to do this?" He said, "Well, you want that pipe that you carried, you're linked to that pipe." I said, "Yes, it carried me through." He said, "Now when you hold that pipe you'll be forever reminded of that experience." I said, "I'll carry that pipe and I'll hold that pipe and that pipe is the most important thing in my life." He said, "Yes. I see that that pipe is the most important thing in your life." I said, "Yes." Then I said, "We'll take that pipe back to the lodge and we'll smoke it together." So he says, "OK."

So we took it back to the lodge and I had my sweats and he pulled me back *really* into my body. Then I had my first sip of water and I choked on it because I wasn't used to it. Finally the people were there and we were all warm and we shared the experiences and we smoked the pipe together. Then he gave the pipe to me and said, "That's the symbol of your experience to be a fearless warrior. And that physical pipe that you hold in your hand is probably the most precious thing that you could ever have." And I said, "Yes. This is the most precious thing in my life." He said, "You have one more test to do." I said, "What is that?" He said, "You are to take that pipe and where you have fasted, you are to bury it." So I went there, took the pipe, dug a hold in the ground and buried it.

I just had a horrible time to let go of it. I felt I was attending my own funeral. The elder said, "You have to understand. You can't have an attachment to the physical world, you have to let go of it. Even the pipe, it's a symbol."

So I got another pipe. But when I turn the pipe to the four directions I sense that there's another pipe turning in the ground that links me with the earth.

I told him of the experiences and asked him what he experienced on his first fast. He said, "Oh, I experienced the same thing." I said, "Why didn't you tell me?" "Then you wouldn't have done it. By telling you, I would have robbed you of the opportunity of learning that experience for yourself. It's yours," he said.

So, that's part of their culture, it's probably been done for thousands of years.

Intervox Q10: *And what kind of difference does having an experience like that make in your life?*

Cardinal R10: Well, you sort of look at things, like they say, from the other side. You know what you're going to have to face when you die. It's a question of whether you're going to be stupid in running your life. You have to think of things from the other side.

Intervox Q11: *You still make mistakes, don't you?*

Cardinal R11: Hundreds of them. Even more so. Because you're willing to be out there and do things, you make mistakes. But you're also willing to forgive yourself because you know you're just a human being.

Intervox Q12: *What does it take in order for someone to risk making mistakes?*

Cardinal R12: It just takes commitment. You say, "I'm going to do this no matter what. And my word is my honour." Keeping your word is like keeping your spirit. Your word is a force that is more than just a physical entity. Your word is eternal, but your body is mortal.

When you have that experience you realize that your integrity is more important than your life. You can give up your life easily but you have to face yourself at your death. The reason we suffer so much is because our integrity is out. I just wince when I see people whose integrity is out because I know what they are going to have to face when they die. I just shudder.

Intervox Q13: *Does everybody know it when their integrity is out? Are they responsible for that?*

Cardinal R13: Yes. You know, but people think they're immortal. We all know. We just fool ourselves. That's why the elders say, "Look at things from the other side." You don't want to go through all that pain that you go through when your integrity is out.

Intervox Q14: *In the native tradition do they believe in reincarnation, or are you a soul that only comes here once or lives for just one lifetime?*

Cardinal R14: They don't deal with those kinds of things too much. It's sort of an experiential thing. Those rituals are designed so you learn whatever you learn.

In their prayers they always talk about their grandfathers, the people in the spiritual world on the other side. Almost like the saints or the guardian angels of Christianity. When you go to the other side, it's like you're guided through the experience. There's something there that helps you.

When you go into the lodge you sometimes get tremendous insights or everyone may have a powerful experience at the same time. So they always say that the grandfathers or grandmothers are there. The grandfathers or grandmothers always walk with the people and so they feel guided. So they just say, "I think I'll go ask my grandfather about that."

Intervox Q15: *And they can?*

Cardinal R15: Yes, they can. Non-Indian people sometimes think that the grandparents are alive, but they're not. They are continually communicating with their grandfathers and grandmothers.

Intervox Q16: *Are these literally their grandparents or are they simply people who have passed on?*

Cardinal R16: They call just about anybody grandmothers or grandfathers. We're all brothers in the sense of spiritual brothers. Some people are blessed, they are the grandfathers and grandmothers. It isn't just Indian people. The lodge is open and almost everybody can come.

Intervox Q17: *Would anybody have similar experiences?*

Cardinal R17: Yes.

Intervox Q18: *There's no preparation necessary?*

Cardinal R18: No. You're there in that pressure cooker and you're going to experience what you experience. And the lodgekeeper isn't a priest, he's in there with you. It ain't easy.

Intervox Q19: *Do you see people becoming more aware of these kinds of issues? Is it a trend?*

Cardinal R19: I think so. It doesn't really matter what other people do. You're entirely 110 percent responsible for what you do and you're cause in the matter and everything that's around you. You have to take 100 percent responsibility for your own life. When you die, you're alone with your own creator.

Intervox Q20: *For someone who wants to participate in one of these sweats, does it matter what motivates them?*

Cardinal R20: I remember so many people would come to the lodge, it was very hard on me. So I went to one of the elders and asked him what to do. He just said to make more offerings [turn up the heat]. So I tried that and very few came back. They were afraid of it. It was too hot, too hot. The ones who came back were committed and got something out of it. The ones who were there to see a museum-in-action kind of thing, they were gone. They couldn't take it. They didn't really want to change.

They know that if you go through it and get some insights and don't do anything about it, when you come back to the lodge you have to face yourself.

Intervox Q21: *If anybody wants to find out about the Indian way how can they do it? It's not really available through books is it?*

Cardinal R21: No. The Christians did everything possible to wipe it out. They took our children away, took our parents away, legislated against our rituals. It was quite a threat. It's very important that societies that are imperialistic or religions that control people and develop empires, have everybody believing that they're powerless victims. That's been instilled in almost every agrarian civilization for 15,000 years. That no one could aspire, everybody had to fit in and everybody was afraid. Fear was instilled so that people would fit into a pyramidal system. Even the pharaohs were afraid. We have built these systems and it's all based on fear.

The aboriginal peoples weren't agrarian. They were hunters and gatherers, they never were "civilized." They never had some being having dominion over them. They had their own creator.

Intervox Q22: *But do you think it's possible to have that kind of world now? We have civilization and it looks like it's here to stay.*

Cardinal R22: The agrarian civilization is over. We live in an information society. We don't have to live in our little pyramidal boxes and be afraid. We live in a free world. We have such things as the American constitution which is totally un–European or Middle Eastern. The American constitution could be spoken by the elders themselves — that every human being has the right to the pursuit of happiness. That kind of thing is native thinking. Now the Russians are changing too. The whole society is much better off if each person takes full responsibility. There are problems, but less order.

Intervox Q23: *I don't think that's the way most white people would see it. Because of our conditioning we would say that the American constitution was a creation of the European settlers.*

Cardinal R23: They forget that when the settlers came over they were changed forever. They saw that they had kings over them and that the savages had more freedom than they did in their societies. That kind of thinking caused the French Revolution.

Intervox Q24: *Yet they still destroyed the whole Indian nation.*

Cardinal R24: One tries to destroy something that one is afraid of. Imperialists that feared the Indian way of thinking did everything possible to destroy it. Like the Brave New World — how one person set out to be different.

Intervox Q25: *But I think most white people believe that they destroyed them because they were savages.*

Cardinal R25: Exactly. They don't know that they destroyed them because they were the spiritual people. Indian people are the spiritual people. They're the human beings. Cherokee's call them the "human beings." "Why are they killing the human beings? The human beings walk with the spirit. Why are they being destroyed by the people that follow their heads rather than their hearts?" The Indian nations didn't know why a lesser being was destroying them.

Intervox Q26: *So how much of the Indian knowledge is lost? Is any of it lost?*

Cardinal R26: No.

Intervox Q27: *Is it time for this knowledge to come out into the world?*

Cardinal R27: The cowboys won over the Indians who had a philosophy of harmony with the earth, but we lost. It's 5 minutes to 12 for mankind and all life on this planet. The Indians have to win or we won't have anything left.

Intervox Q28: *What does that mean?*

Cardinal R28: That attitude of being in harmony with every living creature. Seeing that every living creature has a soul. We have to be in communion with every one. We're part of the life chain, we're not dominion over it. Conquering and all that Biblical stuff. That so called "right," that God gave us dominion over everything. You be dominion over everything and you end up with the mess we're in with the planet.

Intervox Q29: *What does it take, at 5 to 12, to accomplish that?*

Cardinal R29: It will happen anyway. The knowledge is always there. It's when the rest of the world realizes that the aboriginal people have a contribution to make, that they've been living on the planet in harmony for thousands of years. It's happening. It's just holding on to your beliefs and philosophy, and things will change. Realizing that it's not something to be ashamed of. You're able to make a contribution. It's like Gandhi. One person decides to weave his own cloth and defeats the whole British Empire.

Intervox Q30: *This time, though, it's not a matter of defeating the empire but changing it.*

Cardinal R30: I think there is that change. There's more and more people concerned about the environment, more people wanting to live in communion with themselves, in harmony with themselves. Searching for something other than narrow religious concepts. More and more people are doing that, and they ain't killing off the Indians. Except in Brazil.

A lot of people are looking for an alternative way of looking at the world and a lot of Indian people also don't believe what *they* have. They believe all the stuff they have on TV. Everybody's in the same soup.

I think the old knowledge is the new knowledge. I think that is the destiny of the Indian people. We have to teach the immigrant culture to love as we love because our very survival depends on that task.

Intervox Q31: *Can we participate in that?*

Cardinal R31: The Indian people don't see it as a racial thing. We call the white people "mooneyow." It's not a racial term. It means: "somebody who is totally controlled and motivated by money, dollars." It's just a behavior trait.

Intervox Q32: *I don't think that's true for all white people.*

Cardinal R32: That's right. So lots of white people are Indians. I'm saying that the Indian people don't look at people in a racist way. Perhaps we're judging them on their behavior rather than racially. There are just as many assholes in the Indian community as there are in the white community. Maybe more because they're their own worst enemy.

Intervox Q33: *Your path isn't typical of the native spiritual tradition is it? I mean your environment is bureaucratic and concrete.*

Cardinal R33: That's because they bought the bullshit of society. They defined the narrowness of what being a native person is. They've been watching too many John Wayne movies. A lot of people bought that being an Indian is in the past, not in the present.

Intervox Q34: *Is that changing? Are natives becoming more active in the world?*

Cardinal R34: Yes. I think that's happening. People have to realize that maybe they're hanging on to the traditions in a physical way instead of getting underneath it and seeing why these traditions are there. People can get caught up in the ritual. Even Christians, you know they go and pray and do the communion and confession and then they go out and screw everybody else wild. They think that being a good Christian is following the rituals instead of following it as a way of life.

Intervox Q35: *What is it that inspires you to make a contribution, to put yourself "out there"?*

Cardinal R35: You have to realize that you're not only a sensory being but that you have a life force or spirit or whatever that is more than just your complaining human being. To be a man of knowledge in the Indian culture meant that you have to be in touch with that. There were a whole bunch of rituals and ceremonies and things that the elders had for thousands of years that put you in touch with that. The people regard themselves as spiritual beings not as physical beings. They talk in terms of walking with their grandfathers and defeating my worst enemy which is myself. The whole culture is based on those kinds of values. Then the Christians came along and decided to convert them.

Intervox Q36*: I guess I'm still curious as to how many people are following it as a way of life rather than dealing with it superficially?*

Cardinal R36: I suppose a lot of people. It's not that I or they are better, we're probably even worse. We're always screwing up as a human being. When you're not playing it safe you make thousands of mistakes, thousands of screw-ups. You're willing to be wrong a lot. You can't try and be a saint. I think saints probably lead dull lives.

FOUR

Values, Land, and the Integrity of Person

Cross-Cultural Considerations

We begin (and end) this chapter with a discussion of the work of two philosophers, one Canadian and one American, whose arguments when taken together constitute a significant contribution to our understanding of the relationship between Native values, the Native concept of land, and the Native concept of person. These two philosophers are Professor J. T. Stevenson of the University of Toronto and Professor J. Baird Callicott, Regents Professor of Philosophy and Religious Studies, Institute of Applied Sciences, University of North Texas. We discussed some of Callicott's work in regard to certain methodological considerations in our Preface and in developing our defense of ethno-metaphysics in Chapter One. Here we will concentrate on his papers "Traditional American Indian and Western European Attitudes Toward Nature: An Overview" and "American Indian Land Wisdom? Sorting Out the Issues." Though both were published elsewhere they have been reprinted in Callicott's 1989 book *In Defense of the Land Ethic: Essays in Environmental Philosophy.* We begin our discussion, however, not with Callicott but with Stevenson's ground-breaking paper, "Aboriginal Land Rights in Northern Canada."

Person and Place

Jack Stevenson's "Aboriginal Land Rights in Northern Canada" first appeared in 1983 as part of the section on "Aboriginal Rights" in Wesley

Cragg's consciously Canadian book *Contemporary Moral Issues.* Cragg's book was very successful and his publishers, McGraw-Hill Ryerson, brought out several revised editions, all of which, thankfully, still contain Stevenson's important article on aboriginal land rights. Stevenson's paper is hard hitting. He not only argues *that* it is morally wrong to ignore, as has been done in the past, the Native point of view in the discussion of such issues, but he also shows *why* attempting to "settle" Native land claims through the courts, through the Canadian legal system, is in his words "profoundly misguided" (Stevenson 1992, 297). Stevenson notes, quite simply and quite fairly, that the issue is cross-cultural and yet Canada's current culture, including its political and legal system, has been imposed upon the aboriginal people of Canada. Determining whether or not this ought to be the case, or whether or not such an imposition is just, cannot be decided by the very system that has been imposed. To attempt to do so would be to beg the very question at issue. For this reason, though not for this reason alone, Stevenson concentrates on the moral (as opposed to the legal) justification of aboriginal land claims.

In order to avoid any charge of ethnocentric bias, Stevenson searches for moral principles to use in his argument which are as much as possible cross-cultural. He finds one such principle, an extremely useful one from the standpoint of his argument, in Article Three of the United Nations Declaration on Human Rights (1948): "Everyone has the right to life, liberty and the security of person" (Stevenson 1992, 301). What is interesting, and, from our point of view, most important about this, is Stevenson's very detailed interpretation and defense of the "personal-security aspect" of Article Three.

Stevenson argues that the right to security of person is violated not only in cases of physical torture, death, or enslavement but also in cases involving psychological torture using sensory deprivation, hallucinogenic drugs, etc., which more often than not lead to severe personality disorders. He argues that the victims of such torture can end up as human derelicts, alcoholics with feelings of chronic anxiety, guilt, and worthlessness, totally unable to function normally either economically or socially. He notes that these results can also be, and indeed have actually been, brought about quite unintentionally by the European settlers in North America as they disrupted the aboriginal peoples' relationship to their environment, the land and their way of life. He argues that the evidence for this frightening claim is more than apparent on Indian reserves and in cities and towns across Canada, and, we would add, the United States as well.

In order to support his claim, that disruption of their relationship with the land and their traditional way of life is, or can be, a violation of the personal security right of the aboriginal peoples of Canada, Stevenson refers to the best scientific evidence available, including the "research program of cultural materialism" developed by anthropologist Marvin Harris and the work of psychologists Erik Erikson, Jean Piaget and Bruno Bettelheim (Stevenson 1992, 303–306). We will not rehearse the details of these arguments here. However, we do recommend that all those dealing with issues surrounding "Native rights" immerse themselves in Stevenson's article. The piece is truly a watershed. It shows how the North American Indians' right to security of person has been violated, admittedly unintentionally, by economic and political decisions affecting the traditional Indian way of life including their relationship to the land, the way they nurture their children, and the spiritual significance they bestow on certain ceremonies and cultural artifacts. Stevenson argues: "Because of our ignorance, our past wrongs may not be *culpable*, but, since we should now know better, future ones of the same sort would be" (Stevenson 1992, 307, emphasis added). It is this claim which makes Stevenson's argument such a watershed. He has demonstrated beyond any reasonable doubt not only *that,* but also exactly *why,* it would be morally wrong to continue treating the aboriginal peoples of Canada as they have been treated in the past. It would be to violate, knowingly and with malice aforethought, their right to security of person. Stevenson is well aware that "past wrongs" are also morally blameworthy, that people really ought to have known better. Immediately following his discussion of Erikson's study of the psychological damage done to Indian children by U.S. government schools and the parallel that it is possible to draw with Canadian Indian residential schools, there appears in Stevenson's paper the following quite angry statement: "If you wanted a recipe for the destruction of personality, one such would be this: destroy the material basis of a culture; force the people into an environment which provides little means for economic activity; foster the culture of poverty and dependency by means of minimal handouts; make ignorant and racist attacks on the structure and superstructure of what remains of the culture; as the adults disintegrate from these shocks, experiment blindly with their children" (Stevenson 1992, 306).

The one weakness we find in Stevenson's argument is that he provides little evidence for the essential psychological link his argument requires between the concepts of land and person. He does present the following argument with which we agree: "It is important to note ... that the native belief that the natural world forms a complex, interdependent system of which the native peoples are an integral part should not be dismissed as mere primitive or magical thought" (Stevenson 1992, 303). He goes on to point out that the belief is based on "thousands of years of experience and empirical observation" in their struggle for survival. "Although not expressed in our theoretical terms and differing in many details, the general approach is consistent with our most advanced biological science. In their own way, the native peoples got there first" (Stevenson 1992, 303).

Stevenson is arguing, in effect, that long before the modern science of ecology the Native peoples of North America discovered that they and their environment form a kind of ecosystem "connected by a complex web of interdependencies and feedback loops which maintain the system in a delicate balance" (Stevenson 1992, 302–303). In the course of his argument Stevenson goes on to extend this systems approach "from biology to our understanding of society, culture, and the development of personal identity" (303). In our opinion, Stevenson does not provide sufficient evidence to establish his basic claim, the link between the Native person and the land. We hasten to add that we believe that this essential link does indeed exist. However, we think that it is more easily understood by looking at Callicott's arguments rather than at Stevenson's alone. It is for this reason that we are discussing the work of these two thinkers together. Their arguments support one another.

In fairness to Stevenson, it should be noted that the evidence he presents in support of the essential link between the Native peoples and the land could be considered more than adequate if he were simply giving further examples of an uncontroversial, commonly accepted belief. This may well be what he thinks he is doing. He cites a number of statements made by individuals to the Berger Commission as found in its report, *Northern Frontier, Northern Homeland: The Report of the Mackenzie Valley Pipeline Inquiry.* By way of interpretation, Stevenson insists on translating these "Native voices" into more scientific language. He notes, for example, that they "believe that they live in a complex, symbiotic relation with the land and its ecosystems; that is, their environment, culture, and personal identity are closely interwoven in a balanced system" (Stevenson 1992, 300). Although we think that this scientific interpretation is accurate and captures something of the essential link between land and person, the only pieces of evidence Stevenson cites in support of it are the following two statements made to the Berger Commission. The first is by Richard Nerysoo: "To the Indian people our land really is our life. Without our land we cannot — we could no longer exist as people." Stevenson draws attention to the fact that

Nerysoo's exact words are that they could "no longer exist as people," not "as *a* people"—a very important distinction. Nerysoo continues: "If our land is destroyed, we too are destroyed. If you people ever take our land you will be taking our life." The second Native voice cited is that of Georgina Tobac: "Every time the white people come to the North or come to our land and start tearing up the land, I feel as if they are cutting up our own flesh because that's the way we feel about our land. It is our flesh" (cf. Berger 1977; Stevenson 1992, 387). These statements do capture the experienced oneness of land and person, rather better than Stevenson's scientific reinterpretation. Further, what they express does seem to be a commonly held belief. In fact some of our Native students look at us rather skeptically when we tell them that Callicott's arguments are required in order to establish this point beyond a reasonable doubt. This is something that they have experienced. This is something that they know. It is something that Native people have known for thousands of years. They certainly don't see any need to have some academic environmental activist from Texas prove it to them. In a sense, of course, they are quite right. In fact, it has been either a working assumption or one of the general conclusions of many recent studies such as that of the Berger Commission. By way of example we will cite one other such report.

In 1989 Lakehead University's Centre for Northern Studies released a research report by anthropologist Dr. Paul Driben and Native lawyer Donald J. Auger entitled *The Generation of Power and Fear: The Little Jackfish River Hydroelectric Project and The Whitesands Indian Band*. We have chosen to cite this particular report because it discusses not only the economic impact of this huge hydroelectric project but also its sociological and cultural impact. As such it provides some particular, concrete content for some of the more general conceptual claims we have been making concerning the intimate relationship between land and person. Driben and Auger do provide detailed tables showing the amount of income derived from trapping and selling furs (beaver, muskrat, and lynx) and from picking and selling blueberries. The income is not great, but Driben and Auger argue, "Cash is not the only category of wealth that the foragers from the north shore of Lake Nipigon generate from their homeland." They note that hunters of game "also produce a substantial amount of Indian food, particularly meat, including 'beef' from species such as moose, beaver, muskrat, and lynx; 'poultry' in the form of geese, ducks, grouse, and hare; and fish such as pickerel, whitefish, pike, lake trout, and sucker." They conclude that were it not for hunting, fishing, and trapping these "foragers would undoubtedly be hard-pressed to purchase the food which they and their dependents need to survive" (Driben and Auger 1989, 12). But even this is not the most important thing about living off the land. Equally important are the social relationships established, or confirmed and renewed, through the distribution of the food. As Driben and Auger point out, "This is done according to custom — gifts of meat are given to neighbours with the expectation that, someday, such gifts will be returned in kind" (12). Driben and Auger cite a Royal Ontario Museum study, entitled *The Round Lake Ojibwa,* by E. S. Rogers: "When a gift is made a return is expected, but the type of return and the time when it should take place vary with the particular individuals involved" (Driben and Auger 1989, 12; Rogers 1962, C7). Gifts, then, are used not only to indicate feelings, but also to communicate expectations. Further, "gift-giving also functions as the primary way in which Ojibway foragers acquire prestige in the eyes of their kinsmen and friends. In sharp contrast to Eurocanadians [sic], whose prestige is based upon the accumulation of wealth, Ojibway foragers acquire prestige through the distribution of wealth." As Driben and Auger go on to observe: "This is particularly true in the case of wealth in the form of meat. The fact of the matter is that the more meat a forager distributes, the higher his social status" (Driben and Auger 1989, 20).

Driben and Auger also note that although some members of the Whitesands Indian Band are not foragers and in fact live in small towns such as Armstrong, Ontario, nevertheless "according to custom, those who do not live off the land provide the foragers who give them gifts of food with other gifts in return: a place to stay, meals, a ride in a vehicle, and so on." In this way such people "are able to maintain their position in Ojibway society, and, in no small way, reaffirm their membership in Ojibway culture." It is important to note that "if they gave such gifts to the foragers without receiving gifts of food in return, they would shame not only the foragers but also themselves" (Driben and Auger 1989, 31).

The Driben-Auger report does provide some further concrete detail on the basis of which it is possible to acquire a deeper understanding of Stevenson's point that Indian people "live in a complex, symbiotic relation with the land and its ecosystems," that "their environment, culture, and personal identity are closely interwoven in a balanced system" (Stevenson 1992, 300). It also helps us understand more fully the following Native voice we have seen Stevenson quote from the Berger Commission: "If our land is destroyed, we too are destroyed. If you people ever take our land you will be taking our life." However, one thing missing from the Driben-Auger report is anything which would help us interpret Georgina Tobac's statement to the Berger Commission cited above: "Every time the white people come to the North or come to our land and start tearing up the land, I feel as if they are cutting up our own flesh because that's the way we feel about our land. It is our flesh." We attempted to explain this, above, in terms of "the experienced oneness of land and person." Unfortunately such an explanation is far from adequate. It fails to "flesh out" this important belief with further content. Some of this missing content is included in Callicott's two papers, "Traditional American Indian and Western European Attitudes Toward Nature: An Overview" and "American Indian Land Wisdom? Sorting Out the Issues."

Drawing on the work of anthropologist Irving Hallowell, Callicott points out that "the Ojibwa regarded animals, plants, and assorted other natural things and phenomena as persons with whom it was possible to enter into complex social intercourse" (Callicott 1989, 209). In Callicott's original research on the Ojibwa narrative tradition, published with Thomas W. Overholt in *Clothed-in-Fur and Other Tales: An Introduction to an Ojibwa World View,* he came to realize that "Ojibwa narratives consistently represent the natural world as a world of other-than-human persons organized into a congeries of societies" (Callicott 1989, 14). This concept of "other-than-human persons" is an extremely important one. A person is someone with whom our relationships may be, indeed must be, evaluated morally. The concept of "person" is, at least in part, a value concept. Callicott gives further depth and content to this point noting that for the Ojibwa, plants and animals are not really thought of as other species. They are rather more like other tribes or nations. Describing what he found in his study of the Ojibwa narrative tradition, Callicott argues that "human economic intercourse with other species is not represented as the exploitation of impersonal, material natural resources, but as reciprocal gift-giving or bartering, in which both the human and nonhuman parties to the exchange benefit. Game animals give their skins and flesh to human beings, who in return give the animals tobacco and other desirable ... artifacts" (Callicott 1989, 214–215). This is a widespread belief among Algonquian hunters. For example in the Mistassini Cree narrative tradition there is a story of the hunter who marries a caribou. Although to most of the hunters the caribou just appear as caribou, to a chosen hunter one of the caribou appears as a beautiful young woman with whom he falls in love and marries. "During a caribou hunt later on, the hunter who married the caribou maiden watches as the caribou flee and are killed by the humans, but to him it appears as if human beings are running and then throwing off their capes and flying into the air, leaving their capes for the hunters. These 'capes' to the hunters are caribou carcasses" (Kinsley 1995, 17). Other-than-human persons who share their flesh and fur with humans seem to be able to do so, many times in the cycle of life. As Callicott puts it, "The slain animals are reincarnated in the most literal sense of that term — reclothed in flesh and fur — and thus come back to life to enjoy their humanly bestowed benefits" (Callicott 1989, 215).

It is important, here, to remember Stevenson's point that the Native American Indian attitude toward nature, including other animals, is one which "they forged in the struggle for existence and it is based on thousands of years of experience and empirical observation." It is not to be "dismissed as mere primitive or magical thought." As Ojibwa Elder and scholar James Dumont has pointed out in an extremely useful paper entitled "Journey To Daylight-land: Through Ojibwa Eyes," "These legends, these myths are ... no mere childish tales of how a world began, or why human and animal beings have the peculiar features and characteristics they do. Nor are they fanciful explanations for the landscape and the atmosphere being filled with liveliness and strange superhuman beings. Rather, they speak of how meaning and life, that seems of another reality, is brought into the ordinary reality we are born into. 'They make a home out of the world'" (Dumont 1976, 39).

Anyone raised listening to stories embodying the kind of values Callicott and others have isolated in the Ojibwa narrative tradition is bound to have an attitude of respect toward nature, toward plants and animals and their shared homeland. Indeed, such values, such attitudes, "make a home of the land" by providing the deeper meaning which attaches to everything that is. It is this level of meaning which is missing from the Driben-Auger report. That report could be read as saying in effect that the Native foragers want to use the land in one way and Ontario Hydro wants to use it in another. Both groups could be seen as exploiting the land. Yet as Callicott has observed in the Native narrative tradition, "Human economic intercourse with other species is not represented as the exploitation of impersonal, material natural resources, but as reciprocal gift-giving or bartering, in which both the human and nonhuman parties to the exchange benefit." It will be remembered that in the Driben-Auger report it was noted that if the non-foragers "gave gifts to the foragers without receiving gifts of food in return, they would shame not only the foragers but also themselves." Is it not also the case that the members of the Whitesands Indian Band would bring shame upon themselves if they stood by and did nothing while the habitat of those other-than-human persons with whom they exchange gifts is threatened or destroyed? After all, it is through the exchange of gifts that one maintains one's membership in Ojibwa society. Are not these other-than-human persons with whom they exchange gifts members of that society and entitled to the same respect and help accorded to any other member of the community? There is, we suggest, a moral obligation to protect the habitat of the moose, the beaver, the muskrat, and the lynx; the habitat of geese, ducks, grouse and hare, not just because members of the Band wish to continue hunting and trapping, but because these other-than-human persons are also extended members of Ojibwa society. As we noted in the previous chapter, such a view of Nature is strengthened by the experience of the vision quest. In fact we believe that our discussion of nature and Native values makes more sense when read against the background of the phenomenology of the vision quest (cf. Chapter Three). It is for this reason that the chapters appear in the order that they do. Further, we contend that this view of nature, or very similar ones, can be found in most Native American societies.

A useful description of the kind of thing we are trying to get at appears in the famous novel by Margaret Craven, *I Heard the Owl Call My Name*. There, a West Coast Indian describes his village not merely as a "strip of land" but rather "the myths are the village and the winds and the rains." The village is also the river and "the black and white killer whales that herd the fish to the end of the inlet." It is "the salmon who comes up the river to spawn, the seal who follows the salmon and bites off his head." It is the owl, the talking bird, "who calls the name of the man who is going to die." It is "the silver-tipped grizzly" and the bluejay. It is a mountain goat who is "the little white speck" on a mountain in the distance. It is also the totem pole and each of the figures represented in it. The Native protagonist concludes his description by saying that if you go to the village then "from the time you tie up at the float in the inlet, the village is you" (Craven 1984, 12).

Perhaps our original abstract description in terms of the experienced oneness of land and person, of person and place, is not all that inadequate, particularly when supplemented with the content provided by Callicott, Craven and others. The question still remains: Why does this important view of the world not appear in the Driben-Auger report? We suspect that the only reason it was not included is that the authors of the report believed, probably correctly, that no one at Ontario Hydro would understand it. Our major objection to such a situation, if such indeed exists, is that it has now been shown that companies such as Ontario Hydro, whose projects are likely to have a major effect on the condition of land used by Indians, are morally obliged to have people in decision-making positions who are capable of at least understanding the real damage that such projects could bring about. That, surely, was the major point of Stevenson's 1983 paper, "Aboriginal Land Rights in Northern Canada." As Stevenson has so convincingly argued, "Because of our ignorance, our past wrongs may not be culpable, but, since we should now know better, future ones of the same sort would be" (307).

We suggested above that Stevenson's position is strengthened by arguments found in Callicott's two papers. We also suggested that Stevenson does not establish as strongly as he might the essential link between land and person, though as we have now seen Stevenson does so well enough. But what Callicott adds is this. He examines various possible, and actual, counter claims and meets each objection with a reasoned argument. It should be noted, however, that Callicott is not attempting to defend Stevenson's position. There is no evidence that he was even aware of it. Callicott is rather presenting arguments in support of his own thesis, which is that the North American Indian attitude toward nature constitutes a land ethic very close to that proposed by the famous American environmentalist Aldo Leopold. Leopold argues that what is important in making decisions affecting the environment is not the right of the individual, human or otherwise, but rather the good of the biotic community. "A thing is right when it tends to preserve the integrity, stability, and beauty of the biotic community. It is wrong when it tends otherwise" (Leopold 1949, 224–225).

It is our contention that the arguments Callicott presents in support of his environmental thesis also provide conclusive evidence in support of Stevenson's thesis that there is an essential and too often overlooked connection between their land and the psychic as well as physical health of Native American Indian people. Callicott is very much aware that his thesis — the American Indian as native environmentalist — may be dismissed as simply an overly "romantic" view of Native people, the "Noble Savage" all over again. He cites a 1971 article by Daniel Guthrie, entitled "Primitive Man's Relationship to Nature," as typical. Guthrie sees the North American Indian as an example of primitive man and cites conditions on some present day Indian reservations as evidence of environmental insensitivity. Guthrie even suggests that pre-contact Indians lacked both the population and the technology to do very much environmental damage (Guthrie 1971, 721–723). Callicott realizes that it is difficult to counter this sort of "scurrilous" argument by appealing to the testimonials of Native elders. Although Callicott is himself "not unmoved" by such testimonials, he admits that "a less sympathetic critic" could easily dismiss them as not really reflecting any shared cultural value and as merely nostalgic. "As one is forcibly dispossessed of one's ancestral lands, it is natural to feel both outrage at the colonial usurpers and nostalgia for one's rightful natural heritage. The tender sentiments for the environment in the testimonials ... may only be a personal reaction and cultural afterthought, a natural response to cultural oppression and personal dispossession" (Callicott 1989, 211). Guthrie, of course, is virtually the paradigm of that "less sympathetic critic." It should also be obvious that the sort of arguments Guthrie puts forward can be used to short circuit Stevenson's claim that dispossession of traditional land is a violation of the Native American Indians' right to security of person.

Callicott counters Guthrie's "less than sympathetic" position with a critical examination of recent studies using ethnographic description and the findings of ethnohistory to corroborate the testimonials of Indian spokespersons such as Black Elk, Lame Deer, and others. Callicott notes, for example, that Calvin Martin's study, *Keepers of the Game: Indian-Animal Relationships and the Fur Trade,* which itself surveys "a wide range of literature that bears on the subject," and William Cronon's *Changes in the Land: Indians, Colonists, and the Ecology of New England* both agree that Native people, prior to contact, possessed both the population and the means (one should not say the technology) to inflict greater damage on their environment than they in fact did (Callicott 1989, 205; cf. Martin 1978 and Cronon 1983). Callicott also argues that Guthrie, and others, actually contradict themselves; for not only do they claim that pre-contact Indians lacked the technology to do much environmental damage, they also blame these same Indians, or rather their even more "primitive" ancestors, for "the otherwise mysterious extinction of a number of genre of large mammals at the end of the Pleistocene" (Callicott 1989, 206). As Callicott quite rightly points out, Guthrie and company cannot have it both ways: "It cannot both be true that Pre–Columbian American Indian technology was so ineffective as to be incapable of palpable environmental destruction and that a more primitive Paleo-Indian technology was so effective as to have been responsible for more North American extinctions than followed upon the rediscovery of the continent by modern Europeans" (206).

Callicott, we suggest, is successful in defending his thesis concerning the environmental sensitivity of North American Indians. However, we do take exception to some minor points in his argument. Callicott notes that "the *contemporary* institution of the family hunting territory and its division into annually rotated quarters — to permit the recovery of populations of game animals" has been cited as "evidence of conservation among *aboriginal* northern woodland hunter-gathering peoples" (Callicott 1989, 207, italics in the original). He rejects this evidence because current research suggests that such family hunting territory "was a post-contact development" and hence it is at least possible "that conservation was expressly taught to the Indians by whites" (Callicott 1989, 208). Although others have made similar claims (e.g., Bishop 1970), here we suggest that Callicott is being just a little bit too cautious. He is granting too much to the other side, to the skeptic. After all way back in 1992 we celebrated the five hundredth anniversary of contact between Europeans and the aboriginal peoples of the Americas. Just how long does a way of life have to be followed before it becomes a tradition? If a Native person has lived all his life in the family hunting territory where his father lived and his grandfather before him, is this not part of Native American Indian tradition? Whether or not they learned this form of rotation from whites, the fact that they readily accepted it, and have maintained it for generations, suggests that such practices were at least compatible with traditional Native ways.

We do, however, agree with Callicott that the concept of "conservation" does not adequately capture the Native attitude. Native people are not really interested in calculating the optimum sustained yield of natural resources. Doing so would hardly show the appropriate respect for these "other-than-human persons." As Callicott discovered teaching Ojibwa students with fellow philosopher Tom Overholt at the University of Wisconsin: "Animals, plants, and minerals are not ... rightless resources, as is the case in Western economic assumptions.... Human beings must assume appropriate attitudes toward the non-human members of their polymorphous community.... Above all non-human beings must be respected" (Overholt and Callicott 1982, 154–155).

Learning Respect

In order to explore more deeply this important notion of respect, including respect for the other-than-human, we like to compare one well known analysis of the acquisition of respect offered by modern mainstream philosophy with a Native American account of the same thing. Here, we believe the differences, and, interestingly enough, some similarities become most apparent. The non–Native account we use in our comparison was first articulated by the very influential German philosopher Immanuel Kant (1724–1804). He was just analyzing a commonly accepted underlying attitude in Western moral thinking and did not suggest that he was proposing anything new or radical, except perhaps in the philosophical terminology he used to describe it, which is, itself, quite revealing. Kant claims that the concept of person applies only to human beings who can act on universal moral principles that they rationally accept and impose upon themselves. Each person thus becomes, according to Kant, "a law-making member in a universal kingdom of ends" by "always choosing his maxims from the point of view of himself— and also of every other rational being — as a maker of law" and, Kant adds, "this is why they are called persons" (Kant 1964a, 106). In this way, says Kant, human persons (the only kind of persons there are on earth) acquire a "dignity ... above all mere things of nature" (Kant 1964a, 105). This is, of course, very different from the Native American notion of a deep respect, perhaps even a religious respect, for a nature which consists for the most part of other-than-human persons, perhaps even more-than-human persons. Kant has his own reasons for wanting to draw such a sharp distinction between nature and humanity. By his day science had advanced far enough that it was obvious to him that a scientific explanation, i.e., a causal explanation, could ultimately be given for every natural event including the behavior of human beings. But problems arise concerning ascriptions of moral responsibility if causal explanations can be given for moral behavior. After all, how can we blame or praise someone for something if the action in question was caused by prior events completely beyond the agent's control? Science has attempted to show that all human action is subject to this sort of causal explanation. Kant himself thought he had justified the application of causal explanation to everything in what he called the phenomenal world, the world we discover through sense perception. Human beings are, of course, part of this phenomenal world, "*homo phenomenon.*" As such human beings are thus subject to causal laws.

In what sense, then, is our behavior free, as opposed to being causally determined? In what sense can we be held morally responsible for what we do? Kant attempts to answer such questions by speaking of a noumenal world, a world other than the phenomenal. Such a world is so extra-ordinary that Kant argues that it is impossible to describe using our ordinary concepts of reality — thing, substance, causality, etc. This means, of course, that it is very difficult to say anything meaningful about it at all. We discover this noumenal world, not through scientific reason, but through what Kant calls, practical reason, through our moral action. When we act on universal moral principles which we make and impose upon ourselves then, for the first time, we are acting with freedom, with autonomy. Through acting on principle, as opposed simply to giving in to desires, we achieve autonomy and become genuine persons with intrinsic worth, with dignity. We become, in Kant's terms, "*homo noumenon*" as opposed to "*homo phenomenon.*" It is, Kant thinks, this ability to rise above our phenomenal nature, which sets us apart from the other animals and indeed apart from the rest of nature. Insofar as our phenomenal natures are concerned, even though we are rational animals, we are really no better than, have no more moral worth than, the lower animals: "Man in the system of nature (*homo phenomenon, animal rationale*) is a being of slight importance and shares with the rest of the animals, as offspring of the earth, a common value (*pretium vulgare*)" (Kant 1964b, 99). The concept "vulgar," which Kant uses here in its Latin form, originally just meant common, but due to the disdainful attitude Kant is expressing here both the terms "vulgar" and "common" have taken on a negative connotation. He contrasts the common vulgar animals with morally responsible persons. "But man regarded as a person — that is, as the subject of morally practical reason — is exalted above any price; for as such (*homo noumenon*) he is not to be valued as a mere means to the ends of others or even to his own ends, but as an end in himself" (99). Such persons, Kant argues, have "*dignity,*" which he defines as "an absolute inner worth," and therefore a person can and should "extract *respect* for himself from all other rational beings in the world: he can measure himself with every other being of this kind and value himself on a footing of equality with them" (Kant 1964b, 99, italics in the original).

One of the things Kant is doing here is making explicit an implicit and widespread very non–Native, Euro-Western, attitude toward nature. It seems to be one of complete alienation from the earth. The offspring of the earth have only a common value (*pretium vulgare*), whereas man alone (by which Kant means the human or rational animal) has dignity, an intrinsic value worthy of respect. For Kant, it is of course our rational side, not our animal side, that confers upon us intrinsic value or dignity. It is not difficult to see why Callicott, for example, would prefer the Native American worldview as a foundation for an environmental ethics, a land ethic. In spite of this obvious difference, however, a closer examination of Kant's notion of respect will show that it is not all that far removed from what we may call the Native view, though, who or what is thought worthy of respect differs widely. A comparison of the two applications of the concept of respect will provide a deeper understanding of both worldviews.

Kant's concept of respect seems to be closely bound up with his notion of autonomy, with the self as free (*homo noumenon*). The self is free only in so far as it is self-disciplined, i.e., only in so far as it acts for the sake of moral principle instead of giving in to desire. This is the true Western meaning of "autonomy" which comes from the Greek "autos" meaning self, and "nomos" meaning law (think of "astronomy" which is the study of the laws of the heavens). Just as an autos-mobile (automobile) is something that is self-moving, so an autonomous being is one that imposes its own law upon itself. If laws regulate our behavior, then, by imposing such laws upon ourselves, we become self-regulating (autos-nomos), autonomous. We therefore have freedom, provided, of course, that the laws are ones that we freely accept or are of our own making. If the laws that regulate our behavior are imposed on us by someone else, someone other than ourselves, then we have not achieved autonomy. We then have, or rather are under, what Kant insists on calling "heteronomy" (from "heteros" the Greek word for "other," as in heterosexual, being attracted to "the other" sex, for example). Instead of using our own will power, we have submitted ourselves to the will of another, whether that other is society, God, or another person. According to Kant "*Autonomy* is ... the ground of the dignity of human nature and of every rational nature" (Kant 1964a, 103, italics in the original). We are, however, always in danger of losing our autonomy in one of two ways: (1) by giving in to a desire instead of exercising our own will power and acting on principle, on the moral law, in which case we become merely part of the causal order (*homo phenomenon*); or (2) by submitting to a law imposed by another, in which case though our behavior is law-governed, it is not autonomous since the law is not self-imposed. Still, it is important to learn to govern our behavior according to laws or moral principles. As children we are governed by rules imposed by parents, teachers, and so on — by adults. As we achieve adulthood ourselves, having already learned law-like behavior, we continue to impose upon ourselves such laws as we still accept. In short, heteronomy is considered the first step toward autonomy. As John Watson (1847–1939), a famous Kant scholar, puts it: "At first everyone is under apparent bondage to his superiors in the family relation, but in reality this is the means by which a measure of freedom is attained. It is true that he must render implicit obedience to those in authority over him, but in so doing he learns to free himself from an undue accentuation of his own individual desires, and to seek his freedom where alone it can be found — in the subordination of his own will to the good of others" (Watson 1988, 37–38).

Would many Native American Indians agree with Watson on this?

Would any? Certainly beings with freedom deserve respect. Certainly the good of others is at least as important as, and usually more important than, the satisfaction of my individual desires. But could anyone *really* expect to achieve freedom by giving it up? When we put it like that it sounds completely contradictory. Heteronomy may well be an implicit part of the Western philosophical tradition stemming from ancient Greece. However, it most certainly is *not* a concept native to North America. A great deal of research has been done on the education of Native children. One point on which all researchers seem to agree is that Native children are given much more freedom than their non–Native counterparts.

This point, which is crucial to our argument, is well documented in a major book-length study, titled *Native Literacy and Life Skills Curriculum Guidelines* and produced by a special committee of the British Columbia Ministry of Education. The committee (made up of both Native and non–Native members) was charged with "the task of developing guidelines to provide, in addition to basic literacy materials, materials directed toward the teaching of pre-employment skills and life skills, computational skills, and Native cultural awareness" (1989, v). The report contains a sympathetic and well documented discussion of Native culture, particularly as it relates to education. The members of the committee indicate that they are very much aware that "any discussion of cultural learning styles is fraught with danger because of the tendency toward stereotyping" (13). Nevertheless, they do provide a useful comparison of "Indian and non–Indian characteristics that may impinge upon the classroom" (13). Insofar as the different attitudes toward children are concerned, they suggest that "at the age of mobility" the Native Indian child is "considered a person" and is "free to explore his own environment" whereas the non–Indian "is watched and controlled by parents throughout childhood." The word "autonomous" is used to describe the Native American Indian child whereas his or her non–Native counterpart is said to be "dependent." In comparing learning styles, once again the Native American Indian child is said to be "independent and autonomous" while the non–Native child is "dependent and controlled." The "flexible and often non-existent" routines of the Native American Indian child are said to be "child-determined," for example, "meals served on demand, bedtimes vary with sleepiness and family activity." The non–Native child is raised with more rigid routines dominated or controlled by adults. In the extended family of Native American Indian society "rarely is a child punished in a systematic way" whereas the non–Native child can expect "punishment for failure to comply with adult expectations" (14–15). The comparisons between Native American Indians and non–Natives made here by the *Native Literacy and Life Skills Curriculum Guidelines* draw heavily on quite a large number of other classic studies, including: *A Survey of the Contemporary Indians of Canada,* ed. H. B. Hawthorne (Ottawa: Department of Indian Affairs and Northern Development, 1967); R. Barnhardt, *Culture, Community, and the Curriculum* (Fairbanks: University of Alaska, 1981); F. Erickson and G. Mohatt' "Cultural Organization of Participation Structures in Two Classrooms of Indian Students" (1980), an unpublished study cited often in *Native Literacy and Life Skills Curriculum Guidelines*; and S. Philips, "Participation Structures & Communicative Competence: Warm Springs Children in Community and Classroom," in *Functions of Language in the Classroom,* ed. D. Hymes (New York: Teachers' College Press, 1972).

Obviously all these comparisons between Native American Indians and non–Natives contain rather general observations and we would invite readers to agree or disagree on the basis of their own experience. However, we do suggest that the general tendency is clear and is probably in accordance with the experience of most Native American Indians. As *The Native Literacy and Life Skills Curriculum Guidelines* conclude; for the Native American Indian child, his "autonomy allows him his own decisions" (15). It seems to be clear that in the Native American Indian tradition young people do not have to endure a period of heteronomy in order to gain autonomy as is the case in the Western philosophical tradition explained by Watson and Kant.

We have discussed in some detail how, in the Kantian tradition, the individual first acquires autonomy and respect for other persons through "the subordination of his own will to the good of others," through heteronomous relationships with family, teachers, and other adults. How does this occur in the North American Indian tradition(s) where autonomy seems to be granted "at the age of mobility?" How does such an individual learn respect for other persons? Here we cannot turn to, and draw upon, a full philosophical analysis of the problem by a Kant or a Watson. No such philosophical analysis of Native American Indian tradition(s) has been attempted as yet. Indeed, a full analysis lies far beyond even the scope of this study. The best we can do here is suggest what sorts of things ought to be included in the analysis, and hence in the answer to our question about respect for other persons. Certainly the examples set, and the stories told, by elders are of vital importance. As Native elder Ron Geyshick puts it, "In my stories, I try teach young people respect for everything: other people, trees, water and the spirits" (Geyshick and Doyle 1989, 31). Indeed, the entire narrative tradition plays an important role in helping the individual formulate a view of the world and thus decide what sorts of things deserve the respect accorded to "persons." Fortunately the Native American Indian narrative tradition, at least that of the Ojibwa people, has been subjected to a preliminary philosophical analysis in Thomas W. Overholt and J. Baird Callicott's *Clothed-in-Fur and Other Tales: An Introduction to an Ojibwa World View.* This, we believe, makes it a little more accessible to those not raised in the Native tradition. As Callicott has often observed: "Ojibwa narratives consistently represent the natural world as a world of other-than-human persons organized into congeries of societies ... [where] animals give their skins and flesh to human beings, who in return give the animals tobacco" (Callicott 1989, 214–215). It is not difficult to see how children raised on such narratives would gain a natural respect for those other-than-human persons who give themselves willingly to the hunter. They would also learn, from the example of the hunter himself, to share what they had with others: "The fact of the matter is that the more meat a forager distributes the higher his social status" (Driben and Auger 1989, 20).

Finally, we suggest that the vision quest plays an essential role in at least re-enforcing traditional values. In the previous chapter on the phenomenology of the vision quest we noted that one of the things discovered during the vision quest is that we are not really *apart from* the earth and other people. We are rather a *part of* the earth and other people. As Douglas Cardinal put it: "The elders say, 'You ask all the living beings for strength because they are at one with the creator and you are part of creation' ... It seemed like I was part of everything, and I felt very, very powerful" (cf. Chapter Three, R8). With this realization comes the knowledge that willing the good of others is not in any sense a form of self-sacrifice given the enlarged sense of self acquired in the journey into non-ordinary reality. The expression "enlarged sense of self" which we have used here may be a little misleading. This notion may convey a sense of arrogant individualism which is not intended and is certainly not present. After saying, in the passage cited above, "I felt very, very powerful," Cardinal adds, "I just wasn't there." In our phenomenological analysis of the vision quest we suggested that with this mysterious expression Cardinal is attempting to put into words his felt experience that there is just no distinction between the individual and the rest of the community, indeed, the rest of the universe. Even this analysis is still misleading since it is quite wrong to suggest that the individual self dissolves into the greater whole. The exact relationship of the individual and the community, and the greater whole, requires further analysis. As a special instance of this, the relationship, or rather the inter-relationship, between the vision quest itself and the narrative and other traditions also requires further analysis. We noted in the previous chapter that Cardinal did not accept as authentic all the visions that came to him during his fast: "All the sounds at night made you hallucinate. You had all these demons you had to deal with that were just part of your imagination. You couldn't deviate for one second from holding the sacred pipe and always asking for strength. If you let yourself go and let your mind go, you'd be confronted with some nightmare monster in your own head" (cf. Chapter Three). What implicit criteria are being used here to distinguish the nightmare monsters, the hallucinations of one's own imagination, from the authentic visions, from the truly "magical experiences" as Cardinal calls them? Obviously the sacred pipe is an important link to the tradition. Certainly the teachings of the elders play an equally important role: "The elders say, 'You gotta watch because now the forces will turn on you. The bad forces will start sweet-talking you'.... They were trying to sweet-talk me out of my commitment. I just held on, kept that pipe."

In a great many ways, then, which are in need of much more analysis than we can attempt here, the tradition feeds into and to some extent governs the vision quest, just as the vision quest in its turn feeds into and re-enforces the narrative and other traditions. We can, however, say something more about the *result* of this mutual interaction. It results in individual persons who, in active ways, will the good of other persons, both human and other-than-human, in their mutually shared community. Further, these individuals in turn expect each individual in the community to do the same. "When a gift is made a return is expected, but the type of return and the time when it should take place vary with the particular individuals involved" (cf. Driben and Auger 1989, 12; Rogers 1962, C7).

We have been attempting to explain how Native American Indian children arrive at the notion of respect for persons and responsible, morally appropriate behavior without having to endure the heteronomous domination of adults throughout their childhood. The *result* of traditional Native Indian upbringing, through what we might call noninterference, the example of elders, the narrative tradition, the vision quest, and so on, seems not unlike Kant's universal kingdom of ends, though without the emphasis on moral laws. Kant sums up his position in the following words: "[R]ational beings all stand under the *law* that each of them should treat himself and all others, *never merely as a means,* but always *at the same time as an end in himself.* But by so doing there arises a systematic union of rational beings under common objective laws — that is a kingdom. Since these laws are directed precisely to the relation of such beings to one another as ends and means, this kingdom can be called a kingdom of ends (which admittedly is only an ideal)" (Kant 1964a, 101). Kant, of course, has a much more limited notion of person than the Native American concept which includes other-than-human persons. In fact in this passage Kant limits persons, those who deserve respect, to "rational beings." These persons are all law-making members of this kingdom of ends. No one is under the laws of another. They all have autonomy. Since the laws are universal, "common objective laws," it is *as if* each legislates for all. What are these laws of morality all about? They are about treating persons as ends in themselves, as each having their own dignity and intrinsic value. Even though they can be treated as means, according to Kant, persons must never be treated *merely* as means. The laws of morality, for Kant, "are directed precisely to the relation of such beings to one another as ends and means." Such persons cannot be treated *only* as means for they must be treated with respect. In other words, if you are always accepting favors and gifts from people and never do anything for them in return, then you are treating them only as a means to your own happiness, satisfaction, or whatever. Comparatively, the Driben-Auger report, which we discussed above, found, of the members of the Whitesands Indian Band who live in the town of Armstrong, that "if they gave ... gifts to the foragers without receiving gifts of food in return, they would shame not only the foragers but also themselves" (Driben and Auger 1989, 31). The two worldviews share in common a respect for the autonomy, the dignity, of persons. However, as we have seen, they reach this common view by very different paths. The one seems to require heteronomy in order to develop autonomy whereas the other makes no use of heteronomy in any way. It is important to realize that what we have been discussing here is not merely how respect for persons is cultivated, but how the person himself or herself is developed within the particular culture.

There is one interpretation of our position here which is a little misleading. Addressing it will help to clarify our comparison of Native and non–Native worldviews. The interpretation appears in the posthumously published book *How It Is: The Native American Philosophy of V. F. Cordova.* Viola Cordova discusses our paper, "Some Thoughts on Articulating a Native Philosophy," which we presented at the American Philosophical Association (APA) Pacific Division meeting in Seattle in 1996 (McPherson and Rabb 1997, 11–30). Cordova was also presenting in the same session so that we were able to discuss each other's presentations at the time.

As we understand it, although the occasional paper on aboriginal issues had been presented to the APA in the past, this was the first full concurrent session devoted entirely to Native American philosophy ever presented at the APA annual meetings. We are pleased that Dr. Cordova (Apache), the first Native American ever to earn a Ph.D. in philosophy (University of New Mexico, 1992), was able to receive at least this level of recognition from the APA before her untimely death in 2002.

As part of our presentation we did indeed compare Kant with Native American philosophy and child-rearing practices, though not in the detail we have attempted here. Cordova, in her essay "What Is It to Be Human in a Native American Worldview?" which appears in *How It Is,* makes it quite clear that it is our interpretation she is addressing. To be clear, this is not the paper she presented at the APA and does not reflect the discussion that went on there. She begins her argument here by noting that "J. Douglas Rabb and Dennis McPherson, Canadian professors in Native American philosophy at Lakehead University, have written on the method of creating autonomous actors within a Native American society" (Cordova 2007, 148). She then references the published version of our APA paper cited above. She is not attacking our position. She seems largely in agreement with us. She acknowledges that we are more than familiar with Native American child rearing practices, citing, with approval, some of the studies we have also referred to above. She does say that we "make a claim, that on the surface, seems incredible to those who are not familiar with child-raising techniques among Native Americans" (148). That seemingly incredible claim, our claim as detailed in Cordova's book, is "that the methods that eighteenth-century German philosopher Immanuel Kant proposed for making adults into autonomous thinkers and ethical agents are the same methods used in raising Native children, with one very important difference"(148). Now, this is the misleading statement. This is not our position, though we can see how even our presentation above, in which we were trying to be exceedingly careful, might be possibly read as such. Cordova, as might be expected, singles out Kant's use of "heteronomy" as the "one very important difference." As Cordova herself puts it: "According to Kant it is necessary for an individual to go through a period of *heteronomy*—of dependency wherein one is guided by external rules and authorities—before one can become truly autonomous" (148). We agree that this is one important difference. However, Kant's use of heteronomy is not the only important difference. As we made clear above, it is the *result* of traditional American Indian upbringing, noninterference, that we are saying is not unlike Kant's universal kingdom of ends, though without his emphasis on moral laws. It is not, as Cordova seems to suggest, Kant's *methods* for making adults into autonomous thinkers and ethical agents that are the same as those traditionally used in raising Native American children. The *results* may well be similar but what we actually consider incredible is that the *methods* used to achieve said results differ, and differ radically. Certainly the use or non-use of heteronomy is one important difference. But there are other equally important differences as well. There is no place in Kant for the vision quest, for example. In fact he would be against any kind of experiential learning of this kind in moral thinking. As we noted above he argues that ethical thinking involves moral laws, principles laid down by pure practical reason, quite independent of (not polluted by) sensory experience. Kant is a principlist in ethics. There is no place in Kant for the stories told by elders or for modeling behavior based on their example.

Native Ethics as Narrative Ethics

Given the emphasis on story and the narrative tradition we are tempted to say that a narrative ethics, rather than a Kantian or principlist ethics, would be more compatible with a Native American approach. This, we contend, is confirmed by such studies as Keith H. Basso's *Wisdom Sits in Places: Landscape and Language Among the Western Apache*, and David B. Morris's "Narrative Ethics and Pain: Thinking with Stories." In arguing for his rather anti–Kantian thesis that "[t]he emotion implicit in narrative provides a valuable resource ... in the formation of moral knowledge and ethical action" Morris actually cites Basso's study of Apache narratives to lend support to his thesis (Morris 1996, 207). Morris admits that he draws on the Apache tradition in order "to put us in contact with valuable resources for moral thought and action" (Morris 1996, 197). Now, the principal purpose of Basso's study, as the subtitle makes perfectly clear, is to show how story and place, language and landscape, are so interrelated that the "Apache people in the U. S. Southwest live today in a local world richly endowed with narrative meaning—where the reference to specific places (such as Line-of-White-Rocks or Red-Ridge-with-Alder-Trees) instantly evokes tales of what happened there" (Morris 1996, 197; Basso 1996, 80). We discuss the relation between traditional narrative and specific place in more detail in the following chapter. Here we want to concentrate on the role of narrative in ethics, specifically the transformative impact of story. J. T. Banks, in his study of narrative ethics "The Story Inside," observes, "Narrative inevitably expresses and transforms who we are at every level of our being: the organic, the symbolic, the social, and the spiritual" (219). This ties narrative to the transformative nature of ceremonies like the vision quest discussed above, confirming, we contend, how very un–Kantian the Native American narrative traditions really are. Basso notes how in the Western Apache tradition one would never directly criticize another person, regardless of age. That would be considered rude. We should point out that it follows that a Kantian use of heteronomy would also be considered rude. As Morris explains referring to the narrative tradition examined in Basso's study: "In a culture that avoids direct rebuke, these narratives, as Basso demonstrates, provide unobtrusive and gentle but steady moral guidance" (197). Basso cites Apache people explaining how stories can "work on you," "get under your skin," "make you want to change," or "make you want to replace yourself" (Basso 1996, 59). This notion of "replacing yourself" in the face of moral misconduct is obviously transformative. It is a recognition that radical change is required. But these conclusions are arrived at on your own after hearing, and reflecting on, specific stories. No one has told you that you need to change, or even that you have done anything wrong, much less that you have violated one of Kant's moral laws or ethical principles. This is an indirect manner of instruction which is a manifestation of what we might call an ethic of interventive-noninterference, the very opposite of a Kantian ethic. Native elders, for example, are not known for offering advice, at least not directly. In actual fact they have the reputation of never giving a straight answer. You will often be told a story which seems to have nothing whatsoever to do with whatever question you asked or problem you raised. You are given the autonomy, the complete freedom, to discover the relevance of the reply, and hence to work the problem out for yourself. This is a sign of respect. It is also a method of instruction which fosters self-reliance and independent thinking. Further, it is consistent with a narrative ethic, not a Kantian one based on moral principles. As Morris explains: "In contrast to principle alone, narrative in its detailed, emotion-rich representation of experience can help us recognize implicit values and negotiate conflicts of moral action" (213).

One of the first philosophical studies of Native ethics was published by the late Mohawk psychiatrist Clare Brant in the *Canadian Journal of Psychiatry* (Brant 1990, 535–539). The title of his classic paper, "Native Ethics and Rules of Behaviour," is somewhat unfortunate in that it seems to suggest that a Native ethics would be one based on rules or moral principles making it seem closer to a Kantian ethics than it is in fact. This certainly is not

Brant's intent. When he speaks of "rules of behaviour" he is describing protocols he has observed in the various Cree, Ojibwa and Mohawk communities where he has set up a visiting clinical practice. In other words, insofar as rules are concerned, he is doing descriptive ethics, not normative ethics. The rules do not tell the people what to do. They do not set the norms; rather, they describe values, the most prevalent of which seems to be noninterference. In fact it is from Brant's study that we adopted the term "noninterference" as we use it above. In order to understand Native ethics and Native values, Brant's short paper is certainly a good place to start, particularly because his study included remote Cree and Ojibwa communities where the influence of the dominant society might not yet be a distorting factor. However, we think that a great deal more research is required. As more Native American students complete university with training in philosophy, particularly at the graduate level, it will be possible for such members of specific communities to do research on Native values in their home communities where they in fact formed their own sense of values. They can and should assess their own traditions from their own perspectives. As we argue in some detail in our concluding chapter, Native values should be examined empirically and given specific content through community-based research by indigenous scholars, as these scholars themselves begin to gain a better philosophical understanding not only of their own cultures and communities, but also of themselves.

Here we will give just one example of the kind of research we are recommending. Cree-Métis philosopher Dr. Lorraine Mayer (Brundige), in doing research for her Master's thesis, "Continuity of Native Values: Cree and Ojibwa," returned to her mother's home community, the Chemawawin Band of Easterville and Cedar Lake in Northern Manitoba (Brundige 1997a; See also Brundige 1997b). There she interviewed elders, aunts, and other relatives, and spent a considerable time living in the community and just talking to people. This is a community which had a formative influence on her growing up. Though she did not actually live there, she did spend her summers in the community and considered herself a part of it. Her thesis both confirms and refines Brant's discussion of Native values. She explains the value Brant calls noninterference by noting that "an Aboriginal person does not tell another Aboriginal what to do. The act of directly interfering in someone's life is considered rude" (Brundige 1997a, 42). She quite rightly insists, however, that "this is not to say that people never interfere, but when they do, it is an indirect way designed not to offend" (Brundige 1997a, 46). This is certainly consistent with Basso's findings among the Western Apache.

We would like to see this kind of research carried out in Native communities right across North America. As we argue in Chapter Seven, we think it should be done by philosophically trained members of the communities, as they will know what they are looking for and when they have found it. Given the wide variety of documents concerning child rearing practices among Native Americans we discussed above, we suspect that there will be a certain level of consistency throughout contemporary Native American communities, but no one will really know until the research is actually done. It is also necessary to deal with possible influence by the dominant society that might affect the results of this kind of research. As we argued at length in Chapter One, this can be dealt with, at least in part, by examining historical documents written close to the time of contact, before the widespread influence of Euro-Western ideas and practices in Native American communities. Mayer/Brundige deals with this in her thesis by examining in some detail the *Jesuit Relations,* and concludes that: "these values are continuous with precontact values and they exist and are operating in many Native people's lives today in spite of European influence" (Brundige 1997a: 5). We give here only one example from the *Jesuit Relations.* But it is a quotation we have chosen deliberately because it illustrates the widespread influence of what Kant called heteronomy in European thought and practice at the time. The level of complete autonomy granted by Native American Indian parents to their children was something noticed and remarked upon with much astonishment by the early missionaries, such as Father Le Jeune, in the *Jesuit Relations:* "There is nothing for which these people have a greater horror than restraint. The very children cannot endure it, and live as they please in the houses of their parents, without fear of reprimand or of chastisement" (Thwaites 1959, III, 271). The horror at the lack of chastisement sounds very Kantian. But, as we detailed in Chapter Two, the Jesuit philosophy has ancient and mediaeval origins. As we noted above Kant himself believed he was just explaining a widespread European belief as to how best to teach autonomy by imposing rules upon children so they could learn to impose said rules upon themselves as they became adults. Kant probably thought it was a universal truth, or at least a practice not limited to Europe. Though the *Jesuit Relations* cover the time period 1610–1791 no one would want to say they were in any way under the influence of Kant (1724–1804).[1] They both independently exhibit the widespread European belief that autonomy is imposing rules on yourself, and that this is learned by having others impose rules on you in your youth. With this mindset, it is little wonder that the missionaries like Father Le Jeune, when they saw Indian children running about like "little savages" with apparently no parental guidance, thought that it was their Christian duty to impose discipline on these poor children so they could learn autonomy the same way Europeans did.

This may well be the origin of Indian residential schools. They may well have been set up with the best of intentions. But however good the intentions, we would argue that such intentions were misguided, wrong-headed, even. In our discussion of philosopher J. T. Stevenson at the outset of this chapter, we have already made reference to his use of Erik Erikson's study of the psychological damage done to Indian children by U.S. government schools. As we also noted above, Stevenson insists that the analysis of this important issue requires the use of "the best scientific evidence available." Though, as we have seen, Stevenson does well enough, he was writing in the early 1980s and some of his scientific sources were drawn from as far back as the 1950s and '60s, Erikson for example. Science has advanced considerably since then, particularly in the past 30-odd years.

Cognitive Science and Native Narrative Traditions

Of particular relevance to our argument here are advances in what is now called second-generation cognitive science and its impact on the discipline of philosophy itself. One of the leaders in this field, philosopher of cognitive science Mark Johnson, in his 1993 groundbreaking study *Moral Imagination: Implications of Cognitive Science for Ethics*, argues that "there are many things wrong with our received view of moral reasoning as consisting primarily in discerning the appropriate universal moral principle that tells us the single 'right thing to do' in a given situation" (1). Johnson critiques what he calls the "Enlightenment folk theory of Faculty Psychology" which we have inherited from 17th and 18th century science and philosophy (207). It is important to realize that the plausibility of a Kantian ethic — or indeed of any rational ethic based on principles — presupposes this folk theory of faculty psychology which assumes "our mental acts can be broken down into separate and distinct forms of judgment" (207). There are, it is supposed, epistemic or knowledge judgments; theoretical judgments dealing with the way the world is; moral judgments dealing with how we should behave and the way things ought to be; and finally aesthetic judgments "based on *feelings* and *imagination*, expressing our feeling response to certain perceptible forms of natural and artificial objects. It was regarded as crucial not to confuse moral with aesthetic judgments" (Johnson 1993, 207). Morality after all was thought to be based on the faculty of reason, not imagination. According to the "Enlightenment folk theory of Faculty Psychology" and the correlative "Moral Law Folk Theory," in moral judgment the will uses moral principles or ethical maxims derived from the faculty of pure *a priori* practical reason (duty) to rule our emotions, feelings and desires; to keep such passions in line. Some such view is, as we have seen, certainly apparent in the philosophy of Immanuel Kant. It is, however, at least as old as Plato (c. 427–347 B.C.). Although it operates for the most part unconsciously, Johnson observes "this folk theory of Faculty Psychology is shared by virtually everyone in Western culture" (15). What we argue Johnson's work puts beyond dispute is, in his words, that "those folk theories that are based on Enlightenment Faculty Psychology, its distinction among types of judgment, and its correlative distinction among realms of experience (i.e., the theoretical, moral, and aesthetic) are, for the most part, shown to be wrong by cognitive science" (208). This is an extremely important conclusion. It underlines the significance of the subtitle of Johnson's study: *Implications of Cognitive Science for Ethics*. Back in 1993, when the *Moral Imagination: Implications of Cognitive Science for Ethics* was first published, Johnson felt compelled to justify his main title: "I began this book with the observation that many people are likely to regard the term 'moral imagination' as an oxymoron, a juxtaposition of two contradictory concepts." He goes on to explain that "their reason for holding this mistaken view is that they accept the *Moral Law* conception of morality as a system of moral laws derived by pure reason alone, whereas they associate imagination with art, creativity, and our general capacity to *break* rules and transcend our present concepts" (207). Indeed, in striking contrast to the received time honored view that "man is a *rational* animal," Johnson begins his study with the provocative claim: "My central thesis is that human beings are fundamentally *imaginative* moral animals" (1).

In 2006, less than a decade and a half after Johnson's *Moral Imagination*, another internationally recognized ethicist, Margaret Somerville, published a book titled *The Ethical Imagination: Journeys of the Human Spirit*. But Somerville saw no need to justify her title. There is not even a hint that putting the concepts "ethical" and "imagination" together in her title would seem odd, much less ever be regarded as an oxymoron. Of course she too is trying to be provocative in her study. She argues that something more than reason is required in order to deal with complex moral issues, and she says that narrative and myth are important. "From an ethics perspective, we need to pay close attention to myths" (Somerville 2006, 73) because, as she puts it, "[o]ur primary focus on reason may have deprived us of the ability to deal with complexity" (205). But Somerville makes no mention of either cognitive science in general or Mark Johnson's work in particular. Still, we contend something changed, and changed radically, in the field of ethics in the 15 years or so between these two books. This important change makes the notion of an ethical or moral imagination not only intelligible, but actually an acceptable — and indeed necessary and indispensable — concept. This change, we argue, is bound up with groundbreaking findings in the field of cognitive science over the same decade and a half.

In 2003, exactly ten years after the publication of Johnson's *Moral Imagination,* another important study on the moral imagination appeared. This work, *John Dewey and Moral Imagination: Pragmatism in Ethics* by Steven Fesmire, is obviously inspired by Johnson, and argues that recent empirical findings in cognitive science corroborate much of the pragmatic thought of American philosopher John Dewey (1859–1952). This should not come as a great surprise given the pragmatists' emphasis on actual concrete moral experience rather than more abstract moral rules and ethical theories, which we consider of little practical value. What is important in Fesmire's study, from our perspective, is that he provides evidence to show that "moral deliberation is fundamentally imaginative and takes the form of a dramatic rehearsal" (4) which involves imagining possible courses of action without having to physically endure the negative consequences of paths we decide ought not to be taken. Given that this kind of imagining as storytelling or narrative is also an art, Fesmire argues, for the related thesis that "moral conduct is helpfully conceived on the model of aesthetic perception and artistic creation" (4). Although Fesmire develops these theses in the context of a study of the philosophy of John Dewey, he insists that they stand on their own merit. As Fesmire puts it, "Although I hope the emphasis on imagination and art contributes to a more robust understanding of Dewey's ethics than is currently extant, I draw from Dewey to develop theses that stand or fall independent of him" (4). Following Johnson, Fesmire admits that "approaching moral conduct from the standpoint of art and aesthetic experience may still strike some as, at best, incoherent. Worse, it may appear to be an opening for an anything goes relativism" (122). However, by Fesmire's time, this attitude can be and is dismissed as mere prejudice, a hangover from 17th and 18th century thought shown to be false by the findings of cognitive science. "This prejudice is conditioned by our Enlightenment heritage, which teaches that ... aesthetic and moral experiences are discontinuous.... Despite growing disrepute and incompatibility with empirical findings, assumptions about reason dominant in seventeenth and eighteenth century Europe still set the context for moral inquiries, for both the person on the street and the moral philosopher" (122–123). As a result, Fesmire concludes, "any attempt to decompartmentalize the supposedly autonomous spheres of the moral and the aesthetic ... raises a suspicious eyebrow because it is mistakenly taken to radically subjectivize moral reflection" (123).

However, if we can somehow drag moral thought out of the 17th and 18th centuries and into the 21st century, we will discover, as Fesmire puts it, "far from collapsing into extreme subjectivism, decompartmentalization revitalizes moral theory and opens the door to a more responsible ethic" (125). This is also the kind of imaginative narrative ethic we discussed above in relation to Keith Basso and Apache story telling. Basso reports that the Apache use hunting metaphors to explain the role of stories about the long ago which can be said to stalk individuals and hit them like an arrow (Basso 1996, 58). We find that Native American ethics, indeed, Native American philosophy, is confirmed and corroborated by the most recent findings of cognitive science.

Johnson has published a number of studies with George Lakoff of the Institute for Cognitive Studies, University of California at Berkeley, including *Metaphors We Live By* (1980) and *Philosophy in the Flesh: The Embodied Mind and Its Challenge to Western Thought* (1999). Lakoff and Johnson have found that most if not all of our abstract thinking is in metaphors using image schemas, prototypes and so forth to facilitate processing impossibly large amounts of information very quickly. The source domain, the origin of these metaphors, they suggest, turns out to be the human body, in particular the sensorimotor system. On the basis of this, they argue that "there is no ethical system that is not metaphorical" (Lakoff and Johnson 1999, 325). They distinguish between "basic experiential morality," such as "health is good," "everyone ought to be protected from physical harm," and more abstract universal moral concepts such as "justice," "rights," "nurturance," and the like all of which *must* be defined metaphorically. All such moral metaphors, they argue, "are inextricably tied to our embodied experience of well-being: health, strength, wealth, purity, control, nurturance, empathy, and so forth" (331). This is of crucial importance because it avoids the problem of ethical relativism. For Lakoff and Johnson, all moral "metaphors are grounded in the nature of our bodies and social interactions, and they are thus anything but arbitrary and unconstrained" (290). We speak, for example, of taking a balanced approach, or of being an upright citizen, meaning someone of good moral standing. These common expressions are metaphorical. They are based on the fact that we embodied beings literally walk upright on our own two feet and must physically keep our balance. Falling down does not contribute to our well-being, staying upright does. It is easier to find our way in sunlight than in the dark, so we naturally associate light with good and dark with the opposite. When we speak about seeing the point of an argument or grasping a difficult concept, we are not talking about literally seeing and grasping. One cannot literally see a logical implication nor physically grasp with one's hands an abstract concept; nevertheless, literal seeing and physical grasping are the source domains of these conceptual metaphors. That is why cognitive scientists say such metaphors are derived from and dependent upon the sensorimotor system. In recent years, neuroscience has made significant advances using breakthroughs in brain imaging technologies such as positron emission tomography (PET scans) and functional magnetic resonance imaging (fMRIs). Lakoff and colleagues are reported to have found that "when we use a metaphor (like 'grasping' an idea) that involves doing something with our physical bodies ... the same neurons light up as if we were in fact performing that act" (Holland 2009, 98). We use temperature metaphors to describe affection ("She is a warm and loving person" or "She is a cold-hearted bitch") because, according to Lakoff, "temprature is publicly discernible while affection is not" (Lakoff 2008, 84). As children in a family we often experience affection and warmth at the same time, for example "feeling warm while being held affectionately" (Lakoff and Johnson 1999, 50). This is the experiential origin of the "Affection Is Warmth" conceptual metaphor. At least that is how this metaphorical mapping is written in English. "The mapping it names is neural in character" (Lakoff 2008, 83). As Lakoff likes to say: "Neurons that fire together wire together" (83).[2] It should be noted that this neural mapping will only flow one way. Because we experience warmth through the sensorimotor system the temperature synapses fire more often than those associated with affection and are therefore stronger. "As a result, activation will flow from temperature to affection and not in the opposite direction" (Lakoff 2008, 84). That is why it makes sense to say "She warmed up to me" but not "The soup got more affectionate" (cf. Lakoff 2008, 84).

Lakoff and Johnson note that for most of us our first encounter with morality is in the family as children and that therefore most metaphors about morality have their source domain in the family. In other words, much moral thinking is based on family morality (cf. Lakoff and Johnson

1999, 312–313). But as Lakoff and Johnson also argue, the metaphorical construction of morality based on family can take a number of different forms depending on various different conceptions of the family. They contrast, for example, "the strict father family morality" with the more caring nurturant parent family morality, recognizing that both are idealizations and that many families are a combination of both (1999, 313–316). Lakoff and Johnson describe the nurturant parent metaphor as "a morality of caring for others out of compassion and empathy, rather than a "morality of obedience to moral laws given by divine authority" which is much closer to a Kantian account of morality. Kant would, of course, substitute Reason for divine authority (319). Still Kant's is obviously a form of strict father family morality. The strict father is the metaphor for moral authority whether that authority is thought to be God, the Church or pure practical reason. Why do we call priests Father, like Father Le Jeune, the missionary we discussed above who could not tolerate the freedom Indians seemed to grant their children? He was obviously working with a more authoritative model of morality in mind. Priests, like God the Father, are symbols of moral authority in which the strict father family morality metaphor is made quite explicit.

As noted above, we have argued in the past that this strict father family morality in the form of a Kantian heteronomous treatment of children produces equally autonomous, morally responsible adults as those of Native American child rearing practices which employ the value of interventive-noninterference and seem to treat children as autonomous from the moment of mobility. However, Lakoff and Johnson, drawing on current scientific research in three fields of psychology—family violence studies, socialization theory and attachment theory—argue that "strict father family morality tends to produce children who are dependent on the authority of others, cannot chart their own moral course very well, have less of a conscience, are less respectful of others, and have no greater ability to resist temptations" (327). This, of course, is the exact opposite of the autonomous, morally responsible citizens it purports to develop. We suggest that the nurturant parent model, which we believe is much closer to Native American child rearing practices, would be much more successful. Lakoff and Johnson are correct in saying that this is an empirical question that can be decided by research particularly in the cognitive sciences. The evidence to date suggests that strict father family morality may not be the best method of child rearing because it is not all that "successful in developing the kind of moral agents it prizes" (Lakoff and Johnson 1999, 327).

Lakoff might have some problems with the Native American value of noninterference, since he is critical of what he calls permissive family moralities. "The permissive family is what Lakoff calls a 'pathological' form of the nurturant parent family, since it mistakenly thinks that letting the children do whatever they please is an appropriate form of nurturance" (Lakoff and Johnson 1999, 323). But to apply this pathological form to Native American communities (as we have noted missionaries like Father Le Jeune seemed to do) would be to ignore the important role of stories, modeling elders, the vision quest, and many other traditional ceremonies, in their child rearing practices. We agree that many contemporary "urban Indians" may not have access to such community practices. But that is no reason to force their children into schools where Western practices based on strict father family morality predominate. What is needed is something more compatible with Native American values and philosophy. That is precisely why we are encouraging more research in Native American philosophy. That is precisely why we are writing this book.

As we have argued, not only have Western practices based on strict father family morality failed, under empirical scrutiny, to produce the kind of moral agents they prize; but they are also based on outmoded 17th and 18th century Enlightenment folk theories of Faculty Psychology and Moral Law which have been shown to be false by the findings of second-generation cognitive science. It is important to be careful in rejecting Enlightenment assumptions, even obviously outmoded ones, in defending Native American worldviews. There is always the danger that we will be accused of postmodern (pomo) relativism, and have our arguments dismissed as mere "pomospeak" (sometimes equated with George Orwell's "newspeak" from his dystopian novel *Nineteen Eighty-Four*). For instance, Frances Widdowson and Albert Howard, in their dismissal of traditional and contemporary aboriginal views, *Disrobing the Aboriginal Industry: The Deception Behind Indigenous Cultural Preseveration*, assert, "Pomospeak is everywhere in the literature justifying current aboriginal policies" (65). Widdowson and Howard argue that "postmodernism embraces eclecticism; it proudly advocates 'radical scepticism' or anti-authoritarianism ... 'celebrating differences' in opposition to focusing on common principles, claiming that they suppress human freedom and creativity" (64). All this because, in their view, for postmodernism "all assumptions upon which the Enlightenment was based are to be rejected not only because they are supposedly ethnocentric but on the basis that they are oppressive" (64). Now we actually agree with much of what Widdowson and Howard have to say in *Disrobing the Aboriginal Industry* (and we expect this sentence and the next to be quoted extensively out of context). A lot of nonsense *has* been generated in the name of aboriginal advocacy. *Disrobing the Aboriginal Industry* has collected a lot of it. It is a book which should be discussed widely by aboriginal students and scholars. We discuss it further in the next chapter. Here we are interested in showing how it is possible to reject outmoded Enlightenment assumptions in defending Native American philosophy without falling into the trap of postmodern relativism. We saw above how philosopher of cognitive science Steven Fesmire recognized that any rejection of the Enlightenment folk theory of Faculty Psychology is seen as "an opening for an anything goes relativism ... because it is mistakenly taken to radically subjectivize moral reflection" (Fesmire 2003, 122–123). Still, as we have seen, Fesmire concludes that this fear of radical relativism is unfounded. "Far from collapsing into extreme subjectivism, decompartmentalization revitalizes moral theory and opens the door to a more responsible ethic" (125). This is because cognitive science has provided good grounds for rejecting the 17th and 18th century Enlightenment folk theory of Faculty Psychology. Today we have a much better scientific understanding of cognition. Of one thing we can be quite sure. Cognitive science does not support, much less lead to, any kind of postmodern relativism. It has, in actual fact, led to just the opposite. With its emphasis on metaphor and narrative in imaginative rationality, cognitive science has led to the development of a new discipline of study, the cognitive theory of literature, which goes far beyond postmodernism. We find, for example, in Mary Thomas Crane's *Shakespeare's Brain: Reading with Cognitive Theory,* that cognitive science is used to counter the extreme relativism of postmodern literary theory such as that associated with Jacques Derrida (1930–2004). Drawing explicitly on Lakoff and Johnson, Crane argues that "the Derridean 'There is nothing outside the text,'... clearly does not fit a cognitive theory. Indeed, from a cognitive perspective, meaning is anchored ... by a three-way tether: brain, culture, discourse" (24). Crane concludes that "cognitive subjects are not simply determined by the symbolic order in which they exist; instead, they shape (and are also shaped by) meanings that are determined by an interaction of the physical world, culture, and human cognitive systems" (12).

Cognitive science itself finds overwhelming empirical support in the form of the convergent findings of a number of disciplines such as linguistics (including Native languages and linguistics), historical linguistics, cognitive psychology, developmental psychology, and gesture analysis (including studies of Native American sign language) (Lakoff and Johnson 1999, 83). Philosopher Mark Johnson, with cognitive scientist George Lakoff, argues that although it is the virtue of scientific knowledge to be open to revision on the basis of further empirical evidence, the disciplines cited give us converging evidence which make the findings of cognitive science as stable as any scientific knowledge can be: "The methodology of convergent evidence and the masses of different types of evidence minimize the probability that the results will be an artifact of any specific methodology" (89). We suggest that cognitive literary theory, such as that exemplified in the book *Shakespeare's Brain,* and our own work on the narrative character of Native American philosophy, could be added to the convergent evidence corroborating cognitive science. Indeed cognitive science, to its credit, has led to the development of a number of new fields of study. Besides cognitive literary theory, there is now a cognitive theory of medicine, cognitive legal studies, and even a cognitive science of science itself. For example, Theodore L. Brown in *Making Truth: Metaphor in Science,* drawing on the work of Lakoff and Johnson, argues: "The theory of conceptual metaphor provides us with powerful tools for understanding how scientists reason about and communicate abstract ideas" (Brown 2008, 12). In the field of cognitive legal studies Steven L. Winter's *A Clearing in the Forest: Law, Life, and Mind* takes recent advances in the cognitive sciences, such as narrative rationality, radial categories, image schemas and conceptual metaphor, and brings them "in cognitive theory to bear upon the Law" (xi). Winter argues that the narrative or stories that lie behind legislation are what really give the law meaning. "The idealized cognitive models that work in every other aspect of our cognitive and communicative life are no less available to the law. Rights and other legal concepts continue to be meaningful because we can recall and reflect on the lived experience that gave them birth" (Winter 2001, 351). We argue in a forthcoming anthology on aboriginal rights that some of the metaphors that Winter uses, such as "rights are rights of way on a forest path," can be useful in explicating the notion of aboriginal rights (Mayer and Tomsons, forthcoming). We hope that this anthology, based on the 2001 Canadian Philosophical Association international conference *Philosophy and Aboriginal Rights: Critical Dialogues,* will be the beginning of an ongoing cross-cultural dialogue on aboriginal rights.

Here, we will discuss the cognitive science of medicine in more detail because its emphasis on narrative in medicine can be used to give scientific support for the role of stories in Native American teachings. We note in passing that (Western) medically trained Native Americans tend to go back to their traditions to justify using narrative in their medical practice (cf. Mehl-Madrona 1998, 2003, 2007). Physician and cognitive scientist Gary

Wright, in his 2007 book *Means, Ends and Medical Care*, argues that health care professionals need to pay more attention to "the unstructured narratives" of their patients, "to the stories of their illnesses and their efforts to cope ... to their stories of seeking care and trying to find ways to pay for it" (162). To see what he is getting at here, it is helpful to think of diseases and other diagnoses by physicians as metaphors, the way in which cognitive scientists see all abstract thought. Wright notes that some of these metaphors for disease are used in professional conceptualization and discourse, such as "Disease Is Disorder," whereas others, like "Disease Is Being Under Attack," are more prominent in the thinking and conversations of patients and the general public. The important point is that everyone, physicians and patients alike, are speaking metaphorically, not literally. Wright explains, "It is apparent ... that the symptom, such as a 'cut,' a 'bloody nose,' a 'headache,' 'blindness,' 'numbness,' 'vomiting' or 'fever' is the level on which most of us would start to understand the whole system of concepts topped by 'disease in general.' One reason for making this assertion is that symptoms, such as 'stomach ache,' and 'chest pain' are literally embodied, whereas disease entities like 'appendicitis' and 'gastroenteritis' are abstract in that they are a step removed from direct experience" (54). According to Wright, then, patients' symptoms are literally experienced, whereas diseases and diagnoses are metaphorical explanations of these symptoms, pointing to ways of dealing with them.

Wright is stressing narrative and informal clinical judgment because in his over thirty years of medical practice he has learned that "any protocol, guideline or algorithm needs to be supplemented and tempered with compassionate discretion" (158). It is in attempting to counteract what he calls "the creeping formalism in Anglo-American medicine" that Wright calls upon the findings of second-generation cognitive science. Formal protocols and quality of care guidelines require clear classifications and classical categories so that every member of an identified category can be dealt with the under the same protocol. Classical categories are thought of metaphorically as containers, and something is either in the container or outside of it, either a member of said category or not. Given that there are clearly specifiable conditions for category inclusion all members of the category can be treated indiscriminately in the same way, making quality of care guidelines and other such protocols relatively easy to formulate and apply. But, Wright argues, according to cognitive science things are not all that simple. Many of the categories dealt with in medicine are not classical categories. They are rather what cognitive scientists have identified as *radial* categories. Such categories cannot be thought of as simple containers. Membership is "not an all or nothing matter" (14). Members are not treated alike. Some are considered more representative than others. Wright explains the radial nature of such categories: "Representative members ... are metaphorically placed in the centre.... Less and less representative members are imaginatively farther and farther away from the center, giving the category a radial structure" (15).

Wright makes it clear that "the overall 'disease' category is *radial* not classical" (56). At the very core of this radial category are the textbook examples of disease, the prototypical cases, such "as 'pneumonia,' 'colds,' 'bladder infections' and 'gastroenteritis' ('stomach flu')"(57). At the extreme margins of this radial category hover such dubious cases as "'old age,' 'weakness,' 'crime,' 'harm,' 'suffering,' 'eccentricity' and 'infertility'" (56). These and more representative cases of disease metaphorically rotate about the prototypical cases in concentric circles like planets in orbit. This is what gives the category its radial structure. Wright explains: "Analogies and metaphors act cognitively like forces (such as gravity) or links in that the easily identified clear cut central members present a cognitive pull on the marginal examples drawing them into association" (56). Wright's worry is that if disease is dealt with as a classical category rather than a radial one, given the growing number of "guidelines and criteria for establishing diagnoses and protocols for dealing with diseases," there is the danger that more and more clinicians will "have a tendency to force their observations to fit pre-existing categories rather than to admit the existence of the doubtful and to deal with it as such" (70). Protocols may work well for the prototypical cases of disease. But cognitive science has shown that disease is a radial category and the protocols may not work so well with the more marginal members of this category. That is why Wright is calling for the greater use of more informal clinical judgment and narrative in medicine.

Mark Johnson's thesis in the *Moral Imagination,* that ethical thinking requires not moral laws but imaginative narrative, is making a point similar to Wright's thesis in regard to medicine. "If a good many of our basic moral concepts (such as person, rights, harm, justice, love) and many of the concepts that define kinds of action (e.g., murder, lie, educate, natural, sex) have internal prototype structure, then Moral Law theories must be rejected" (Johnson 1993, 189). Cognitive science has shown that moral principles like medical protocalls really apply only to prototypes. Johnson explains, "They 'work' for the prototypical cases — the nonproblematic ones — about which there is widespread agreement within moral traditions. What moral laws we have are precisely those that are formulated to fit the prototypical cases, the central members of a category" (190). To deal with more problematic cases in ethical thinking we do not need more moral rules and principles but imaginative narrative, the ability to tell and contemplate stories. Johnson has learned from cognitive science "that narrative characterizes the synthetic character of our very experience.... The stories we tell emerge from, and can then refigure, the narrative structure of our experience ... because we are imaginative narrative creatures, we can also configure our lives in novel ways" (Johnson 1993, 163). This sounds not unlike the Apache notion of the transformative impact of story reported by Basso which we discussed above. We think cognitive science lends empirical support to such Native American practices. In fact we suspect that if, *per impossible*, science and Western philosophy had achieved this level of sophistication by the time of first contact with the Americas, the history of European-Native relations might well have been very different. The narratives and stories told by Native elders might have been recognized as a legitimate form of philosophy. At the very least, the Indigenous peoples of the Americas might have been recognized as human beings and perhaps even treated with (a little) more respect. But of course the European explorers of the 17th and 18th century were not so sophisticated and, as we detailed in Chapter Two, they brought their own prejudices with them (what we called outside view predicates). Such Eurocentric preconceptions were imposed on the indigenous peoples of the Americas. Such pre-judgments, such Eurocentric expectations had been forged in a Europe with a history of the Spanish Inquisition. Under the notorious *Malleus Maleficarum*, or *Hammer of Witches,* Europeans had been trying and convicting women of witchcraft for years. It was widely believed that such women actually consorted with devils and demons in forest wilderness: "Under torture, suspected witches admitted to all sorts of encounters with Satan and his cohorts ... taking place in the woods far from public view. The image of the devil that emerged from such confessions is often that of a being with a dark or red visage, and if not naked, clothed in the skins of animals or decorated with feathers" (Hoxie 568, cf. Wilson 2002, 10). It is little wonder that European explorers, when they encountered half-naked, dark-skinned beings partly clothed in animal skins and bedecked with feathers, thought the vast forests of the Americas were the homelands of demons and devils, perhaps even of Satan himself. Robert F. Berkhofer, Jr., confirms this in *The White Man's Indian: Images of the American Indian from Columbus to the Present,* citing early exploration literature such as *The Principal Navigations, Voyages, Traffiques, and Discoveries of the English Nation*

(1598–1600). There we find the first-hand description of an encounter between some European sailors and an old "Eskimo" woman. The Europeans clearly believed she might be a witch or a devil. They even examined her with the expectation that her feet might be cloven like the Devil's: "The old wretch, whom divers of our saylers supposed to be eyther a devill, or a witch, had her buskins plucked off, to see if she were cloven footed, and for her ugly hue and deformity we let her goe" (Berkhofer 17).

Cognitive Science, Stereotypes, and the Polycentric Perspective

One of the few philosophers to recognize and use the discoveries of cognitive science in discussing negative stereotyping of Native Americans is Agnes B. Curry in her article "We Don't Say 'Indian': On the Paradoxical Construction of the Reavers." In this critique of the use of the savage redskin stereotype in film and popular culture Curry draws on the schemas and prototypes of cognitive science. She acknowledges that the brain's use of such cognitive shortcuts is normal: "As widely-held cognitive and evaluative schemas linking people to characteristics because of their membership in specific social groups, social stereotypes are results of normal cognitive process" (par. 12). She does, however, warn that this knowledge of the normal working of the human brain should make us cautious: "Stereotypes speed up mental processing, but prompt overgeneralization and foster inaccurate perception of individual cases" (par. 12). We think Curry is quite correct and we agree with her that Hollywood with its B-Westerns has much to answer for. Since cognitive science has shown that the brain naturally uses prototypes and radial categories, how do we avoid stereotyping, racial profiling and other such morally questionable but seemingly natural practices? As Curry explains: "When stereotypical elements operate without foregrounding, at the edge of awareness, with no critical space opened up, they merely trigger pre-existing schemas" (Par. 15). But we can make such pre-existing schemas conscious. In this context we can draw attention to the fact that these particular stereotypes, for example, were brought to the Americas from Europe and tended to frame the observations made by early explorers. We have given a concrete example of this above in which the explorers were actually looking for cloven hooves on the indigenous inhabitants. This is one way to counter negative stereotypes (by making people aware of how they are using them). Cognitive science has shown that it makes no sense to demand that everyone just give up their prejudices and be objective and unbiased. That goes completely counter to what we now know about how our brains function. Yet this is what is still taught in many of the social sciences. As Lawrence Neuman, in *Social Research Methods: Quantitative and Qualitative Approaches,* critically reports, "Science is value free, unbiased, and objective... free of prejudice.... With complete value freedom and objectivity, science reveals the one and only, unified, unambiguous truth" (Neuman 2000; 116–117). What is called for is a realistic definition of scientific objectivity, one more consistent with the findings of cognitive science. Philosopher of cognitive science Mark Johnson suggests becoming what he calls transperspectival, by allowing one prototype (or stereotype) to confront another, thus enlarging the overall perspective (in cross-cultural conversations for example): "Here is a vision of a realistic human objectivity. It involves understanding, and being able to criticize, the way in which you and others have constructed their worlds, and it involves ... a limited freedom to imagine other values and points of view and to change one's world in light of possibilities revealed by those alternative viewpoints" (Johnson 1993, 241). Johnson admits that it may well seem odd to combine "imagination" and "objectivity," but he argues it is this kind of "imaginative rationality" discovered by cognitive science which makes human objectivity possible, by allowing us to take up the perspective of others in order to understand their experience (242). As Johnson argues, citing the German philosopher Hans Georg Gadamer, "Our prejudgments are conditions for our being able to make sense of things. Without them, we can understand nothing.... Rather than overthrowing all our prejudgments, we need to open them up to possible transformation through our encounters with others, whose prejudgments may confront our own" (131–132). We think it is significant, in this context, that Johnson's notion of the transperspectival, what we called in Chapter One and elsewhere polycentrism or the polycentric perspective, also turns out to be a traditional Native American value closely related to interventive-noninterference and respect for difference (Rabb 1989, 1992; McPherson and Rabb 2001). This polycentrism is illustrated in an account of the traditional "sharing circle" by Cree scholar Michael A. Hart. He suggests since everyone is sitting in a circle "they will each have a different perspective of the topic" which is metaphorically located in the centre of the circle. "Everyone expresses their views so that a full picture of the topic is developed. Individual views are blended until consensus on the topic is reached. A community view is developed and knowledge is shared for the benefit of all members" (Hart 1996; 65).

We believe this notion of polycentrism to be fairly pervasive in Indigenous philosophy. The concept was picked up by Cherokee philosopher Jace Weaver. Citing the first edition of our *Indian from the Inside,* he argues: "Given the diversity of Indian cultures and worldviews, Native theology is what McPherson and Rabb call 'polycentric'" (Weaver 1997, 32). He goes on to explain the polycentric perspective with the help of a story by Osage scholar George Tinker. In Tinker's story, an anthropologist visits two tribal communities separated by a mountain. In one she learns "that the tribes' council fire is the center of the universe and creation myths are told to demonstrate this concept" (Weaver 1997, 33). She then visits the other community guided by elders from the first and is told the same thing, to which her guides from the first community "nod their assent" (33). When she says to her guide from the first tribe, "I thought you said that your fire was the center," she receives the reply "When we're there, that is the center of the universe. When we are here: this is the center" (33). This story is taken from Tinker's article "An American Indian Theological Response to Eco-justice." It is said to "illustrate the polycentric approach" (Weaver 1997, 33). Weaver cites with approval Tinker's conclusion "sometimes a single truth is not enough to explain the balance of the world around us" (33). As only Jace Weaver can put it, "Ultimate reality, which we see through a glass darkly, is like a child's kaleidoscope. How it is perceived depends on how the cylinder is held, even though the bits of glass that form the picture are unchanging. The task must be to learn as much as one can not only about the given pattern but about the individual bits of glass, so that when the cylinder is shaken we can know something about the new image when it forms.... We need to examine as many different cultural codes as we can to re-create the structure of human life — self, community, spirit, and the world as we perceive it" (Weaver 1997, 33).

Husband and wife team Marie Battiste (Mi'kmaq) and Sa'ke'j Henderson (Chichasaw) confirm that "indigenous communities accept more diversity than most linguistic communities" (Battiste and Henderson 2000, 105). This, of course, follows from the Native American values of noninterference and polycentrism. We argued above that cognitive science avoids any kind of postmodern relativism. It is important to note here that the polycentrism or indigenous pluralism defended by Hart, Tinker, Weaver, Battisie, Henderson, and ourselves, also avoids the charge of relativism. As historian Michael Ignatieff argues, defending what he calls his "patchwork-quilt vision" of Canadian identity: "Pluralism does not mean relativism. It means humility" (Ignatieff 2000, 104).

We think it is significant that Ignatieff, in his discussion of Canadian identity, feels compelled "to acknowledge that it is the very essence of nation-states that they harbor within them incompatible visions of the national story" (2000, 136). Though he does not mention Native American historians like George Tinker and Jace Weaver, like them Ignatieff sees no need to reconcile such inconsistent stories: "Holding a nation together does not require us to force these incompatible stories into one, but simply to keep them in dialogue with each other and, if possible, learning from each other" (2000, 136). We seem to find here the respect for difference we identified above as a traditional Native American value. In fact Ignatieff argues that what he calls the "rights revolution" in Canada "has made us all aware how different we are, both as individuals and as peoples" (2000, 137). Ignatieff claims that differences rather than similarities are of most importance. "Our differences, small as they may seem, are the basis of our identity" (Ignatieff 2000, 137). He seems to attribute this respect for difference and for the rights of the other, at least in part to our Native American (First Nation) heritage: "We are a community forged by the primal experience of negotiating terms of settlement among three peoples: the English, the French, and the aboriginal First Nations. This gives us a particular rights culture and it is this rights culture that makes us different" (Ignatieff 2000, 14). His thesis is not unlike that of John Ralston Saul in *A Fair Country: Telling Truths About Canada,* which we discussed briefly in Chapter Two. Saul, like Ignatieff, also argues that Canada has "a triangular foundation of Aboriginals, francophones and anglophones" (Saul 2008, 119). But Saul goes much further. He wants to argue that the wording of some of the foundation documents of Canada such as the Royal Proclamation and the Quebec Act were actually influenced by Native American (First Nation) values like noninterference and respect of difference. On the face of it, this claim does not seem all that plausible. At the time Canada was under British control, France having surrendered its claim at the end of the seven-years'-war. These documents, the Royal Proclamation and the Quebec Act would have been written in Britain and sent over to and imposed upon "the colonies." Where, then, is the opportunity for aboriginal influence? With the large francophone population, all such documents were translated into French, and that was done in Canada by local officials, many of whom Saul repeatedly tells us had aboriginal wives. Saul argues, "If you want to understand the intent of eighteenth- and nineteenth-century Canadian legal documents, read the French versions" (123). These documents seemed to contain an aboriginal respect for difference. Saul notes that the first British governor, James Murry, "was a Catholic

Scot, a great supporter of the francophones and an opponent of the Boston traders and the few English traders who arrived from England. This alliance of English-descent Protestants in Boston and English Protestants in England thought it should inherit all business in Canada — a reward for the fall of France in the Americas" (123–124). Saul correctly notes that they were furious that the Quebec Act gave the Catholics full rights of citizenship and religion, that the welfare of these Papists was protected. This would not have been the case back in England (124). In the French version of the Quebec Act, "*welfare* became *bonheur* and *le bonheur future.* So *welfare* meant happiness in the eighteenth-century sense ... the fulfillment of the self within the shared well-being of society" (Saul 2008 124). As Saul points out, "This was the *happiness* of the American Declaration of Independance and the *bonheur* of the French *Declaration des droits de l'homme"* (124). Of course the legal terms "peace, tranquilité, welfare, bien-etre, bonheur, good government" were being used in documents around the world, not just in Canada. But as Saul says, "Whether they were empty formulae or took root with real local meaning depended on the society and its situation" (124–125). Though Saul does not say so, this is reminiscent of the methodology used in the field of cognitive legal studies and Steven Winter's point in *A Clearing in the Forest: Law, Life, and Mind,* that it is the story behind the legislation and not the written document itself that is important in the interpretation of local meaning. Concerning the use of these important terms according to Saul, "in Canada they fed directly into the debate over how to build a non-monolithic and atypical system ... and ... the need for some sort of fair arrangement in Canada" (125). This helps to explain the title of Saul's book: *A Fair Country.* This is also why Saul claims that Canada, with its bilingual documents, leans more toward an oral culture. The meaning hovers just over the page somewhere between the English and French written versions. So, for example, a legal loophole based on the "letter of the law" in one language "tends to evaporate in the other" (cf. Saul 2008, 128). As Saul astutely points out, in the Canadian courtroom "only an argument of substance stands up.... Reality seen through two languages can protect us from the demeaning of justice by technical acrobatics. As a result, the meaning of the law in Canada floats slightly off the page in an almost oral manner" (128).

We think the distinction between written and oral cultures is interesting and important in understanding Native American philosophy. We discuss it at some length in the next chapter. However, Saul's thesis about the influence of Native values on Canada's semi-oral bilingual culture requires a good deal more research into the nature and intent of these values before it is possible to discuss the plausibility of his claim in any meaningful way. For example, the whole notion of respect for difference and noninterference including polycentrism or indigenous pluralism, is still not fully understood. As we will see, these concepts are still regarded by some as, to say the least, somewhat controversial.

Callicott and the "Savages"

We began this chapter discussing two philosophers, J. T. Stevenson and J. B. Callicott. We argued that their work taken together contributes to our understanding of the relationship between Native values, the Native concept of land and the Native concept of person. It is our belief that the arguments Callicott presents in support of his Leopoldian land ethic also provide evidence in support of Stevenson's thesis that there is an essential and too often overlooked connection between the Native American concept of land and the psychological as well as physical health of the indigenous peoples of North America. We also believe that Stevenson goes well beyond Callicott in insisting "that the native belief that the natural world forms a complex, interdependent system of which the native peoples are an integral part should not be dismissed as mere primitive or magical thought.... Although not expressed in our theoretical terms and differing in many details, the general approach is consistent with our most advanced biological science. In their own way, the native peoples got there first" (Stevenson 1992, 303). Callicott has been criticized by what he calls his '"indigenous' critics" for insisting that "indigenous thought is *validated* by the land ethic" (Hester et al. 2000, 278). This, of course, devalues indigenous views. "The task of indigenous thought is [only] to *express* the abstractions of the land ethic in the 'rich vocabulary' of indigenous cultures.... Indigenous thought [merely] provides the color commentary in the local vernacular, and indigenous practices show how to put the land ethic into practice in the local bioregions" (Hester et al. 2000, 278). Callicott's response is to amend the position he adopted in his book, *Earth's Insights,* saying: "In retrospect, I wish I had suggested that the ecological insights I found in prescientific religious and indigenous world views and the contemporary scientific world view were *mutually validating.* Indeed they are, I think, mutually reinforcing" (Callicott 2000, 308).

This change puts Callicott much closer to Stevenson than he was in his two 1980s articles we discussed at the beginning of this chapter, or even in his more recent book, *Earth's Insights* (1994), which was the target of his "indigenous" critics, though he is still not saying, as Stevenson was willing to admit, that the indigenous peoples got there first. But this is nothing compared to Callicott's complete failure to understand the full philosophical significance of such Native values as respect, noninterference and polycentrism. This complete lack of understanding is inadvertently revealed in Callicott's *Environmental Ethics* paper "Many Indigenous Worlds or *the* Indigenous World? A Reply to My 'Indigenous' Critics" (Callicott 2000, 291–310). It is actually reiterated in his contribution to the 2002 book *Land, Value, Community: Callicott and Environmental Philosophy* edited by Wayne Ouderkirk and Jim Hill. This book, a collection of seventeen essays on Callicott's environmental philosophy by a wide variety of scholars followed by a reply by Callicott as the concluding chapter, is a volume in the State University of New York (SUNY) series in Environmental Philosophy and Ethics of which Callicott himself is a series editor. We will concentrate on Callicott's reply to his "indigenous" critics in the journal *Environmental Ethics* cited above because there he discusses the article "Indigenous Worlds and Callicott's Land Ethic," by Lee Hester, Dennis McPherson, Annie Booth and Jim Cheney which appeared in the same issue of that journal. Callicott also takes issue with a paper by Viola Cordova entitled "Eco-Indian: A Response to J. Baird Callicott," which appeared in *Ayaangwaamizin: The International Journal of Indigenous Philosophy.* In these articles we have three Native American philosophers, Cordova (Apache), Hester (Choctaw) and McPherson (Ojibwa), all critiquing Callicott's Leopoldian land ethic. Callicott's reply to them is important from the standpoint of Native American philosophy, because, as we have shown above, he is one of very few Western philosophers sympathetic to Native American philosophy. His use of Hallowell's concept "other than human persons" to explain Ojibwa respect for animals and the land is a case in point. He is a Western philosopher who seems, at least on occasion, to "get it." Discovering where he does not "get it," and why, gives us a good place to start in trying to analyze and explicate such Native American values as noninterference, polycentrism and respect, as well as the interrelation between these values and the Native American concepts of land and person.

Callicott complains that, "according to Hester et al., the environmental ethic that I recommend, the Leopold land ethic, is grounded in a 'metaphysic of morals' while '[all] indigenous peoples [everywhere] give primacy to the grounding practice of respect' (p. 281)" (Callicott 2000, 304; square brackets by Callicott and cited page reference is to Hester et al.) Now, if this somewhat ambiguous statement is meant to suggest that Hester et al. criticize Callicott for attempting to ground both Leopold's land ethic and indigenous worldviews in a metaphysics of morals, and that they object to such grounding or validating of indigenous values, then it seems accurate enough. If, however, the statement is read as suggesting that his "indigenous" critics think Callicott believes that both Leopold and indigenous people attempted to offer some metaphysical foundation for their somewhat similar land ethics, this, we suggest, would be an inaccurate reading, a misreading, of the critique offered by Hester et al. Unfortunately, as his reply to the criticism suggests, Callicott seems to have in mind the second, the inaccurate interpretation. He says in apparent rebuttal: "I did not argue that the Ojibwa subscribed to a full-blown metaphysic in the philosophical sense (nor, for that matter do I argue that Leopold did)" (304). However, so far as we can see, no one has suggested that Callicott has argued anything of the sort. What Hester and company do object to, as we explained above, is Callicott's claim that by providing the missing metaphysical foundation he thus validates the indigenous worldview. Grounding an indigenous philosophy in a Western metaphysical foundation tends to distort the indigenous position. They argue, "Callicott's view that we need a *single* environmental ethic to function as a standard for evaluating environmental attitudes and values on the grounds that 'untempered pluralism ... courts conflict rather than mutual understanding and cooperation' flies in the face of the historical fact that hundreds of indigenous cultures have existed side by side on this continent 'forever' without the 'violent ethnic conflict now plaguing the world' about which Callicott is so concerned" (Hester et al. 2000, 278).

It is Callicott's reaction to this argument which, more than anything else, reveals that he does not quite "get" Indigenous pluralism (polycentrism) and respect for difference. Hester et al. are making the historical claim that tolerance of diversity was a feature of life in pre–Columbian America. "It was, in fact, the acceptance (and even *celebration*) of a rich cultural and ethical diversity, of the *differences* between cultures, that made it possible for hundreds of cultures to flourish side by side 'forever'" (Hester et al. 2000, 278). Callicott obviously does not regard this claim as trying to correct the historical record, or trying to present a more accurate account, one not based on the savage redskin stereotype: "A concrete instance of assertive historical revisionism is Hester et al.'s claim that ethnic conflict on the North American continent prior to European contact was not ferocious and horrific, that, to the contrary, precontact American Indians accepted and celebrated the differences between their cultures" (Callicott 2000, 302). We should note in passing that Callicott ignores the fact that Hester et al. always put the term "forever" in quotation marks when they say or imply Native Americans have been in the Americas "forever." They are simply acknowledging that this is what is said. They are simply paying respect to what the elders often say. They are not making a literal historical claim. Their argument works whether or not indigenous people have been here forever or just for a very long time. In using the term "forever" they are simply being nonjudgmental, and acknowledging the elders. As we have seen above even Canadian historian and politician Michael Ignatieff, in acknowledging indigenous influence in Canada, argues that it is normal and healthy to live with incompatible stories, and he sees no need to reconcile them. Again, this is the Native value of noninterference and the acceptance of difference. But Callicott insists on taking Hester and company, and Cordova as well, quite literally, condemning them for making false, indeed ridiculous, historical claims: "If, however, public evidence is forgone in favor of a personal racial-cultural authority to declare truth in the absence of public evidence, then indigenous historical claims become epistemically indistinguishable from fanatical historical claims.... For example, both Cordova and Hester et al. claim that indigenous people, whom they now represent, have been in North America 'forever' [sic.]. The rationale, I suppose, for this ridiculous claim is political. If contemporary American Indian peoples acknowledged that they were the descendants of Asian immigrants — albeit immigrants who first arrived at least twenty times longer ago than the first immigrants from Europe — they fear that their claim to ancestral lands might be disputed" (301). Callicott puts the term "forever" in quotation marks here. But that is simply because he is quoting (actually misquoting) Hester et al. as if they were using it without quotation marks. It is more than obvious that Callicott is accusing them of using it literally and thus making patently ridiculous historical claims based only on the fact that they are Natives and feel that thereby they can and do represent and can speak for all Native people. Callicott then argues that it is equally ridiculous to claim that pre–Columbian America was not "ferocious and horrific." Of Hester and company's contrary view he says, "no historical evidence whatever for this claim is offered; and the evidence that does exist supports an opposite conclusion" (302)

Callicott presents three arguments using the promised evidence. We like to call them "Three Arguments for a More Ferocious and Horrific America." This is an important issue with implications for the philosophical significance of Native values such as noninterference, pluralism and respect for difference. We will, therefore, critically examine each of the three arguments in turn from an "indigenous" perspective. First, Callicott cites the nineteenth century Ojibwa historian William Warren, claiming that the word "Ojibwa" is derived from "*O-jib*, 'pucker up,' and *ub-way,* 'to roast.'" This is supposed to suggest that "the Ojibwa were widely renowned for the way they 'tortured by fire in various ways' their indigenous enemies" (302). Callicott is hardly presenting a balanced picture here. He simply ignores the host of alternative, equally plausible, names for these people. As historian Peter Schmalz documents in *The Ojibwa of Southern Ontario*: "The *Handbook of Indians of Canada* lists over one hundred different names for Ojibwa; indeed, the etymology of the word has not been determined to the satisfaction of many scholars. Almost all of the ethnic groups which came into contact with the Ojibwa gave them a different name; for example, the French called them Achipoue; the English, Chepawa; the Germans, Schipuwe; the Mohawk, Dewaganna; the Huron, Eskiaeronnon; the Caughawaga, Dwakane; the Sioux, Hahatonwa; the Fox, Kutaki; the Winnebago, Negatee; the Tuscarora, Nwaka; the Oneida, Twakanah; the Assiniboine, Wahkahtowah; and the Ottawa, Ojibbewaig" (Schmalz 1991, 3). Schmalz does not even mention Callicott's "pucker up" story, nor the equally implausible widely told story about how traditional Ojibwa moccasins are supposed to look "puckered up," *O-jib.* During the traditional "brain tanning" process the hides could be said to be roasted, *ub-way.* Given that scholars are not agreed on the etymology of the word, it is best not to put much faith in stories like these. Besides, Callicott ignores the explicit warning of his source, William Warren, that traditional story tellers are as likely to make up something to tell an ethnologist, or to unconsciously incorporate things "which they have borrowed or imbibed from the whites." According to Warren, it follows from this that it is necessary to be well acquainted with individual story tellers and their language and customs if you are "to procure their real beliefs" (Warren 1984, 58). Warren's warning of course applies to his own book, *History of the Ojibway People,* as well. It can be regarded as a paradoxical self-referential statement designed to refute itself. Callicott seems not to grasp this kind of Indian humor. For example, a revised and expanded version of the Hester et al. article appears in the Ouderkirk and Hill volume *Land, Value, Community: Callicott and Environmental Philosophy* under the title "Callicott's Last Stand." Their title reflects what they call "Callicott's attempted intellectual coup d'état of Indigenous thought" (Hester et al. 2002, 253). Callicott does not see any humor in the title. In his reply to his critics he says, "Unlike all the other authors in this volume Hester et al.

mount a mean-spirited personal attack on me. Their title rhetorically associates me with George Armstrong Custer" (Callicott 2002, 325). We are truly sorry that Callicott took offense. It was not intended. We do regard him as one of the "good guys." Callicott in his "Reply" says he has met Lee Hester in person. One of the most noticeable things about Lee, besides his full Fidel Castro–like beard, is his large western belt buckle which has the numbers 1876 emblazoned prominently on it. June 25, 1876 is, of course, the date of Custer's Last Stand, one of the most famous battles in the "Indian wars." When *we* asked Hester about the date on his belt buckle he replied with his characteristic little chuckle: "That's the year the Indians won." The Indians had so few victories, it seems a shame not to celebrate this one, at least in little ways, like with belt buckles or the title of an academic article, particularly when the article is about someone who seems to ground indigenous respect for the land in a Western metaphysics of morals, and then, inadvertently, spreads a negative stereotype of Native Americans as the savage redskins of the Hollywood B-Western movies.

The second of Callicott's "Three Arguments for a More Ferocious and Horrific America" begins with a story derived from Frank Waters' *Book of the Hopi,* about the Hopi's name for their fierce enemy, the Navajo. "Pre-Columbian Hopis called the Navajo 'Tusavutah (*tu*—person, *savutah*—to pound) because they killed or captured an enemy [sic. read 'killed a captured enemy'] by pounding his head in with a rock [or stone ax]" (Callicott 2000, 302–303). Corrections in square brackets our own from Waters 1963, 312. Waters actually says the Navajo were called "Tasavuh" from the word "tusavutah"). Now, it is important to remember that the purpose of Callicott's second argument is to show that, contrary to Hester et al., precontact Indians were not disposed to living in peace and harmony with their neighbors, to celebrate difference by practicing noninterference or cooperation. Citing Waters' *Book of the Hopi* as his authority, Callicott asserts that "the bitter conflict, lasting to this day, between the Navahos and the Hopis antedates European contact" (Callicott 2000, 302). We feel compelled to point out that even the pages in Waters' book which Callicott cites do not unequivocally support this contention. Callicott neglects to mention two things which Waters tells us in those pages, both of which actually count against Callicott's contention. When did the Navajo arrive in Hopi country? What Waters actually says is: "Shortly before or after the coming of the Castillas [the "gentlemen of Castile," the Spanish] a strange tribe of barbarians began to trickle into the Hopi villages. Today they are known as Navajos" (Waters 1963, 312). This statement does not unequivocally support Callicott's position. It is equally consistent with the claim that the Navajo may well have been forced into Hopi country by the advancing Spanish. It would follow that any conflict between the Navajo and Hopi could have been the *result* of European contact, not, as Callicott would have us believe, antedate such contact. But how were the Navajo or Tasavuh, as the Hopi came to call them, first received by their Hopi hosts? We think we are justified in using the word "hosts" here. The Hopi did indeed play host to their Navajo neighbors. "They fed and sheltered them. They taught them to work in the fields, to weave baskets, and to spin cotton" (Waters 1963, 312). Yet these Navajo were so different from the more civilized Hopi that Waters, at least, feels justified in using the term "barbarians" to describe them: "At first only one stranger came, hungry and without weapons, his long hair uncombed, clothed only in the skin of a wild animal. Then little bands of men, women and children came, all dressed the same way, all hungry and homeless. The Hopi were good to these barbarians" (312). We are tempted to use this passage to support the Hester et al. position that respect for difference and pluralism are traditional Native American precontact values. The Hopi were good to the Navajo who were so very different from themselves that they saw them as barbarians. Yet they cared for them, fed and clothed them, taught them skills. Given Hester et al.'s account of precontact Indigenous values, this is exactly how we should expect Native people to behave in such a situation. We do wonder why Callicott would cite Waters at all in support of his contrary position. Waters goes on to describe in some detail two other tribes of strangers who arrived to trade for corn. They, however, "always left when the harvesting and trading were over" (313). The Navajo, Waters tells us, did not leave, and by stealing corn and so forth, began to outstay their welcome. Perhaps, we might suggest, thanks to the Spanish they had nowhere to go? At any rate hostilities did break out. But when? Was it prior to European contact as Callicott would like us to believe, to support his contention that pre–Columbian America was ferocious and horrific? On this point Waters is unambiguous. He reports: "Bad feelings grew up between the Hopi and the Tasavuh. This changed to war when the Tasavuh burned Hopi cornfields and killed some Hopi men, which happened soon after the Castillas were driven out of Oraibi" (313). In this passage Waters is making reference to the Pueblo Revolt. He actually gives the date of this famous revolt on the previous page: "The Pueblo Revolt of 1680 ... completely ejected for a time all the hated Castillas" (312). From this it is clear that, at least in Waters' account, war between the Navajo and Hopi happened around or soon after 1680, not in pre–Columbian times as Callicott contends. Callicott also neglects to mention that Waters goes on to report that although victorious "the Hopi were left with a great sadness. They were a people of Peace who did not believe in war, yet they had been forced into killing both Tasavuh and the Castillas in order to protect their homes and their religion" (314). That the Hopi were a people of peace and did not believe in war nicely supports the argument of Hester et al. that precontact Native Americans preferred to live in peace and harmony with their neighbors, however different they might be. This evidence alone, of course, is not conclusive but it is sufficient, from the standpoint of formal logic, to entirely and completely refute Callicott's contention that "the evidence that does exist supports an opposite conclusion" (Callicott 2000, 302). It is also interesting to note that the Hopi were driven to war to protect their home and their religion. They did not go to war to impose their religion on anyone else. This suggests to us that we are dealing with a distinctly non–Western culture here.

As the final part of his second argument for a more ferocious and horrific America, Callicott notes that "the name the Navahos called themselves, *Diné,* means 'The People.'" The conclusion he wants to draw from this he leaves in the form of a (presumably rhetorical) question: "If you are not *Diné*—a person among the People — then who (or what) are you?" (Callicott 2000, 303). Callicott, of course, is presupposing classical binary categories rather than the radial categories of second-generation cognitive science we discussed above. This is somewhat surprising from someone who supports the use of Hallowell's concept of other-than-human persons to explicate Native American respect for animals and the land. But that aside, as Callicott well knows many indigenous peoples, e.g., the Anishnabe and Inuit, refer to themselves as "the People." But given the Native values of noninterference and respect this is just what we should expect: acceptance of different incompatible stories with no felt need to reconcile them, as in, for example, the Tinker/Weaver account of the different stories of the center of the universe which we have discussed. "When we're there, that is the center of the universe. When we are here, this is the center" (Weaver 1997, 33). Callicott seems to think that calling oneself "the People" excludes all others which, in his mind, leads to hostilities. We think that much more research needs to be done with all these different peoples. The Anishnabe, for example, have two words meaning "us" or "we," one which includes you, *giinawind,* and one which excludes you, *niinawind,* as in: "Won't you join us (*niinawind*) and share what we (*giinawind*) have?" (Ningewance et al. 6, 95, 105 and 148). It is difficult to see how Callicott can make a case for hostilities based on this kind of exclusion. But, as we said, a great deal more research into the philosophical implications of the use of such inclusive and exclusive terms in various Native languages needs to be done before any meaningful conclusions can be drawn.

Callicott's third and final argument for a more ferocious and horrific America is equally inconclusive. As a further "line of evidence for the existence of mortal ethnic conflict between North American Indian tribes" he cites anthropologist Harold Hickerson's 1965 claim that there must have been "a war zone between the Ojibwa and the Lakota somewhere in northwestern Wisconsin and eastern Minnesota" (Callicott 2000, 303). This, it turns out, is Hickerson's, and by implication Callicott's, only possible explanation for the reported variation in deer population in very similar habitat. Callicott summarizes the argument: "In the lethally contested territory between these two peoples, who spoke mutually unintelligible languages, deer abounded because hunters didn't go there for fear of falling victim to enemy war parties. In the security of their own territories, hunters reduced the number of deer" (Callicott 2000, 303; see also Hickerson 1965). Now, we don't want to minimize the animosity between the Anishnabe and the Lakota, some legendary examples of which we discuss in the next chapter. Here we want to ask what evidence does Callicott have for a war zone between the Ojibwa and Lakota? Would not a nonaggression buffer zone be equally consistent with the evidence and also support Hester et al.'s assumption that noninterference is a traditional indigenous value? We have no doubt that anyone hunting in such a zone would be killed. But this begs the question about the fate of someone alone, unarmed, disoriented, hungry and in need of help. It is, surely, as likely that such a person would not be killed, but if found, might well be adopted by the opposing tribe, taught their language, and be available to interpret at various negotiations between these peoples. Callicott's point about mutually unintelligible languages is simply beside the point. In fact, if Callicott is implying that these peoples are so antithetical as to find one another "mutually unintelligible," then he is just wrong. As we argue at length in the next chapter, "There is not the radical incommensurability between Lakota and Ojibwa worldviews that inevitably arises between Native American and Western worldviews generally." Callicott's argument here seems to confirm our point about the radical incommensurability between Native American and Western worldviews. Even the fact that he is unable to imagine any explanation for a variation in the deer population other than a war zone between the Lakota and Ojibwa reveals a lack of understanding of traditional hunting territories. Callicott would have us imagine two stable precontact communities with a war zone between them where the deer run free. But, at that time, these were semi-nomadic hunting societies, that expand and contract like an accordion, depending on the season and so forth. A summer gathering group might involve as many as 1500 people trading and visiting by a lake or river. In the winter 35–75 people might hunt together; if the game was scarce this could be reduced to one or two extended families hunting together, as few as ten people, though they would always remain in contact with other groups who could be of help. As current scholarship confirms: "Algonquian social organization is not one of random movement on land but of an accordion, a process of subsistence-motivated expansion and contraction of social groups in relation to resource exploitation" (Darnell 1999, 99). The point is, on this accordion model of social organization; that "in traditional times there was apparently no single place where a band lived, although there was certainly a territory known well which was exploited, used, during different parts of the year" (Darnell 1999, 99). In our discussion of Callicott at the beginning of this chapter we took him to task for claiming that family hunting territories were a post contact development and that therefore "conservation was expressly taught to the Indians by whites." This is not relevant here as we are talking about the whole society, not family hunting territories which may well have been a result of the imposition of more individualistic economic attitudes. The point we are making here is that, contrary to the precontact world imagined by Callicott; "there were no precise boundaries."

Callicott's only historical evidence for his "war zone hypothesis" is the report by some early explorers that "the number of deer sighted ... varied remarkably in similar habitat" (Callicott 2000, 303). This is, as it were, a single snapshot in time, from which, given the accordion nature of semi-nomadic traditional hunting societies, Callicott is really not entitled to conclude anything about the possible reasons for the number of deer in a particular location at a particular time. Callicott seems to be trying to interpret the historical record in the light of his assumption that human relations in precontact times were "ferocious and horrific." He does not seem to understand that Hester, McPherson, Cordova and other indigenous scholars are arguing that more sense can be made of the historical record if it is seen in the light of traditional indigenous values. For example Cordova suggests that the indigenous sense of belonging to a particular place and respect for the "sanctified" homelands of others is not likely to be understood by European colonists intent on spreading across a new continent. In her paper "Eco-Indian: A Response to J. Baird Callicott" Cordova argues that "even today, each Native American knows the boundaries of his group. It might be a series of mountains in one direction, a river or a gorge in another" (34). Referring to the traditional notion of the four directions she argues that "the sanctity of the directions might have come about through a recognition that others lived beyond them, in their own 'sanctified' homelands" (34). She concludes by asking: "How can a non–Native American, a European with a very general 'sense of place,' understand the sense of a boundary? Their god gave them an entire planet in which to 'multiply' and 'dominate': 'one world, one people.' If they do not come equipped with a sense of bounded space, how can they come to recognize and respect the sense of place of the other?" (35). Although Cordova speaks of boundaries in this passage, they are rather nebulous, a series of mountains in one direction or beyond a gorge in another. What is important here is belonging to the land. This is not inconsistent with our claim that in the accordion model of semi-nomadic hunting societies there is a sense in which "there were no precise boundaries." Even for the Ojibwa and other hunters in the woodlands of northern Wisconsin, the area Callicott is talking about, the "ties to the land are foundational, but the particular piece of land to which people are tied can change; ties to a new land require that individuals forge relationships to a particular local environment, continuing a pattern of mutual entailment between the social and the natural worlds" (Darnell 1999, 91).

It is important to realize that the precontact traditional accordion-like social organization of peoples like the Ojibwa is currently being used to understand Native identity and the continuity of Native values in the present day. Regna Darnell, on whose research we have been drawing in this section, shows just how fruitful this approach can be. In her paper "Rethinking the Concepts of Band and Tribe, Community and Nation: An Accordion Model of Nomadic Native American Social Organization," Darnell argues: "It is clear that Algonquian band-level societies have been adapting their traditional cultures to rapidly changing conditions since contact.... It is crucial to recognize, however, that the *process* has not been altered, merely the level of organization which is functional under particular circumstances" (99). Here we find recognition of the continuity of Native values, identity and even social organization. The process is the same; the underlying philosophy has not changed since precontact times. As Darnell explains: "The system looks different in terms of the number of people living together, but the underlying assumptions about repeated subsistence-driven changes in who lives with whom and why have not changed" (99). Of course in the modern world different options are available. Besides fur trapping, "cash labour, whaling, mercenary soldiering, crafts, and other occupations motivated geographical mobility without loss of perceived ties to home place and home people" (99). Darnell adds that "in northern Canada, logging and oil rigs provided additional seasonal employment opportunities" (99). We would argue that it may well be this very kind of social organization which makes Native cultures so resistant to assimilation, which allows Native values to be so resilient. Even if only a relative few families are continuing to teach and practice Native values, traditional ways can always be re-established. As Darnell concludes: "This accordion-like system has a considerable advantage under stress conditions because it can regenerate complexity from any component part" (99). Of course colonial policies of assimilation are probably the most stressful conditions these societies have had to endure. Yet Native values have survived them. Darnell's research may have uncovered one of the principal mechanisms of this survival.

Callicott, it seems, is just unable to believe that precontact indigenous values such as noninterference, respect, polycentrism and cooperativeness could have survived more than five hundred years of oppression and attempted assimilation. Expressing incredulity, he says of the contrary view, "Core cultural values have been passed down from generation to generation — despite a concerted European-American effort, endorsed by the U.S. government, to eradicate American-Indian culture and assimilate Indians into European-American culture over several decades spanning the last third of the nineteenth century and the first third of the twentieth" (Callicott 2000, 298). He certainly seems to believe most contemporary Indigenous people have been assimilated. Speaking explicitly of policies of assimilation, Callicott suggests that "such efforts may have been to some extent successful" (298). He really is quite convinced that Native Americans living in a modern technological society would have great difficulty maintaining anything like traditional values: "I also suggest that adopting nonnative technologies (such as the automobile and the television) and the replacement of native languages by European languages (such as Spanish and English) as mother tongues, might have further attenuated the process of cultural transmission and reproduction" (293). As we have seen in his earlier article, "American Indian Land Wisdom? Sorting Out the Issues," Callicott proclaimed: "To buy guns, motors, and mackinaw jackets is to buy, however unintentionally, a world view to boot" (212). But in this same article he is willing to use contemporary ethnographic accounts to overcome the Eurocentric bias of early contact accounts and historical documents. As Callicott puts it himself: "The often casual and unsystematic and always ethnocentric and distorted quality of these early documents can ... be compared and cross-checked with the more systematic and objective, but always relatively recent, ethnographic accounts in such a way that ideally they mutually correct, supplement, enrich, and illuminate one another" (213). Why is he so willing to dismiss contemporary Native voices? Who does he think contemporary ethnographers talk to? If their work can be used to "mutually correct, supplement, enrich, and illuminate" historical documents and cultural artifacts, surely contemporary Native people might also be useful in this exercise in ethno-metaphysics, particularly philosophically trained scholars like Hester, McPherson and Cordova. Even Cordova admits that "there are surely Native Americans that have been assimilated 'into the mainstream.'" She says, "I can identify them after a very short conversation." But she also notes that "there are also those who have not been and they can as certainly be identified" (Cordova 1997, 33). As we have seen above, Cordova endorses various traditional Native child rearing practices. Callicott, on the other hand, seems not to buy into any of it. In fact, given his belief in the success of assimilation policies, it is not surprising that he responds negatively to Cordova's humorous suggestion that by spending time with her traditionally raised grandchildren Callicott could learn something about Native American values. As Callicott sees it: "V. F. Cordova is menacingly personal in her attack on me — more so than Hester et al. 'Were I a judge,' she concludes, 'assigned the task of sentencing J. Baird Callicott to an 'educational course' for his transgressions (the presentation of incomplete images of Native Americans), I would decree he spend some time with preschool Native American children' — her own grandchildren more particularly — from whom I might learn something authentic about American Indian environmental values prior to European contact" (Callicott 2000, 297). Callicott does not see what he could possibly learn from contemporary Native people, much less from traditionally raised Apache children. His own words make this perfectly clear: "My philosophical engagement with American Indian traditions of thought, in Cordova's view, is a crime: 'The [sic] contemporary Native American is robbed of his [sic] own voice' by me.... Yet we certainly hear her voice loudly and clearly. I *rob* contemporary Native Americans (plural — I would prefer not to essentialize by repeating Cordova's *the*) of their (I would also prefer to be gender inclusive) own voices by suggesting that we can get a better idea about American Indian environmental attitudes and values prior to European contact by consulting stories of precontact provenance rather than, say, Cordova or her grandchildren. Values, she appears to believe, are in the blood" (Callicott 2000, 297; brackets and sarcastic remarks in original).

Contrary to Callicott, we believe that he does *not* hear Dr. Cordova "loudly and clearly." He does not hear her at all. He is not even listening. Callicott is confronted with a traditional way of teaching and does not even realize it. He corrects her non-inclusive language but fails to ask why she might be using it. He cites her as if she were in error (using "sic") and then proclaims that *he* is above making such politically incorrect mistakes. Such language, however, is a feature of Cordova's writing (cf. Cordova 1996, 13–18; 1997, 31; 1998, 26–32; 2007). Might she not be making a point? Might she not be trying to *show* something, as opposed to merely saying it? Might she not be trying to make us think? To reflect? Perhaps she is trying to get us to realize that inclusive language has not always included Cordova and her daughters and granddaughters — women of color. Perhaps she thinks that women in the dominant society are really rather privileged compared to members of racial minorities. Perhaps she thinks that their struggle is not her struggle, that the oppression is just different. Might she not be trying, with her unique use of language, to get us to stop and think about such things? Callicott seems too busy defending his careful research based on his "carefully amassed cultural artifacts" to stop and listen, to stop and think. But, he should know that nowadays most academic journals and editorial boards correct such "politically incorrect language" automatically. We can only imagine the battles Cordova must have had to keep them from changing it. Her use of such language must have some point. This kind of typically indigenous indirect teaching is not the only thing Callicott misses in Cordova's argument. As we have seen above, he accuses her of believing that "values ... are in the blood." But this is not her position. This is not what she says. Callicott simply cannot comprehend how there could possibly be a continuity of traditional values from precontact times to the present. Cordova, as we have seen above, explains clearly and in detail how Native values are passed down and preserved from one generation to the next, if Callicott would only listen. Although the continuing generations are more or less dependent upon genes, the continuity of traditional values has nothing to do with blood. Stories, particularly stories about place, and traditional language and ceremony are the important elements.

Callicott is one of the few Western trained philosophers sympathetic to Native American philosophy. As we said above, he really is one of the good guys. His critique of his "indigenous" critics suggests to us that a great deal more work needs to be done if we are to get Western philosophy to listen to Native American philosophy in such a way that Native American philosophy has at least a chance to influence, change, or adjust Western philosophy by entering into serious dialogue with it. In the next chapter we will illustrate the kind of research which still remains to be done if we are to enter into this sort of cross-cultural dialogue. It involves the relation between language and place as well as a much more in-depth analysis of the nature of place itself.

FIVE

Language and Metaphysics

Native American Ontology and Transformative Philosophy

To insist that one must be fluent in a relevant Native language in order to do Native philosophy or to understand a Native culture is to deprive far too many Native students today of the opportunity to discover who they are and to contribute to the development of their culture. Of course, every effort should be made to preserve Native American languages and to encourage Native youth to learn their language. One way to accomplish this is to encourage the study of Native philosophy, first in English, then, as interest grows and students want to explore their culture and their philosophy in more and more depth, we suggest they will also develop a genuine interest in learning their own languages. It is not their fault that they do not have their language, or, in far too many cases, even an interest in learning it. In Canada, the government has accepted responsibility for doing this to the Native people of Canada; has admitted that it was wrong to do so; and has issued a formal apology.

The Apology

On June 11, 2008, the prime minister of Canada issued a formal Statement of Apology to former students of Indian residential schools, on behalf of the government of Canada. The full text is available on the government of Canada web site "Indian and Northern Affairs Canada" (http://www.ainc-inac.gc.ca/ai/rqpi/apo/index-eng.asp). In this historic statement it is acknowledged that for over a century, mainly "as 'joint ventures' with Anglican, Catholic, Presbyterian or United Churches," 132 government-supported residential schools "separated over 150,000 Aboriginal children from their families and communities." It goes on to state that the "government of Canada now recognizes that it was wrong to forcibly remove children from their homes and we apologize for having done this. We now recognize that it was wrong to separate children from rich and vibrant cultures and traditions that it created a void in many lives and communities, and we apologize for having done this. We now recognize that, in separating children from their families, we undermined the ability of many to adequately parent their own children and sowed the seeds for generations to follow, and we apologize for having done this. We now recognize that, far too often, these institutions gave rise to abuse or neglect and were inadequately controlled, and we apologize for failing to protect you."

In its Statement of Apology the government of Canada actually admits that the two principal objectives of the residential school system were "to remove and isolate children from the influence of their homes, families, traditions and cultures, and to assimilate them into the dominant culture." It goes on to admit further that "these objectives were based on the assumption aboriginal cultures and spiritual beliefs were inferior and unequal." Though it does not acknowledge in so many words that aboriginal cultures and spiritual beliefs are not inferior and unequal to those of the dominant society, it does go on to state: "Today, we recognize that this policy of assimilation was wrong, has caused great harm, and has no place in our country."

In the context of Indian residential schools in the United States, Apache philosopher Viola Cordova notes that not only were students not permitted to speak their own language (talk Indian) but they were also "forcibly placed with children of another tribe so that they could not communicate in any language other than English" (Cordova 2007, 79). It is, she argues, due to this policy of attempted "total assimilation" that "today there are very few Native Americans who can speak their own languages" (28). The policy of assimilation was never intended just to teach Indian children English and "facilitate assimilation into the mainstream" (65). Though that was the rationale usually given, Cordova argues that "in actuality, it was to eradicate a way of being" (65). As the government of Canada Apology recognized, it was, in so many words, intended "to kill the Indian in the child." In this both the governments of Canada and the United States, as well as the churches that implemented the attempted eradication, failed miserably. As this study of Native American philosophy makes perfectly clear, Native cultures and Native ways of being in the world are alive and well here and now in the 21st century. We do not mean to say that Native American people are flourishing, some obviously are not, but they are fighting back, recovering from years of marginalization.

We maintain that it is the nature of Native American philosophy that gives Native people the strength to maintain their ways of being in the world in the face of systematic attempts by government-sponsored residential schools to eradicate Native cultures. Cordova also suggests a further reason the imposition of English as their only language did not eradicate young Native students' unique way of being in the world. She argues that there is "beyond language, a *context* to being 'Indian' that eludes attempts at eradication" (79). Well before the children were "abducted" and forced into residential schools at around the age of six, they had already established a uniquely aboriginal relation to their families, to their communities and, indeed, to the land itself (herself). As Cordova puts it, "Behind language there is a 'pattern system' of 'forms and categories' that could be taught without full knowledge of the language. The 'pattern' consisted of more than words and speech; it included also a way of being in the world" (79). As we saw in the previous chapter, her claim is supported by recent findings in contemporary cognitive science concerning the neurological (prelinguistic) basis of conceptual metaphor. Cordova's point is also confirmed by Leslie Nawagesic, a residential school survivor, in his 2001 Masters thesis in Native Philosophy, *Yuma State: A Philosophical Study of the Indian Residential School Experience* (55–58). He was able to maintain his own language, perhaps, he suggests, because he was allowed to return to his home community every summer where he had the opportunity to speak the language and participate in traditional Ojibwa life with family and community. A sample of his account of the contrast between life on the rez and life as a student in residential school has been published in *American Indian Thought: Philosophical Essays* under the title "Phenomenology of a Mugwump Type of Life in an Autobiographical Snippet" (Waters 2004, 140–152).

Nawagesic confirms Cordova's point about learning "Indian ways" well before, or at least while, learning his first language. He says he is able to relate to a personal story Cordova is fond of telling (Nawagesic 2001, 29). The story involves Cordova watching her married daughter and a non-Native friend playing with their respective infants on the lawn. The non-Native mother supplies a blanket and plastic toys for her child and hovers over him to make sure he does not stray off the clean blanket onto the dirty ground which she tells him to avoid, the tone of voice suggesting revulsion more than the strict meaning of the words "dirty" and "filthy" themselves. Cordova is obviously pleased to observe her grandchild being raised in a much more Native way, no blanket, encouraged to play in the dirt, taste the grass and explore the earth with natural curiosity. Cordova in fact expresses pride and some surprise that she has somehow unconsciously passed on Native values such as noninterference to her daughter and partially through her to her grandchild (Cordova 1997, 33–34). Of course her descriptions of both the children (Native and non–Native) are in a sense stereotypical. Still Cordova's story does help us understand how ways of being in the world can be learned prior to language acquisition, and lends plausibility to her claim, and that of Nawagesic, that such ways were firmly entrenched prior to the residential school experience and might well survive such an experience.

If the policy of total assimilation had been successful, there would really be no perceived need for an apology for the residential schools. But as we have seen, the Canadian government makes more than clear that an apology is most definitely called for: "The Government of Canada sincerely apologizes and asks the forgiveness of the Aboriginal peoples of this country for failing them so profoundly. Nous le regrettons. We are sorry. Nimitataynan. Niminchinowesamin. Mamiattugut." It is somewhat ironic, or should we say tragic, that so many Native people would not be able to read these last words of apology except in the English or possibly the French. We do not see the Canadian government doing enough to rectify this situation, a situation they admit they caused, is wrong, and for which they have apologized. At least the Americans have attempted to address the problem directly.

As far back as 1992, Congress passed the Native American Languages Act. Though ridiculously underfunded, it was intended to "assure the survival of and continuing vitality of Native American Languages" (cited in Manatowa-Bailey 2007, 15). The historic Esther Martinez Native American Language Preservation Act, which Congress passed unanimously in 2006, has the potential to add an additional ten million dollars to the cause (Lutz 2007a, 3). But even this is really just a drop in the bucket. As Ellen L. Lutz, executive director of *Cultural Survival Quarterly,* puts it, "But with 562 federally recognized tribes and many nonrecongized indigenous communities with urgent language needs, much more funding is needed" (3). Jacob Manatowa-Bailey, in "On the Brink: An Overview of the Disappearance of

America's First Languages: How It Happened and What We Need to Do About It," keeps the (under)funding issue in perspective by pointing out that "the operational cost of the Cherokee Nation immersion program for three-to-six-year-olds [alone] is more than $2.5 million annually" (16).

The Canadian government, through Indian and Northern Affairs Canada, does not even come close to anything like this. It does provide for primary schools and/or school teachers on some Indian reserves under treaty obligations and The Indian Act as we explained in Chapter Two. It does provide minimal federal funds to its provincial universities for Aboriginal programming. The government apology provides for cash payments to individual former residential school students, the exact dollar amount depending on a number of factors, including the number of years spent attending residential school and the degree of abuse inflicted. This, "The Indian Residential Schools Settlement Agreement," is really in response to a class action lawsuit against the federal government, and various churches involved, brought by former students of Canadian Indian residential schools (and they say Americans are litigious). As stated in the Statement of Apology: "A cornerstone of the Settlement Agreement is the Indian Residential Schools Truth and Reconciliation Commission." Yes, it does sound not unlike South Africa. This commission is still meeting, hearing first-hand accounts of the residential school experience told by former students appearing before the commission. According to the Statement of Apology, "This Commission presents a unique opportunity to educate all Canadians on the Indian Residential Schools system. It will be a positive step in forging a new relationship between Aboriginal peoples and other Canadians, a relationship based on the knowledge of our shared history, a respect for each other and a desire to move forward together with a renewed understanding that strong families, strong communities and vibrant cultures and traditions will contribute to a stronger Canada for all of us." We fail to see how this will lead to the preservation of a single Native language. Perhaps we will have to await the final report of the commission, though we have no idea how many endangered Native languages will have become extinct by the time the Truth and Reconciliation Commission submits its report.

Language and Philosophy

Cordova vacillates between claiming, as we have seen above, that "there are very few Native Americans who can speak their own languages" (28), and that "not all American indigenous peoples are fluent in their native language" (79), which does not seem quite so bad, does not in itself imply that there is a crisis, that we are in immanent danger of losing fluent speakers of many Native American languages. Let us be perfectly clear. There *is* a crisis! Many Native American languages may well be extinct in less than a decade (Anderton 2007, 21). To be a little more precise than Cordova, according to the Indigenous Languages Institute in the United States: "Of 2 million American Indians, only 18 percent still speak their tribal language, and the vast majority of these are elderly. Moreover, almost half of the 18 percent belong to a single tribe: the Dine (Navajo) Nation" (Manatowa-Bailey 2007, 16). The Indigenous Languages Institute concludes that "86 percent of all North American Languages are in danger of extinction" (Manatowa-Bailey 2007, 16). Though we are arguing that Native American philosophy can, with some difficulty, be discussed in English, we also agree that "when a language dies, everything that is attached to it — prayer, song, stories, dances, ceremonies and every other aspect of a tribal system — becomes more difficult if not impossible to sustain" (Manatowa-Bailey 2007, 16). We would therefore encourage every effort to teach young children their Native language. Such efforts include various immersion programs, one-to-one master apprentice and other intergenerational formats, Native-controlled tribal schools, and so forth (cf. Lutz 2007a, 3). We particularly like the "language nest" format imported from New Zealand and Hawaii. "In language nests, community members form regular speaking groups with friends and family and a more fluent mentor. As group members attain mastery, they then take on the responsibility for mentoring another less fluent group" (Lutz 2007b, 7). The reason we like these language nests is that they provide an ideal environment for discussing Native American philosophy. Of course, all language learning involves implicitly the values and worldviews of the culture. We suggest that making this discussion more explicit can have a beneficial effect on language learning, and, as we have argued above, encourage more interest in learning the language. Young children do not really require further motivation; they naturally, willingly and happily acquire the language in almost any immersion setting. But older teens and students in their early twenties often find language acquisition difficult. They are also often embarrassed by the fact they find it so difficult; after all, it is their own language. They tend to feel it is, in some sense, who they are. It is to this and older age groups that we have been offering classes in Native Canadian worldviews over the past 20-some years. We have found that students can become very excited about discussing Native values and worldviews and often begin to take an active interest in the structure of their language in order to learn more about their philosophy. They are encouraged when we discuss Apache philosopher Viola Cordova's argument that to do Native American philosophy "it is not, perhaps, necessary to become fluent in the language, but it is necessary to know at least how the language works, its structure" (Cordova 2007, 57).

A Philosophical Question

Let us illustrate by posing and discussing one of our favorite philosophical questions, one that involves at least three languages. "If the Lakota describe the atmosphere of a sweat lodge, the sacred steam, as 'wakanda,' and if the Ojibwa characterize it as 'manitu,' are we entitled to conclude that these terms mean roughly the same thing? (cf. Hallowell 1978, 69, and Radin 1914, 349–50)" (McPherson and Rabb 1999, 202). Generally speaking, anthropologists seem to have drawn just such conclusions. Barbara and Dennis Tedlock, for example, in their sympathetic study *Teachings from the American Earth: Indian Religion and Philosophy,* are more than comfortable in equating these terms with the Western concepts of sacredness and holiness. They assert: "The Sioux call this holiness *wakan,* the Ojibwa and other Algonkian peoples call it *manitu* " (Tedlock and Tedlock 1978, xviii). But they don't stop there. They go on to assert that "the Iroquois call it *orenda*" (xviii). We suggest, however, that great care really needs to be taken here. Comparing, say, Ojibwa and Lakota worldviews with one another is just as much a cross-cultural study as comparing either with Western worldviews. Actually comparing these two Native worldviews would be, in a sense, doubly cross-cultural since any such comparative study is inevitably Western, particularly one done and written up in the English language. Cordova points out that for the Native American one of the first problems in cross cultural communication is "determining which of the possible audiences one is writing for ... a Native American audience or a Euro-American" (Cordova 2007, 75). She notes that Euro-American scholars seldom consider this "cross cultural or 'perspectival' approach" (75). At most they might have to decide if they are writing for a specialist or generalist type of audience, but the whole notion of what we call, in chapters one and two, the polycentric perspective is generally ignored by mainstream scholarship (75).

The Incommensurability Problem

In undertaking comparative or cross-cultural studies it is important to deal at the outset with the possibility of the incommensurability of worldviews. As Cordova puts it, "A dialogue with an alien other requires, first of all, an acceptance that there is the possibility of an other as *other* (and not simply a distortion of oneself)" (75). Leroy Meyer and Tony Ramirez, non–Native and Native philosophers from the University of South Dakota, in their paper "Wakinyan Hotan, The Thunder Beings Call Out: The Inscrutability of Lakota/Dakota Metaphysics," argue that the incommensurability problem is much more than a simple problem of translating from the Native language. "Although translation from one disparate way of thinking to another is difficult, coming to understand another way of thinking is not a question of overcoming the difficulties of translation. Coming to understand another world view is 'learning how to reason' in the style of the other world view" (Meyer and Ramirez 1996, 92). Meyer and Ramirez illustrate this with the Lakota concept of "Wakinyan hotan," which admittedly presents the translator with considerable ambiguity. They note that it "could be rendered as 'The Thunder Beings cry out!' or 'The thunder speaks!' or simply 'Thunder!'" (Meyer and Ramirez 1996, 92). However, they argue that what is actually important in attempting to comprehend traditional Lakota/Dakota worldviews here is the philosophical requirement "to discover the network of inferential associations between the Lakota/Dakota concept of *Wakinyan* and the other conceptual phenomena perceived from the perspective of this particular world view" (Meyer and Ramirez 1996, 92). In other words, what is important is thinking and reasoning "in the style of" a particular worldview.

We were once convinced that it is also important to remember that in comparing Lakota and Ojibwa philosophy the networks of inferential associations of interest are, in the first instance, those between Lakota concepts, and, in the second, those between Ojibwa concepts. We should not be looking for networks of inferential associations between Lakota and Ojibwa concepts. Any such inferential associations between Lakota and Ojibwa concepts would likely be imposed by the investigator (McPherson and Rabb 1999, 202–210). However, we now believe there is one important exception to this. It has to do with what Cordova calls the extensive pre-contact practice of "exogamy." This concept, marriage outside the group, Cordova introduces as part of her argument objecting to the stereotype of pre-contact Native Americans "as 'nomadic' groups that existed in a continual state of war with one another" (Cordova 2007, 223). This stereotype, perpetuated through Hollywood B-Westerns, is rejected by Cordova in the strongest possible terms: "This is absolutely not the case. There was an extensive trading system of goods between the groups" (223). She goes on to point out that among the trade items were "marriageable youths." In fact, she argues that "all groups practiced exogamy to a large extent" (223). This meant that "each group had at least one member that could speak the language of some other group" (223). This, of course, created a kind of bond between said groups, even if they were sometimes considered enemies.

The Exceptional Piapot (1816–1908) and Vine Deloria, Jr. (1933–2005)

Let us illustrate this exception to the incommensurability of worldviews with a relevant example, the story of the Cree leader and traditional elder known as Piapot. Piapot is famous for, among other things, defying the Canadian government ban on traditional ceremonies such as the Sun Dance. His story is told with some sympathy by journalist D'Arcy Jenish in his book *Indian Fall: The Last Great Days of the Plains Cree and the Blackfoot Confederacy.* Jenish rightly notes in the introduction that "where the opening of the West was a triumph for Canadians of European descent, it was a catastrophe for the original inhabitants — the Plains Cree, the Sarcee, the Assiniboines, the Saulteaux and the tribes of the Blackfoot Confederacy (the Bloods, Piegans and Blackfoot)" (Jenish 1999, 5). He attempts to present the story of these Indian nations and their leaders from their own perspective rather than that of the colonizers, the victors, as is usually done in history texts. We suggest that he is not entirely successful in presenting the Native perspective; however, he does bring their story to life, though, as we will show, at the expense of reinforcing some negative stereotypes. It is Jenish's story of the early life of Piapot that interests us here.

As a young child Piapot was captured by a Lakota hunting party and adopted by a family in their community. Jenish tells the story in some detail, helping his readers to imagine what it must have been like to be a Cree captured by the Lakota. The Cree, like the Ojibwa, are, Algonkian (Algonquian) speakers whereas the Lakota and Dakota speak dialects of the totally unrelated Siouan language, and are sometimes called Sioux Indians though this is not a term of respect. When captured, Piapot and his grandmother were alone together on the vast open prairie, having fled their home community because it had been devastated by an outbreak of smallpox. At this time Piapot was known by his given name, Kisikawasan, which literally means flash of light, but might be translated into English as anything from Falling Star to Northern Lights or, we would add, Lightening Bolt (Jenish 1999, 20). Negative stereotypes start to creep in when Jenish, seemingly out of his own imagination, attempts to recount what the grandmother must be worried about, caring for Kisikawasan alone and unprotected on the vast and empty prairie. Although smoke on the horizon could signify a Cree encampment or the equally "friendly Assiniboines," the presence of horsemen could mean "either friends or enemies." She obviously fears scouts from possible Lakota war parties. "And scouts are men who specialize in stealth, who can appear out of nowhere, brandishing knives or clubs and ready to use them" (Jenish 1999, 17). She eventually does see horsemen on the horizon, and they may have spotted her and the boy as well for they seem to ride straight toward them. "These men could be triumphant Cree braves on their way home from plundering and pillaging an enemy village. Or they might be warriors from an enemy tribe looking to inflict havoc and mayhem on a Cree band" (Jenish 1999, 18). Now we would be the first to admit that there is little love lost between the Cree or Ojibwa and the Lakota/Dakota but "plundering and pillaging," inflicting "havoc and mayhem"? This is the kind of savage stereotype we have seen Cordova, for example, reject out of hand as "absolutely not the case" (Cordova 2007, 223). Sure, they would raid each others' villages and they steal horses (perhaps still do sometimes), but Jenish portrays them as blood-thirsty savages from a Hollywood B-Western. When the grandmother finally recognizes the horsemen as Lakota, according to Jenish, "she goes cold from head to foot. These men are Sioux hunters. This, she is certain, means death" (Jenish 1999, 19). We are tempted to criticize Jenish's book, here, the same way he himself criticizes "Hollywood westerns, which got the basics right (time and place, winners and losers) but not much else" (Jenish 1999, 1). Why would Sioux hunters, why would anyone, want to kill a little boy and his grandmother who are not a threat to anyone, and seem abandoned and in need of help? Where is the honor in that? As we established in Chapter Four, traditional Native values suggest that taking the life of any animal must be done with respect and for some reason, purpose, or need, not just for the fun of it. We agree the grandmother could well be afraid, but not of death — capture, more likely, and being taken away from her people. That is, of course, exactly what happens. After almost four days of riding into Sioux country they arrive at their new home where the boy is adopted by a family and is raised as one of their own. His grandmother is given in marriage to a "prosperous male," becoming one of his several wives. As Cordova said, exogamy was widely practiced. Jenish is not entirely consistent, given his account of the reception these Cree captives received in the Lakota village. Having gone into great detail about the grandmother's fear of death at the hands of these Sioux savages, Jenish actually says, "And the Sioux welcomed the newcomers because it is not uncommon for parties of warriors or hunters to bring back people they have found lost or abandoned on the prairie" (Jenish 1999, 19). The savage stereotype is so at odds with reality that even Jenish cannot maintain it consistently. Still, his story does help us imagine what it must have been like growing up in a Lakota village knowing you are a captured Cree. Jenish makes it clear that Kisikawasan's grandmother never lets him forget that he is Cree and not Sioux. However, the boy also "learned the language of his captors and adopted their ways" acquiring, according to Jenish, their "four core values — bravery, fortitude, generosity and wisdom" (Jenish 1999, 20). Kisikawasan and his grandmother spent about fourteen years with this Lakota nation which, according to Jenish, "controlled thousands of square miles of land" in the Missouri River basin, a large part of what is now North and South Dakota. Kisikawasan and his grandmother are eventually rescued by a Cree raiding party intent on stealing horses. More mayhem, in the midst of which Kisikawasan and his grandmother are, with considerable difficulty and this time genuine danger, able to identify themselves as Cree to the raiding party and escape with their lives (Jenish 1999, 21–22). They return with them to a Cree community in the Qu'Appelle Valley in what is present-day Saskatchewan. This is where Kisikawasan acquires the name "Payipwat — Hole in the Sioux" (Jenish 1999, 23). The name was anglicized as "Piapot" by Hudson's Bay traders for ease of pronunciation. He became an admired leader among the Cree. "Piapot was no longer Hole in the Sioux. He had become One Who Knows the Secrets of the Sioux" (Jenish 1999, 31). Having participated in traditional ceremonies in both communities, he would certainly be in a good position to bring a unique understanding to both. He would be able for example "to discover the network of inferential associations between the Lakota/Dakota concept of *Wakinyan* and the other conceptual phenomena perceived from the perspective of this particular world view" (Meyer and Ramirez 1996, 92). But he would also be able to relate the Lakota concepts to Cree concepts concerning similar ceremonies as well, providing a deeper understanding of both Cree and Lakota philosophy.

Piapot's position is not all that unique. Given the widespread practice of exogamy by Native communities it follows that not only would it be the case that "each group had at least one member that could speak the language of some other group" (Cordova 2007, 223), but these adopted members would also be in a position to provide a deeper understanding of the values and worldviews implicit in their ceremonies and traditions.

In fact, the famous version of Lakota metaphysics (ontology) developed by Vine Deloria Jr. has been admirably analyzed and defended using concepts drawn from both Algonquian and Iroquoian traditions. This analysis appears in the memorial issue of the *American Philosophical Association Newsletter on American Indians in Philosophy* (Fall 2006) in honor of the life and work of the late Vine Deloria Jr. In the issue's major article, titled "Persons in Place: The Agent Ontology of Vine Deloria, Jr.," University of Oregon philosopher Scott L. Pratt uses both the concepts "Manitou" and "orenda" to explicate Deloria's Lakota derived ontology (theory of reality), and defend it against the usual out of hand rejection by European and American science and philosophy. Drawing principally on *The Metaphysics of Modern Existence* (Deloria 1979) and *Power and Place: Indian Education in America* (Deloria and Wildcat 2001), the article attempts to clarify Deloria's interrelated concepts of power and place. "Power, Deloria says, is defined as 'the living energy that inhabits and/or composes the universe,' place is defined as 'the relationship of things to each other ... the universe is alive' ... it is also a vast collection of persons made distinct through their interactions with each other, that is they are persons through their interactions in place" (Pratt 2006, 5). Persons here include, of course, other-than-human persons, and not just animals, but trees, rocks and entire ecosystems as well. To show how all persons are related and yet individuated by and through power and place, Pratt calls upon the concept of Manitou: "William Jones, a Mesquakie Indian and a student of Franz Boas at Columbia University, argued that the notion of power, here called '*Manitou*,' is an idea held by traditional Algonquian people that marks both what is common among things and what makes things different from one another ... *Manitou* provides a ground for fostering diverse personalities even as it makes understanding and unification an ongoing possibility" (Pratt 2006, 6).

We like the way Pratt draws on writings by traditional speakers like William Jones (1871–1909) for the analysis of Native concepts. Jones was raised in the Mesquakie woodlands tradition by his grandmother speaking a dialect of Algonquian closely related to Cree and Ojibway (cf. Heck 1996 and Hinsley 1996). We think Pratt might have mentioned that Jones not only studied with Boas, but he also earned his Ph.D. at Columbia in 1904.

Jones was quite familiar with Ojibwa and in fact translated numerous Ojibwa narratives into English, many of which he collected from communities in our location in Northern Ontario, from our place. As we have said, we use these indigenous narratives in our Native Canadian worldview classes, thus permitting many of our local students to study narratives that are derived from their home communities, from their sense of place. If the Deloria-Pratt analysis is correct, this means that these Native students are in the unique position of being able to maintain and reinforce their self-defining relationship with their communities through these narratives while studying at a mainstream university (at least for one course).

Pratt also draws on the writings of the famous Tuscarora ethnologist John Napoleon Briton Hewitt (1859–1937). Unlike his younger contemporary, William Jones, Hewitt did not have a university education. Nevertheless, after serving as a summer assistant he was hired as an ethnologist for what became the Bureau of American Ethnology to study Iroquois myths and languages (Tooker 1996, 244). Also unlike Jones, he was not raised speaking his Native language. Though both his parents were fluent in Tuscarora, they did not teach their children to speak it. We suspect this may partially explain why Iroquois linguistics became a lifelong passion for Hewitt. It is said he learned the language at about the age of eleven from classmates at the district school (Tooker 1996, 244). He spent more than fifty years writing about the Iroquois and compiling dictionaries. Pratt draws upon one of Hewitt's more famous articles, "Orenda and a Definition of Religion," which appeared in volume four of *The American Anthropologist* (1902). We are intrigued by the way in which Pratt used the concept of "orenda" to clarify his discussion of "Manitou." Both, it seems, perform the function of differentiation for individuals while showing how said individuals are related to one another and hence to a greater whole, to *place*. "Like *Manitou, orenda* is understood as a kind of unifying notion. Everyone has *orenda*, but it is also differentiating in that different people have different *orendas*" (Pratt 2006, 6). This is explained further through reference to the root of the word "orenda," through its etymology. "One way to understand this concept is suggested by the linguistic root for *orenda—ren—*, which is also the root for the terms for 'songs,' 'to sing,' and 'voice' or 'speech' ... *orenda* marks the song or voice of particular things" (Pratt 2006, 6). We are talking identity here. Voices and songs are metaphors for persons, including, always, other-than-human persons. We are who we are, we are the individuals we are because our voices resonate with those of others in our wider community, the ecosystems in which we live, or rather through which we interrelate. Such interrelations should be thought of as *place*. "'Place' is also an important term in that it implies ... land, rivers, ecosystems, even farm fields, hills, and mountain ranges are also persons in their own right in interaction with other persons, human and otherwise" (Pratt 2006, 7). Think of all these interrelations as voices in harmony. The singers around a pow wow drum, for example, are all individuals in their own right but when they sing together their individual voices take on a character, a resonance they could not have on their own. Or take the drums themselves, say at a large pow wow, a five-drum pow wow. "Listening to the sound together, the resonating drums are a unity of sound; listening for the characteristic expression of a single drum makes individuals emerge from the collective sound. It is important to note that while each drum has its own sound, it is both a sound dependent upon the drum's origin (the skin and wood of which it is made) and its interaction with other agents — the drummer, the listeners, even the other drums in its hearing" (Pratt 2006, 6–7). The resonance with other drums is important for it is that resonance which is a metaphor for our own identity as the persons we are. We would not be the persons we are without this resonance, our interrelations or interactions with others in our extended community. As Pratt puts it, following Deloria, "a person *is* only in place" (Pratt 2006, 7).

This gives us an insight into the deeper philosophical meaning of some of Deloria's earlier work. In *God Is Red* Deloria laments: "A good deal of the political turmoil on the reservations today is between traditional people and more assimilated people over the use of the land and resources. Traditional people generally want to use land in the same way as their ancestors while the more assimilated people want to use it as an economic resource" (212). He goes on to ask "whether land is a 'thing' to be used to generate income or a homeland on which people are supposed to live in a sacred manner" (212). As we have seen above, in his later works Deloria clarifies what he means by living with the land "in a sacred manner." More assimilated tribal members seem to have lost touch with their relation to the land, to place, and have adopted a more Western mechanistic attitude toward the land, regarding it merely as a resource, a commodity, to be exploited for economic gain.

We suggest that Pratt's defense of Deloria's agent ontology against the more obvious criticisms of it leveled by Western philosophy and science can be used to help resolve this widespread dispute which is occurring within far too many Native communities today. Widdowson and Howard, in their 2008 book *Disrobing the Aboriginal Industry: The Deception Behind Indige-*

nous Cultural Preservation, dismiss traditional aboriginal views in general and Deloria's in particular as primitive and unscientific. "For Deloria scientific research that attempts to obtain abstract knowledge is 'useless' and 'should be utterly rejected by Indian people.' He shares with postmodernism the charge that this knowledge is being used to oppress aboriginal peoples.... Deloria, after all, represents the 'voice' of an oppressed group, and postmodernism dictates that his views must be considered 'equally valid' in comparison to 'Eurocentric' (i.e. scientific) scholarship" (68, parentheses in original). The assumption is that Deloria's opinions, like all Native views, are unscientific, primitive, stone age, even. Native people are allowed a hearing only on the totally unjustified grounds of political correctness. "Conservation of obsolete customs deters development.... Many of the activities held as destructive to aboriginal peoples — the teaching of English, the discouraging of animistic superstitions, and encouraging of self-discipline — were positive measures intended to overcome the social isolation and economic dependency that was (and continues to be) so debilitating to the native population" (Widdowson and Howard 2008, 25, parentheses in original). At first contact, according to Widdowson and Howard, the Aboriginal cultures in the Americas were either paleolithic or neolithic societies whereas the European explorers were of course civilized. Widdowson and Howard go on to explain that "the stages of 'savagery' and 'barbarism' refer to hunter-gatherers and horticulturists respectively, and these types of societies roughly correspond to the paleolithic (in the case of savagery) and the neolithic (in the case of barbarism) periods" (12, parentheses in original). Widdowson and Howard do actually admit that aboriginal people today do not remain at these stages of savagery and barbarism since many of them have assimilated into the mainstream, i.e., become civilized, even using cell phones, computers and pickup trucks (their examples, 13). However, Widdowson and Howard go on to issue the warning that since the collapse of the fur trade in North America, Aboriginal people have participated in the economy primarily as consumers, not as producers. At contact their neolithic technologies did not even enable them to turn natural resources into commodities (76). Though many today have become civilized, many others have not and still attempt to maintain traditional beliefs. What this means to the Widdowson and Howards of this world is that "isolation from economic processes has meant that a number of neolithic cultural features, including undisciplined work habits, tribal forms of political identification, animistic beliefs, and difficulties in developing abstract reasoning, persist despite hundreds of years of contact" (Widdowson and Howard 2008, 13). We would argue that Widdowson and Howard's book is a perfect example of what happens when Native philosophy is ignored. Pratt, though he does not mention Widdowson and Howard, is more than aware of the widespread dismissive attitude they represent. Citing various philosophers of science Pratt describes this kind of characterization of traditional Native views as "the mythological explanation of nature which interpreted the objects of nature anthropomorphically, viewing the roaring winds and the babbling brook as living things and perceiving in a thunder storm the wrath of god ... ignorant of what lies behind various biological processes" (Pratt 2006, 5). Modern science, of course, attempts to understand what lies behind various biological processes through the ongoing reduction of biology to physics and chemistry. Pratt would be the first to admit "from this perspective ... Deloria's agent ontology can get no serious consideration at all ... the expectation that living organisms can be accounted for in physico–chemical terms alone, becomes a 'heuristic maxim,' 'a principle for the guidance of research' ... [so that Deloria's agent ontology] can be set aside for the moment since its proof will turn on the failure of a program of research that assumes the opposite and itself shows no signs of failure" (Pratt 2006, 5).

The other principal objection to Deloria's agent ontology is that, unlike scientific explanation, it does not have predictive value. Any description of rocks, for example, which includes life force or active agency would add little to our understanding of the same phenomenon in terms of, say, mass and velocity, laws of motion and so forth. "At the same time, the presence of a living force makes no claims on how the rock will behave in the future.... If Indian metaphysics leads to claims that rocks are alive, it is, one might easily conclude, no wonder that European-descended culture rejects such indigenous philosophy" (Pratt 2006, 6). In defense of Deloria, Pratt does argue that what agency adds to our understanding of nature is that these other than human persons deserve moral consideration. "If, as Deloria argues, the universe is made up of persons, and if interactions among persons are moral relations, then all relations in the universe have a moral character" (Pratt 2006, 7). As we saw in the previous chapter, the traditional Native hunter thinks of the animal as giving itself to the hunter, and in recognition of this life-giving sacrifice the hunter shows respect by offering tobacco, or returning some parts of the animal to its natural habitat, and so forth. Whether or not animals really do willingly give their flesh and fur to respectful aboriginal hunters is not a straightforward empirical question as those who would dismiss the whole idea as primitive animism or anthropomorphism might contend. We regard this sort of question more as a phenomenological/hermeneutical question (Rabb 2002, 290). As we explained in Chapter Three, phenomenology deals with descriptions of raw experience. Hermeneutics is concerned with interpretation (of texts, experience, cultures, etc.), as we explain in more detail in Chapter Seven. In order to fully understand the claim that animals, for example, exhibit agency, it may well be necessary to have certain kinds of experience and the cultural background both to notice and to interpret such experience. Deloria, in *God Is Red*, tries to explain communion with other-than-human persons by drawing attention to the fact that "some non–Indian families who have lived continuously in isolated rural areas tell stories about birds and animals similar to the traditions of many tribes indicating that lands and the 'other peoples' do seek intimacy with our species" (274–275). As we have seen above with Pratt's philosophical discussion of Deloria's agent ontology, this is far more sophisticated than any simplistic animism. Pratt also argues that just as we can predict the decisions and actions of a long-time friend with whom we are very well acquainted, so agent ontology can make as accurate predictions as those made using causal laws, though they lack the expected necessity of scientific law, since agency involves choice and even a good friend can on occasion surprise us by behaving out of character. Pratt, following Deloria, argues: "As quantum theory ... becomes the more or less standard way of understanding the physical world, Western science comes close to a model where even the most stable relations can break down" (9). Still, for the most part, "physical laws are simply expressions of a broad category of well-established interactions ... Deloria's agent ontology can include the accounts and predictions of Western science as claims about very stable relations" (Pratt 2006, 9). Very good friends do not usually behave out of character. Predictability is preserved; however, these very stable relations are for Deloria relations between agents, between persons, including other-than-human persons so "the separation of moral judgment from the work and claims of Western science" must be rejected (9). One thing we can and must learn from Native philosophy is that there is an ethical or moral dimension to empirical or scientific judgments.

How do we get the Widdowsons and Howards to give agent ontology or Lakota/Dakota metaphysics a fair hearing, or indeed any hearing at all? We have seen, with the examples of Piapot and Pratt's defense of Deloria's Lakota metaphysics using Algonquian and Iroquoian concepts, that there is not the radical incommensurability between these Indigenous world views that inevitably arises between Native American and Western world views generally. In other words, as we have seen, although the Lakota/Dakota

(Siouan), Algonquian and Iroquoian languages differ, their modes of reasoning, at least, seem mutually intelligible.

Meyer and Ramirez, in their discussion of the "Inscrutability of Lakota/Dakota Metaphysics," characterize the traditional Lakota/Dakota worldview as what they call "spiritual holism." They go on to explain: "Reality, in the Lakota/Dakota world view, comprises one integrated spiritual whole; what might otherwise be regarded as components of that reality are inseparable manifestations of the unified whole. Furthermore, everything has spirit in some appropriate sense of that term.... The physical appearance of 'hard things' is simply one manifestation of the spiritual reality which underlies everything" (Meyer and Ramirez 100). It is not too difficult to see the foundations of Deloria's agent ontology in this description.

Some scholars from the dominant society, in attempting to understand this Native perspective, have argued that one major difference between this kind of Lakota or Dakota metaphysics and that of the Ojibwa and Cree is that the Lakota involves a more sacred or religious attitude. Such arguments, we maintain, are wrongheaded. For example, environmental philosopher J. Baird Callicott, whose views on Ojibwa values we discussed at length in the previous chapter, argues that "human life in nature from the perspective of the Lakota organization of experience as portrayed in *Black Elk Speaks* ... might more accurately be characterized as religious or holy, since prayers and worshipful rites seem to figure more prominently in the Lakota ideal of human-nature relationships than in the Algonkian" (Callicott 1989, 218). As we said above, we disagree. We argue that the Ojibwa, an Algonkian people like the Cree, are every bit as spiritual as the Lakota. Callicott seems to think that it is misleading "to characterize the means of communication with nature spirits — dreams, visions, divination, and ceremonials — as 'religious rites,' given the usual connotation of the term" (Callicott 1989, 218). Callicott seems to be assuming that the concept "religious" necessarily has otherworldly connotations. As Meyer and Ramirez, not to mention Deloria and Pratt, have shown, Lakota/Dakota spiritual holism is hardly otherworldly. It is this world which has spiritual significance. This, we would argue, is also true of, for example, Ojibwa metaphysics. As Ojibwa philosopher and traditional elder James Dumont puts it, discussing the "religious significance" of both dreams and the vision quest: "Ojibwa man is always *religious man* because he knows that as a 'soul/body' he moves about in both ordinary and non-ordinary reality. The Ojibwa is raised in this awareness from his beginning, and, realizes, further, that at the critical time of approaching independence and manhood, he must establish, once and for all, absolute contact with the spirit world. He will live the remainder of his life in a balance of these two realities" (Dumont 1976, 39).

Dumont's account is confirmed by traditional Ojibwa healer Ron Geyshick in his 1989 book with Judith Doyle, titled *Te Bwe Win* [Truth]. *Te Bwe Win* is an interesting collection of stories Geyshick has heard from elders, as well as his own accounts of personal experiences growing up on the isolated (and hence insulated) Lac La Croix reserve in northern Ontario. He includes descriptions of his first vision quests. These, he tells us, he began at the age of nine. At that age he was left alone on an island to fast for four days and four nights. His father instructed him to avoid drinking water and not even to chew on twigs no matter how thirsty he became. If he started to feel cold, which in all likelihood he would since the ice had just gone from the lake, it was suggested that he run around the island or place a large flat rock on his chest to warm up. That first year, he tells us, he heard no spirits: "For four days and four nights, the only sound I heard was from my grumbling tummy" (Geyshick and Doyle 1989, 42). He tried the vision quest again the following year. This time he did not get so hungry. He reports hearing the trees talking. The third year his fasting became "full of dreams and visions." On the fourth year he says he "began to travel with the spirits, around the world in four directions" (Geyshick and Doyle 1989, 42). Through these experiences Geyshick "learned to be an Indian." He certainly, as Dumont might put it, made "absolute contact with the spirit world." The main point here is that through the vision quest one is transformed. We saw this also in the phenomenological description of the vision quest in Chapter Three. One begins to see the world in a different way, in a way which has a profound influence on thought and action, in a way which makes one truly religious. As Geyshick explains: "In my stories, I try to teach young people respect for everything: other people, trees, water and the spirits. I want them to know that the Creator is in you or me" (Geyshick and Doyle 1989, 31).

Transformative Philosophy and the Incommensurable

What both Dumont and Geyshick are describing can usefully be characterized as a form of what has been called "transformative philosophy." We suggest that Lakota and Ojibwa metaphysics, indeed Native American Indian worldviews generally, are best understood and compared with one another as types of transformative philosophy.

Transformative philosophy has proven extremely useful in cross-cultural comparisons of Western and non–Western philosophies. We draw upon the excellent study by John Taber entitled *Transformative Philosophy: A Study of Sankara, Fichte, and Heidegger,* which is based on his doctoral dissertation at the University of Hawaii, a major center for East–West comparative work in philosophy. Taber establishes "the transformative pattern as a distinct type of philosophy" which can be discovered in very different cultures and compared. He argues that "we are ... able to ascertain *types* of philosophical systems, and by contrasting systems of the same type from different cultures we are often better able to understand them" (Taber 1983, 2), and explains that "transformative Philosophy ... does not stand on its own as a theoretical edifice but requires a certain transformation in the student to be intelligible, which transformation it in turn finalizes" (Taber 1983, 65). This he illustrates with the 8th or 9th century East Indian philosopher Sankara. According to Sankara, in order to fully understand union with Brahman (a principal teaching of Hindu philosophy), it is necessary to acquire a certain kind of "precognitive knowledge," an experiential state attained through purification. "This purity is marked by certain qualities which it seems proper to label 'spiritual'—dispassion, tranquility, control, and so forth. It is to be cultivated by the regular observance of religious and social ritual ... and by spiritual disciplines such as celibacy, austerity, meditation, and restraint of the senses" (Taber 1983, 55). These observances are expected to bring about a kind of transformation in consciousness, producing, for example, feelings of unity or oneness. Then it supposedly follows that "having, so to speak, already achieved union with Brahman on a precognitive level, the explicit statement that one *is* Brahman is all that is needed to precipitate a clear consciousness of that union and bring it into being as such for the first time" (Taber 1983, 55).

The transformative role of traditional Lakota ceremony, its role in putting participants in touch with their own spirituality, is confirmed by Deloria in *God Is Red.* Explaining the importance of ceremonies Deloria suggests that "traditional Indian people experience spiritual activity as the whole of creation becomes active participants in ceremonial life" (Deloria 1994, 274). He argues that we should understand that such ceremonies "act to complete and renew the entire and complete cycle of life, ultimately including the whole cosmos present in its specific realizations, so that in the last analysis one might describe ceremonials as the cosmos becoming thankfully aware of itself" (Deloria 1994, 276–277). To dance at a pow wow, for example, and understand that the dance itself is a specific realization of the whole cosmos, to think of your dancing-self as "the cosmos becoming thankfully aware of itself," is to experience a transformation of consciousness. It is, in a very real sense, to be transported from the mundane to the spiritual. Only after such a transformation are we really in a position to understand, for example, the insight of Lakota spiritual holism that "everything is ultimately of one continuous spirit" (Meyer and Ramirez 100). As Opaskwayak Cree scholar Shawn Wilson concludes in his important little book on research, relationships and community, titled *Research Is Ceremony: Indigenous Research Methods, "If research doesn't change you as a person, then you haven't done it right"* (Wilson 2008, 135, italics in the original).

Failure to recognize the transformative nature of Native American philosophies often leads to profound misunderstandings. To give one example: Ojibwa medicine societies such as the Midewiwin are usually described, we would say misdescribed, as secret societies. Again we cite the Tedlocks' *Teachings from the American Earth,* because it really was quite a sympathetic book for its day. They state categorically that "throughout North America, there are secret societies in which holy men share the power of their visions with a group of initiates, sometimes their former patients: the Iroquois Society of the Mystic Animals, the Midewiwin of the Ojibwa, the numerous medicine societies of the Pueblos, and many others" (Tedlock and Tedlock 1978, xix). Interestingly enough the Tedlocks seem to recognize the importance of the *personal* vision quest. "But it is not enough to share the visions of others. Over much of North America, young Indians are encouraged and even expected to seek their own visionary encounters with the other world. Indeed, the seeking is prerequisite for adulthood itself. In some tribes, the first attempts may be made as early as the age of five, and in most it has to be made before adolescence" (Tedlock and Tedlock 1978, xix). Unfortunately, the Tedlocks fail to relate this form of consciousness transformation, the need for this kind of experience, to the ability to understand the teachings of the so-called secret societies. What is missing in their account seems to be any insight into the nature of the teachings of these alleged "secret" societies. The teachings are not really secret. Rather they simply cannot be understood by someone who has not undertaken the appropriate forms of purification. There is nothing mysterious or mystical about this. It is simply not having the experience necessary in order to understand what is said to you. This is exactly what is to be expected when dealing with a form of transformative philosophy. The point we are attempting to make here about the transformative nature of Ojibwa and Lakota philosophy (Native American philosophy) is illustrated beautifully by "Anishinahbœótjibway elder"

Wub-e-ke-niew from the Red Lake Reservation in Northern Minnesota. In his book with the pointed title *We Have a Right to Exist* he makes the following quite humorous observation about scholars from the dominant society researching the Midewiwin: "The *Midé* is not a secret — but enculturation into Western European civilization usually prevents people from seeing or understanding it. I have been present when *Midé* elders told interested and open-minded White people things about the *Midé*, in English, and the person to whom the elder was talking did not realize they were being told anything" (Wub-e-ke-niew 1995, 8).

This returns us inevitably to the incommensurability problem. What kind of transformations do non–Natives have to undergo in order to understand Native worldviews? It has long been recognized that non–Natives who take Native views seriously often experience profound emotional and psychological change. Even the Tedlocks write about "whites who have tried to hear Indians and were changed in the process" (Tedlock and Tedlock 1978, x).

Meyer and Ramirez also recognize that for most of us to fully understand Lakota/Dakota spiritual holism we will have to undergo some form of transformation, though they use the term "gestalt switch" rather than transformative philosophy. "To *say* that the Lakota and Dakota see the world holistically as one spirit is not the same as to *see* the world that way. For another to see the world that way would require a kind of gestalt switch involving a shift in 'styles of reasoning' as well as ways of perception. It would entail responding to the world according to the exhortation; Mitakuye oyasin! — 'We are all related!'" (Meyer and Ramirez 1996, 105). Widdowson and Howard's study *Disrobing the Aboriginal Industry* is a good example of the nonsense that results when Native America philosophy and its transformative nature are ignored. They give, for example, a most unsympathetic response to presentations of traditional knowledge (TK) they heard at a 1996 Federal Environmental Assessment Review in Yellowknife, Northwest Territories. They report hearing elders explain how you must live in a certain "spiritual" manner in order to be worthy to "hold" traditional knowledge, e.g., "giving offerings to the land, holding potlatches, and thinking in a cyclical fashion" (Widdowson and Howard 2008, 6). They cite an elder claiming: "My father taught me many spiritual things. One thing he said is that rock moves. You have a tough time understanding and believing that.... It takes a lifetime to understand. What I am sharing with you is just touching the surface. I have witnessed all of the things I've talked about" (Widdowson and Howard 2008, 6). Widdowson and Howard have no time for the use of TK in environmental hearings, concluding that "unlike physical science, traditional knowledge assumes that all objects in the universe are governed by spiritual forces that cannot be seen by a white man.... Scientific understanding does not rely on the alleged 'spiritual qualities' of a scientist, or processes that are visible only to people of a certain racial ancestry" (Widdowson and Howard 2008, 6–7). It is not just Widdowson and Howard who are ignoring Native American philosophy; many elders, including the ones they heard making presentations in Yellowknife, have a responsibility to think through what they are saying and at least try to communicate to the (often unsympathetic) audience that confronts them. In other words they too need to engage in Native philosophy while recognizing the incommensurability problem, at least if they want to do any good at environmental assessment hearings. We suspect that, in many cases, they have indeed taken their audience into consideration and realize that whatever they say, many of the non–Native members of the audience, like the Widdowsons and Howards, are just not going to get it, ever.

We suggest that a principal cause of the incommensurability problem, at least in this context, is, as Wub-e-ke-niew puts it, "enculturation into Western European civilization." More precisely it has something to do with the difference between oral and literate cultures. But even this is not sufficiently precise. Many North American and certainly Meso-American cultures had their own unique forms of writing as well as oral traditions long before contact with Europeans (see for example Coe 1992, Doxtator 2001). More precisely, then, what is it about literate cultures rooted in Western European civilization which makes it difficult for their descendants to come to grips with the indigenous oral traditions and traditional knowledge of North America? This may seem like an impossible question. But one possible answer is suggested in a study by philosopher David Abram entitled *The Spell of the Sensuous: Perception and Language in a More–Than-Human World.*

We will outline this answer, and suggest one unforeseen and rather startling implication it has for the teaching and preservation of Native languages. As the subtitle of the book suggests, human language developed in concert with our perceptual encounter with a meaningful, animate more-than-human world. This perceptual encounter is essentially relational and indeed interpersonal. We see it as reminiscent of Deloria's agent ontology. As Abram explains: "Our bodies have formed themselves in delicate reciprocity with the manifold textures, sounds, and shapes of an animate earth — our eyes have evolved in subtle interaction with *other* eyes, as our ears are attuned by their very structure to the howling of wolves and the honking of geese" (Abram 1996, 22). It is not just the earth, including the two- and the four-legged animals which, as other-than-human persons, speak to us, thus in effect giving us the gift of language, but the air itself in which we are all immersed, is animate relating us to one another, both human and more-than-human. Abram actually gives a Lakota example. Noting that "the sacred pipe is smoked in ritual fashion during all of the diverse Lakota ceremonies, from the sweat lodge to the Sun Dance," Abram draws our attention to the important fact that the "pipe smoke makes the invisible breath visible, and as it rises from the pipe, it makes visible the flows and currents in the air itself, makes visible the unseen connections between those who smoke the pipe in offering and all other entities that dwell within the world: the winged people, the other walking and crawling peoples, and the multiple rooted beings — trees, grasses, shrubs, mosses" (Abram 1996, 229). He also notes that the Lakota believe that the smoke as it floats upwards carries prayers "to the sky beings — to the sun and the moon, to the stars, to the thunder beings and the clouds, to all those powers embraced by *woniya wakan,* the holy air" (229).

Language and Alienation

Now, as we said above, all this would sound to the Widdowsons and the Howards like so much primitive animism, childish and simplistic. To Christian missionaries in the last century, and unfortunately to some even today, it would be nothing less than heathenism, something to be eradicated, something from which primitive people need to be saved. To counter these typically Eurocentric responses Abram asks the following rather revealing questions: "If human discourse is experienced by indigenous, oral peoples to be participant with the speech of birds, of wolves, and even of the wind, how could it ever have become severed from that vaster life? How could we ever have become so *deaf* to these other voices...?" (Abram 1996, 91).

The answer he gives to these questions is almost as startling as the questions themselves. Our alienation from the meaningful, natural life-world of other-than-human persons is, he argues, due, among other things, to the development and widespread application of the phonetic alphabet. "Only ... with the advent and spread of phonetic writing did the rest of nature begin to lose its voice" (Abram 1996, 138). Abram examines the historical development of the phonetic alphabet in some detail, demonstrating how we began to relate *only* to the all too human sound of the written letters of the alphabet. Among the first peoples to shift to a purely phonetic alphabet were the ancient Hebrews who became known as the people of the Book. "They were perhaps the first nation to so thoroughly shift their sensory participation away from the forms of surrounding nature to a purely phonetic set of signs, and so to experience the profound epistemological independence from the natural environment that was made possible by this potent new technology" (Abram 1996, 240). To represent certain natural forms in statues and imagery became the sin of "*idolatry!*" The ancient Hebrews were becoming totally alienated from the land so much so that "*it was not the land but the written letters that now carried the ancestral wisdom*" (240, italics in the original). This ancestral wisdom contains many stories of alienation from the land, from place: Adam and Eve's banishment from the Garden of Eden, the Israelites' exodus from Egypt, and their wandering in the desert looking for the "promised land." Abram argues somewhat contentiously that there is a sense in which they are still looking. "The Jewish sense of exile was never merely a state of separation from a specific locale, from a particular ground; it was (and is) also a sense of separation from the very *possibility* of being placed, from the very possibility of being entirely at home" (196). This kind of deep displacement Abram argues is really "inseparable ... from alphabetic literacy ... of which the Hebrews were the first real caretakers" (196). Perhaps because they were the first to be so "dis-placed" they also continue to feel a lingering yearning for the "sensory nourishment" of an all but forgotten personal relationship with the living land, with place as person. Abram is not alone in this assessment of his people. He cites in support the Jewish poet Edmond Jabes (1912–1991): for whom "*being Jewish ... means exiling yourself in the word and, at the same time, weeping for your exile*" (Abram 1996, 196, Jabes 1974, 72, italics in Abram). Despite the alienating influence of their phonetic alphabet, Abram admits they still to this day retain an understanding of, and deep respect for, sacred sites. Still, as quoted above, "*it was not the land but the written letters that now carried the ancestral wisdom*" (240, italics in the original). This represents a move from animism to a more abstract religion in which the sacred is, like the air, invisible. Not unlike the Lakota, who, as we saw above, regard the air itself as "wakanda," the ancient Hebrews maintained a religious respect for the air, the wind, breath. Abram sees the absence of written vowels in the ancient Hebrew "*aleph-beth*" as supporting this claim. Given that the vowel sounds are "made by the unimpeded breath itself" while consonants are made by using the tongue, throat, palate, and so on to momentarily "obstruct the flow of breath" Abram argues that "it is possible, then, that the Hebrew scribes refrained from creating distinct letters for the vowel-sounds in order to avoid making a visible representation of the invisible" (241). To do so would be a form of idolatry. "It would have been to make a visible representation of a mystery whose very essence was to be invisible and hence unknowable — the sacred breath, the holy wind" (241). After drawing attention to various etymologies such as the Greek word meaning both soul and breath found at the root of such terms as "psychology," the Latin for both breath and wind giving rise to such terms as "spirit" and "respiration," and the Sanskrit *atman* "which signified 'soul' as well as the 'air' and the 'breath'" manifesting itself in the word "atmosphere," Abram concludes "that for ancient Mediterranean cultures no less than for the Lakota and the Navajo, the air was once a singularly sacred presence" (238). Noting the importance of "the breath itself" within Kabbalistic mysticism, Abram goes so far as to suggest that a Jewish prayer beginning with the Rabbi's exhorting "the wind to come from all four directions and fill his breath" is "startlingly reminiscent of a Navajo or a Lakota ceremony" (247). Yet he argues as the phonetic representation of purely human sounds in the Hebrew *aleph-beth* and the Greek and Roman alphabets began to dominate, particularly after the printing press and widespread literacy, the Western intellect would increasingly fail to recognize an animate earth and sacred air. "*Only as the written text began to speak would the voices of the forest, and of the river, begin to fade. And only then would language loosen its ancient association with the invisible breath, the spirit sever itself from the wind, the psyche dissociate itself from the environing air.* The air, once the very medium of expressive interchange, would become an increasingly empty and unnoticed phenomenon, displaced by the strange *new* medium of the written word" (254, italics in the original).

It is important to recognize that Abram is not arguing that we should give up literacy, or that we should turn our backs on the written word, which has dis-placed an agent ontology of living place. Rather, he is arguing that "the written word carries a pivotal magic — the same magic that once sparkled for us in the eyes of an owl and the glide of an otter" (Abram 1996, 273). Abram sees his task as that of "*taking up* the written word, with all its potency, and patiently, carefully, writing language back into the land" (Abram 1996, 273). However, before we look at how it is even possible to write language back into the land, it is important to examine other factors which are also responsible for this dis-placement, this enculturation into a Western European mind set. These factors are mentioned only briefly in passing by Abram and include particularly the agricultural revolution and urbanization (185–184, 263–264). The effect of urbanization is not difficult to imagine. Once we surround ourselves with houses and other buildings, roads and bridges, things of our own construction, it does not take very long for the wilderness to fall silent to our ears. From this perspective nature, as we heard one urbane professor once quip only half in jest, is just something to keep buildings apart. He also let it be known that he felt that the closer they are together the better. His attitude may reflect the long cold winters we experience in this part of the world. Still, it is our place; or rather we are of this place.

Time and Place

The impact of the agricultural revolution is considerably more complicated than that of urbanization. The agricultural revolution has been described as "a process of truly earthshaking proportions ... the shift from merely gathering wild food to actually engineering it into being. The neolithic" (Martin 1992, 37). This neolithic revolution brought about a radical change in cosmology, an alienation from our true selves and a related disengagement from the earth. This kind of dis-placement seems to be a hallmark of Western civilization. Historian Calvin Luther Martin, much to the consternation of fellow historians, puts it this way: "Mankind now serves two masters, and they are in direct opposition to one another. One is the amnesiac of neolithic historical consciousness, who ... appears in many masks and beguiles us with the liquor of detached rationality, fear, and unsustainable dreams. The other is the great, brooding presence of earthly process, whose songs and multitudinous creations no longer harmonize with *Homo' s* neolithically derailed speech and artifice" (130). Why does Martin characterize the "historical consciousness" as an "amnesiac"? Amnesia has something to do with lack of memory, especially about who you are, your identity. Martin is convinced that our identity is closely related to a genuine relation to place, that this is something that hunter gatherers intuitively understood, but which seems to have been forgotten in the neolithic revolution. "One of the great insights of hunter societies is that words and artifice of specific place and place-beings (animal and plant) constitute humanity's primary instruments of self-location, the computation of where, in the deepest sense, one is in the biosphere.... Only by learning ... about these things, can one hope to become, in turn, a genuine person" (103–104). Though Martin does not mention Deloria in this context, Martin's position does sound very much like Deolria's agent ontology or, in actual fact,

Lakota/Dakota metaphysics. Ever since the first edition of *God Is Red,* in 1978, Deloria has been consistently drawing attention to this fundamental difference between Native American and Euro-Western ways of understanding place and self. "American Indians hold their lands — place — as having the highest possible meaning.... Immigrants review the movement of their ancestors across the continent as a steady progression of basically good events and experiences, thereby placing history — time — in the best possible light" (Deloria 1994, 62–63). This could well be considered one of the principal roots of the incommensurability problem. "When the one group is concerned with the philosophical problem of space and the other with the philosophical problem of time, then the statements of either group do not make much sense when transferred from one context to the other..." (Deloria 1994, 63).

Calvin Martin with the publication of his *The American Indian and the Problem of History* back in 1987 shocked his fellow historians by drawing attention to a scandalous deficiency apparent in histories of North America, which Martin attributes to the fact that historians writing about Native American Indians "have only the most rudimentary understanding of native phenomenology, epistemology, and ontology" (27). In his more recent book, *In the Spirit of the Earth,* Martin, like Deloria, draws a distinction between the metaphysics of place and those of time, between what he calls mythological consciousness and historical consciousness. Martin discusses, for example, the "lesson taught by mythology and familiar to hunter-gatherer societies, this being that words of place and place-beings, such as animal and plant beings, are instruments for triangulating our true selves within the cosmos" (100). This is, he argues, a lesson all but forgotten by Western civilization after the neolithic revolution and the rise of historical consciousness. "The Greek rationalists who scorned the singing poets substituted one kind of truth for another; they exalted the truth of written history (logos) over the very different order of truth we call myth (mythos), which was sung" (95). His reference to the ancient Greeks here links his argument nicely with that of Abram, discussed above, since the Greeks, like the ancient Hebrews, were among the first to use a purely phonetic alphabet. Martin maintains, quite rightly in our opinion, that historical consciousness "has no song. History uttered and history written have replaced the songs of where and who that are taught by a singing earth" (94). As we explained in Chapter Two, citing Thomas Carlyle, one of the great nineteenth century historians, written history, historical narrative, is necessarily "linear" (Carlyle 1901, 89). The time which comes into being with history is also, of course, linear time, not the cyclical processes of hunter-gatherer *mythos*. Bear in mind that the move from the metaphysics of place to the metaphysics of time is due at least in part to the Neolithic, the agricultural, revolution. But farming also depends on seasonal cycles. With this in mind Martin asks, "Why lay hands on the cycle and straighten it into a vector?" (Martin 1992, 67). It turns out that time and the control of nature are closely related. "For the secret to the riddle of plant and even animal production and reproduction was timing: time which became a clock.... A careful watch of the heavens ... revealed such a gigantic mechanism ... mathematically precise and beautiful, and computable by those who made it their business to attend to such things: priest-astronomers" (Martin 1992, 57). On the basis of this, Martin argues that the Neolithic saw the emergence of the priest-king "as a special rank of individual uniquely qualified in the art of cosmic divination and, more subtly and dangerously, time itself, on behalf of a society now increasingly committed to engineering food into existence" (56). History, Martin suggests, "was initially royal history, dynastic history: the story, more the recording, of a single ruler or his family, generation to generation, and their divine mission — order out of chaos" (60). This turns out to be, of course, the linear narrative of written history. These priest-kings saw themselves "as the anointed, lineal, dynastic keepers of order — essentially, their fear of what they imagined as chaos" (67).

Martin, Deloria and Abram, quite independently of one another, all reach the conclusion that there is disturbing documentation for this Neolithic consciousness in "the Judeo-Christian historical trajectory." Martin concentrates on "Jews and Christians as a people with a mission; history being punctuated by episodes of violent destruction; the death of god [the crucifixion] changing the terms of history; the god's blood as symbolic of our salvation; Christians reminding themselves of their redemption and mission by drinking the god's blood and eating his flesh (Holy Communion); Christians hastening the end through their proselytization, so as to end human history and inaugurate eternity; mankind influencing time, in this case collapsing it; Christians as conquest societies with a noble goal" (65). It is significant that Deloria too, with his critique of Christianity, in *God Is Red,* seizes on this same notion of "Christians as conquest societies with a noble goal." As Deloria puts it, "In the first several centuries of Christian existence, one of the most popular justifications for the failure of Jesus to return to earth was his alleged admonition to his disciples to preach the message of his life to all nations" (107). Deloria goes on to suggest that a great many Christians believed Jesus would not return, that the second coming could not happen, until the Christian message had been preached to every nation on earth. "In almost every generation of Christians, there was somewhere a militant missionary force seeking to convert non–Christian peoples, and this propensity to expand the religion's influence meant in realistic terms an expansion of control by the church structure over non–Christian peoples" (107). Though he does not mention Deloria, Martin quotes Mark 16:15: "Go ye into the world, and preach the gospel to every creature." Martin then goes on to express what is essentially Deloria's concern: "With this, Christ's followers also become a people with a mission: to convert the pagan and the infidel.... Christians have been exemplary as missionary people: to convert the nonbeliever, wherever he or she may be, and so to hasten Christ's return" (64). Martin also seizes upon the Exodus story, Abraham's offspring, the children of Israel launching themselves on their own special history to establish themselves in the Promised Land. "They were Jehovah's people, and their wars of conquest against resident and neighboring peoples were pronounced holy" (Martin 1992, 63). Martin challenges historical narrative itself by challenging these historical religions, asking: "Who, then, was this Jehovah?" He concludes: "In my opinion, a frank and virulently potent icon of a newly emergent historical consciousness; essentially a spokesman for the conviction held by a nucleus of individuals that the destiny of the Children of Israel should not be frittered away in parochial issues, such as those which consumed the energies of the animal idols one witnessed in profusion among the pagan societies throughout the ancient Middle East" (59). David Abram also recognizes the role of Christian missions in the spreading of historical consciousness, adding his own contribution about the spread of the phonetic alphabet: "Christian missions and missionaries were by far the greatest factor in the advancement of alphabetic literacy.... It was not enough to preach the Christian faith: one had to induce the unlettered, tribal peoples to begin to use the technology upon which that faith depended" (Abram 1996, 254).

We began this chapter with a discussion of the damage done to Native people by the missionary-run residential schools. It is with Abram's research what we can begin to see the real depth of that damage: "Only by training the senses to participate with the written word could one hope to break their spontaneous participation with the animate terrain" (Abram 1996, 254). Everything we discussed in this chapter, from Meyer and Ramirez's Lakota/Dakota metaphysics to Pratt and Deloria's agent ontology, from Native American language to the transformative nature of traditional Native American ceremony, the residential school experience seemed designed to eradicate from the consciousness, from the perceptual awareness of Native American children. Worse still, in an attempt to preserve Native languages, we now write Native languages using the Roman alphabet, thus representing the sound of the language purely phonetically separating the language from living place and place beings, the other-than-human persons addressed, spoken to, by various tribes in terms of "Mitakuye oyasin!—'We are all related!'" (Meyer and Ramirez 1996, 105), or "GAKINA-AWIIYA — We Are All Related" (Peacok and Wisuri 2002, 39). We have just cited two examples, Lakota and Ojibwa, respectively, of representing the sound of Native languages purely phonetically using the Roman alphabet. If Abram's thesis is correct, and we think he is certainly on the right track, any representation of sound by arbitrary abstract symbol runs the risk of separating language from the living land, from place, perhaps not in the first few generations, but eventually. After all, as Abram has shown, it took over two thousand years for the West to do it to itself.

Syllabics

We see here some important implications concerning the use of various writing systems, particularly syllabics, to maintain Native American languages and cultures. In fact, the year after the publication of Abram's book, we presented a paper drawing on his research to the Annual Algonquian Conference arguing that "alienating Native languages from the land through the introduction of such writing systems may well be the most pernicious, most potent technology of assimilation ever devised" (McPherson and Rabb 1999, 210). Algonquian syllabics were developed by Methodist missionary James Evans (1801–1846) and based in part on stenographers' shorthand. He ensured that translations of the Bible, various church hymns and so forth were published in syllabics. Known as Indian writing, it became quite popular among Cree and Ojibwa before the introduction of residential schools and the decline in the use of their languages. At one time this form of Indian writing was so popular that the story was told that Kisemanito (the Great Spirit) gave the syllabic system to his people simultaneously through two prophets, Cree elders, Mistanaskowew (Badger Bull) in Western Canada and Machiminahtik (Hunting Rod) in Eastern Canada (http://www.creeculture.ca/e/language/syllabics.html).

With modern attempts to preserve Native languages, syllabics are now being taught as part of a strategy to encourage the use of Algonquian languages. Syllabics for reading and writing are relatively easy to learn. Characteristic sounds are represented by an arbitrary symbol which in turn can represent related sounds by a simple change of orientation. For example the sound “pe” is represented by a wedge “v.” Turn it upside down and it represents the sound “pi.” Turn it on its side—“>”—and it becomes “pu.” Turn if its on other side—“<”—and it says “pa.” All this is, of course, purely arbitrary with no relation to the land or place. Even the ancient Hebrew *aleph-beth* began with some morphological resemblance to the world of which it spoke. Abram goes into some detail describing the “pictographic inheritance” of the “ancient Semitic *aleph-beth*” (Abram 1996, 101). For example, its first letter, Aleph, turns out to mean “ox” in ancient Hebrew. It was written somewhat like a “v” with a strike through, “ꝟ,” thus having some resemblance to the head of an ox, long face, horns above the line. It was actually written on more of a slant as if the ox had its head turned slightly to the side. The point is, the resemblance to the animal it names, and thus its pictographic inheritance, is evident. As alphabets develop, this inheritance is increasingly lost. Turned further on its side and slightly more stylized it becomes the first letter of the Greek alphabet, “alpha.” Turned completely upside down, it, in fact, became the letter “A” in the Roman or Latin alphabet, the alphabet we use in English today. The original link to the animal, to the other-than-human world, has been completely lost. Deloria’s agent ontology, which we discussed in some detail above, is but one illustration of how much this kind of loss can mean to Indigenous peoples. Abram gives many examples of this move away from the pictographic inheritance of the Hebrew *aleph-beth*. Two further examples should be sufficient to make the point here. The Hebrew letter “mem” which was also their word for “water” they depicted as a series of waves on a lake or sea. It eventually became the letter “M” in the Latin (English) alphabet. The waves are still there in stylized form, but any reference to water is completely absent. Finally, the letter “Q” could be said to look not unlike a monkey seen from behind, its tail dangling from its round body. It is derived from the Semitic “qoph” which also means monkey in their language and was written as a circle with a tail, thus resembling the animal. As Abram has shown in some detail, as phonetic alphabets developed, this pictographic inheritance, and thus any link to the animate other-than-human world, was completely lost in the process.

In a paper author Rabb presented with Cree philosopher Lorraine Mayer at the University of Oregon to David Abram, and to which Abram himself responded, this process was called “Phonicating Mother Earth”

(Brundige and Rabb 1997, 78–88). Abram's principal concern is with environmental issues. He is trying to understand how we could possibly have become so alienated from the earth that it is now regarded primarily as a rightless resource which can be exploited for solely human purposes. His answer involves the story of the development of the phonetic alphabet discussed above. We on the other hand are more concerned with the impact of the development of the phonetic alphabet on the worldviews of indigenous peoples. We see it as an attack on their very indigeneity. This is precisely why we argued before the Algonquian Conference that "the introduction of such writing systems may well be the most pernicious, most potent technology of assimilation ever devised" (McPherson and Rabb 1999, 210). The Algonquian Conference annual meeting is the largest regular gathering of Native language teachers in North America. These are the folks who make their living teaching syllabics, and honestly believe that in doing so they are contributing to the preservation of Native languages and culture. They hold their annual conference at various universities throughout North America. For example, prior to our presentation on the implications of Abram's thesis for syllabics it was held in Chapel Hill, North Carolina (1995), and Toronto, Ontario (1996). In 1997 it was held in Thunder Bay, Ontario, organized by our own university which has a large Native language teachers' program. That is when we first questioned the use of syllabics in the teaching of Native languages, though the proceedings were not published until 1999. In that year the annual conference was held in LaFayette, Indiana. It has also been held in, for example, Boston, Massachusetts (1998), Berkeley, California (2001), Madison, Wisconsin (2004), Vancouver, British Columbia (2006), Minneapolis, Minnesota (2008) and Montreal, Quebec (2009 and 2000). The point is that this important conference of Algonquian scholars circulates through major universities across North America on both sides of the Canada/U.S. border. Needless to say the Native language teachers among them were not entirely pleased with our warning that their use of syllabics may well be doing more harm than good. We now admit that we may have exaggerated just a little in describing syllabics as "the most pernicious, most potent technology of assimilation ever devised" (McPherson and Rabb 1999, 210). We were of course attempting to stimulate discussion. We succeeded. However, much of the discussion revolved around hoping that Abram's thesis about impact of the phonetic alphabet was mistaken. As we noted above, his book, *The Spell of the Sensuous*, had just come out and most of the audience were hearing about it for the first time. However, Abram's thesis is not easily dismissed. For example, *The Utne Reader,* in recognition of his work, has named him "one of a hundred visionaries currently transforming the world" (http://www.wildethics.com). Abram also has had a section devoted to him in *Visionaries: The 20th Century's 100 Most Inspirational Leaders* (Satish and Whitefield 2007, 20–21). He is certainly becoming very well known. Film clips of him dancing in dialogue with a fast flowing Norwegian mountain river are on the internet (http://www.wildethics.org/projects/norway_06.html). There is growing support for Abram's thesis, particularly among environmental activists. He founded, and is currently the creative director of, the Alliance for Wild Ethics (AWE), "a consortium of individuals and organizations working to ease the spreading devastation of the animate earth through a rapid transformation of culture" (http://www.wild ethics.com). We think it is fair to say that Abram's thesis is indeed bringing about a "transformation of culture," though we are not sure how rapid it actually is. We would also argue that the growing acceptance of Native American philosophy is helping to facilitate, or is at least contributing to, this transformation. Given that this is the case, we have to concede that our presentation to Algonquian language teachers characterizing syllabics as "the most pernicious, most potent technology of assimilation ever devised" was more than a little contentious, mischievous, even. It was, we admit, needlessly upsetting. Still, the Algonquian conference participants did, in a sense, get their own back, with the help of the syllabics teachers at our own university. The summer immediately after we made our presentation to the Algonquian Conference, syllabics appeared on new signs at the main entrances to our university (see, for example, the photo at the end of this chapter). At the same time numerous signposts were erected on campus pointing directions to the student centre, library and various academic buildings. On each post directly below the English sign was another written in syllabics. We felt this was a kind of bureaucratic, albeit somewhat amusing, rejection of our warning about the dire consequences of using syllabics. The new signs came as a complete surprise to us. No one had consulted McPherson or anyone else in the Department of Indigenous Learning, the main academic unit dealing with Native students and research on campus. No one had consulted us as principal researchers in the Native Philosophy Project. Had we been consulted we no doubt would have shared our concerns, but in the end we would have told them to go ahead with the new signs as we recognize that our thesis is controversial.[1] In fact, we see Abram's entire book *The Spell of the Sensuous* as an exercise in transformative philosophy intended to help us write language back into the land and by doing so to get in touch with, and learn to respect, place, the living world of other-than-human persons our Western technological society is in danger of destroying (Abram 1996, 273). If we can write language back into the land, then we should be able to write syllabics back into the land as well. We are therefore not rejecting syllabics; rather we are warning that care needs to be taken using syllabics in the attempt to restore and/or preserve traditional Native culture. Of course to write language, including syllabics, back into the land, to rediscover the primordial meaning of hawk, wolf, rock, and wind will require a major transformation of consciousness for those of us enculturated into Western European civilization.

Viola's Egg: Reanimating the Earth

How It Is: The Native American Philosophy of V. F. Cordova outlines a thought experiment designed to transform the thinking of those who believe or act like "the Earth is an inanimate form of dumb matter ... simply there, requiring no second thought ... as we step onto its 'surface'" (Cordova 2007, 77). On this view, which Viola Cordova admits is her caricature of the "Standard Average European," the earth is not something we need to respect or even care for; it is "a simple hard surface that we need not take into consideration when we plan our actions" (77). Of course it supports life, but this ball in empty space is not itself alive. Any care or consideration we give it needs to be justified by pragmatic or utilitarian arguments to the effect that the care is required in order to maintain life as we know it, or even more crassly, to maintain the growth of Western economies. This is not a characterization of a caring, other-regarding, society. Does the Western economist, for example, care about the widow in Somalia, or some far off place, who has to decide which of her three children to feed because she does not have enough food to keep all three alive?[2] There are really two questions involved here. One is respect for, moral consideration of, other persons. The other has to do with who counts as a person, which is raised in particular by the Native concept of other-than-human persons. Cordova wants to help the SAE (Standard Average European) come to grips with Native worldviews common in the American southwest which "envision the female Earth as surrounded by a male fertilizing 'sky' ... the Sky-Father and Earth-Mother in an unavoidable and eternal embrace" (78). Such a view not only regards the Earth and Sky as in some sense persons in their own right, but also implies that all of us, including other animals, plants, and so forth are in some way like brothers and sisters caring for one another as close relatives. With respect to the earth herself, as Calvin Martin has argued, we need to "relearn what hunter-gatherers knew to the core of their being, that this place and its processes (even in our death) always takes care of us" (Martin 1992, 130). This view of an animate, caring Earth is a complete paradigm shift away from that of the SAE. A first step in bringing about this transformation is Cordova's thought experiment which we designated at the beginning of this section, Viola's egg.

Cordova asks us to think of the earth not so much as a ball floating in empty space, but more like, of all things, the inside of a raw egg. "The Earth is the yoke, swimming in the egg white — which we know commonly as the 'atmosphere,' but usually disregard as part of the Earth" (77). For this thought experiment we need to remember that the egg white is only white in a cooked egg. In the raw egg it is, like the atmosphere, more transparent though somewhat thicker. Here, "we do not so much walk on the surface of the Earth as swim in a narrow area surrounding the skin of 'the yoke'" (77). We begin to see the earth as much more fragile. "Its permeability is exposed, its 'surface' becomes less sure" (77). Cordova compares us to sea creatures living on the ocean floor and speculates that perhaps these fish may be "as unaware of water as we are of the atmosphere that sustains us" (78). Her egg experiment, like the transformative Lakota pipe ceremonies discussed above, is intended to draw our attention to, and increase our respect for, the sustaining atmosphere in which we are all immersed relating us to one another both human and other-than-human. Some find her thought experiment helpful. Others do not, finding the egg analogy a little far fetched wondering, for example, what part the shell might play. It sometimes helps to point out the little known fact that the egg shell is not actually made by the chicken. The egg itself in effect makes its own shell. "The membrane surrounding the yolk and white attracts calcite that is floating freely in the chicken's body, and causes it to form a shell, in a process that is similar to how crystals are formed" (Paterson and Kelly 2006, 9). Since the shell is a protective layer we can compare it to the protective ozone layer surrounding the earth and attracted to it by the gravitational pull of the earth itself, not unlike the way the calcite is attracted to and by the egg. Whether or not Viola's egg helps us think of the earth as animate, along the lines of Deloria's agent ontology, we have to admit that her insistence on contrasting such a view with that of the Standard Average European is a little misleading. Similar views arguing that the earth is a living, breathing being have been developed by Western thinkers, for example, James Lovelocke's famous Gaia hypothesis (Satish and Whitefield 2007, 12ff). David Abram, himself, is a Western-trained philosopher, though, as we have seen, he draws inspiration from Indigenous thinkers and Native worldviews. He does, however, also draw on the philosophy of other Western thinkers as well. For example, Abram supports his conclusions through a careful examination of the phenomenology of French philosopher Maurice Merleau-Ponty (1907–1961) as much as he does by appealing to Indigenous philosophies. Abram's main argument, that there is a correct respectful relationship with the land that the West has somehow lost, draws upon Merleau-Ponty's phenomenology of perception which suggests that below the level of our verbal awareness our bodies are in dialogue with the land, that there is a sense in which everything seems capable of speaking and hearing. "The clear sense that the animate terrain is not just speaking to us but also *listening* to us ... bears out Merleau-Ponty's thesis of perceptual reciprocity; to listen to the forest is also, primordially, to feel oneself listened to *by* the forest, just as to gaze at the surrounding forest is to feel oneself exposed and visible, to feel oneself watched *by* the forest" (Abram 1996, 153).

If we are to write language back into the land we need to experience this perceptual reciprocity with the animate more-than-human world. Abram describes the process as "releasing the budding, earthly intelligence of our words, freeing them to respond to the speech of the things themselves — to the green uttering-forth leaves from the spring branches" (273). But it is also telling stories about place and place beings, stories "that have the rhythm and lilt of the local sound scape" (273). Abram concludes that returning language to the land involves "planting words, like seeds, under rocks and fallen logs — letting language take root, once again, in the earthen silence of shadow and bone and leaf" (274). This is a difficult concept to grasp. Calvin Martin can add some clarification. He argues, "Words are too precious ... too inherently powerful be left unmoored, unaffiliated with place and the sentient beings there" (Martin 1992, 94). Martin concludes that language must be "rooted in precise place and learned from such place ... learned in song from place beings" (94). Both Martin and Abram, then, argue — correctly, we believe — that language must somehow be linked in this special way to the land. Neither of them goes into any more detail about how this is possible. As we have seen it involves the song of "place beings" and, in story, the "rhythm and lilt of the local sound scape." We believe we can provide further clarification by examining, through example, how it is possible to write *music* back into the land.

Ojibwa Landscapes

We were most fortunate to have heard the world premiere of *Ojibwe Landscapes,* a choral composition by contemporary Canadian composer Brian Hubelit. The piece was commissioned and performed by Dulcisono Women's Choir of Thunder Bay, Canada, under the direction of Susan Marrier. The choir was accompanied by tympani evoking thunder and the constant slow beating of the waves of Lake Superior, French horn and some unusual instruments: tuned Lake Superior rocks and rainsticks which sound oddly like gentle waves on the pebbled beaches of the big lake. The tuned rocks were gathered from the shore of Lake Superior, the largest of the Great Lakes and one of the largest bodies of fresh water in the world. The stones were gathered in pairs: a large one which produces a unique pitch and a smaller one used as a striker. Tuning forks were used to help select the appropriate rocks. We are told that there was some difficulty finding one of the exact pitches that was needed. At one point during the search someone stepped on or kicked a stone striking it against another and the choir realized that it sounded the exact pitch they were looking for. They then had to find the rock they heard from among those they were walking on. They like to say that they felt the stones were calling out to them.

The choir was also accompanied by a narrator, Ian Bannon of Fort William First Nation, who presented local Ojibwa legends about place, as appropriate photographs appeared on a huge screen above the choir. The use of the photographs of Lake Superior and significant landmarks by local photographer Lois Nuttal was suggested by choir director Susan Marrier. For our purposes this is an inspired addition. The projected photographs provide visual representation of the places the narrations are about. As we have seen above, in oral cultures significant places brought to mind particular stories associated with the site. One significance of *place* is that each place, in a sense, has its own story (tells its own story?).

Our concern about syllabics as a phonetic writing system for Algonquian and other Native languages is that it has the potential to convey story independent of place, as Abram has shown with other phonetic writing systems. We think it is significant that though the Cherokee have had their own syllabary for over a hundred years they have never used it to record their stories of place, their important myths (Fogelson 1996, 579–580). They have actually been criticized for this. At least Raymond Fogelson, in his article "Sequoyah (c. 1770–1843): Inventor of the Cherokee Syllabary" for Hoxie's *Encyclopedia of North American Indians,* says "we must also recognize what Cherokees did *not* do with writing. They did not suddenly blossom into a nation of poets; they did not write short stories, novels, biographies, and autobiographies or other genres recognized as literature in the West; they did not record their myths or the oratory of their great leaders, although they did record ceremonies of great eloquence and style" (582). We read this as criticism because Fogelson goes on to say: "But the Cherokee's failure to develop an indigenous literature should not demean the magnitude of Sequoyah's achievement" (582). Fogelson also argues that "while for some theorists the advent of literacy marks a watershed in cultural evolution and brings about a dramatic restructuring of thought ... writing for the Cherokees tended to be more of an advanced mnemonic system and a device for focusing thought rather than a mental move into a more enlightened level of cultural development" (581–582). We think this kind of criticism is entirely misplaced. It ignores the important philosophical connection between story and place which, as Abram has clearly shown, any phonetic writing system threatens to destroy. Here we have a phonetic writing system, Sequoyah's syllabary, developed by the Cherokee themselves. They way they use it, or more importantly, the ways in which they *do not* use it, can show us something important about their philosophy of place and the relation of story and culture to the land. However, much more work in Native philosophy needs to be done to corroborate this. All we are doing here is pointing out one direction research in Native philosophy needs to move in the future. Cherokee philosophers might do for Cherokee philosophy what Deloria started to do for the Lakota philosophy of place with his analysis of agent ontology. As Pratt, Meyer and Ramirez have shown, much more work remains to be done in Lakota/Dakota metaphysics as well. We all are still just scratching the surface. Though not all Native American peoples have the same philosophy of place, we strongly suspect that place plays a paramount role in all their philosophies.

The narration of Ojibwa legends in *Ojibwe Landscapes* certainly illustrates the importance of the link between story and place for the Ojibwa. The photographs accompanying Ian Bannon's narrations serve as a visual reminder of the place responsible for the story being told. But the music the choir sings itself also invokes place, the specific place of the particular narrative. They sing, for example, of the legendary giant Nanabijou who helped the Great Spirit, Gitchi Manitou, create the world.[3] Actually, to say they sing *of* Nanabijou is somewhat misleading. The voices of the choir do not tell the story. The story is told by Bannon in the narration. The choir sings the Ojibwa words Gitchigumi, Nanabijou over and over, alternating parts of the words between different parts of the choir, altos and sopranos, for example. Together with the rainsticks and the striking of the tuned rocks, as they sing, stretching out the words, they sound like the wind and waves of Lake Superior (Gitchigumi). Though the words are written phonetically in the score the singing voices through onomatopoeia are invoking a particular place, the place represented in the projected photographs, the place the narration is about. The place is of course Lake Superior, Gitchigumi, specifically, here, the land mass called The Sleeping Giant, Nanabijou, forming part of Thunder Bay harbor at the head of the Lake. The landmark is in fact part of the Sibley peninsula. The large rock formation really does resemble a giant sleeping on his back arms folded across his chest.

The haunting sound of the choir, due also in part to the unique use of Ojibwa terms and onomatopoeia, makes the familiar landmarks of the photographs and narration feel oddly unfamiliar, makes these ordinary places seem somehow extraordinary. We would say that the sound evokes the spiritual significance of these places, but for the fact that the term "spiritual" often suggests "*other* worldly" thanks in part to our "enculturation into Western European civilization" (Wub-e-ke-niew 1995, 8). Here we want to emphasize the point that for the Ojibwa it is *this* world that is spiritual. That, we believe, is what this unique choral composition is attempting to capture by writing music back into the land.

According to the first Ojibwa legend narrated in *Ojibwe Landscapes,* after Nanabijou helps Gitchi Manitou create the world, he is sent north for a well deserved rest, where we see him still sleeping to this very day. The narrative of *Ojibwe Landscapes* continues with the legend of Nanabijou. As the choir sings "Nanabijou! Help us" the narration tells the story of how

The Sleeping Giant, Nanabijou. Drawing by Mary and Sarah McPherson.

Gitchi Manitou assures the Ojibwa people that Nanabijou would awaken to help them if they call upon him for help. The story goes on to say that as the years passed the Ojibwa people mixed with the Europeans and the younger ones ceased to practice traditional ways. Finally the Europeans began to take Ojibwa lands and lakes for themselves. The elders tried to summon Nanabijou for help. Though they danced to show respect in the traditional way and sang for him there were too few elders left and Nanabijou did not hear them. "The young ones did not know the traditions and could not help.... Eventually the last elder died and no one was left to call." This section of the narrative ends with these ominous words: "Nanabijou is still there today, sleeping, waiting for his People to call him so he can help them."

Though this is obviously a post contact narrative, it does nevertheless illustrate how the traditional Ojibwa narrative functions as a teaching device. The land formation, the Sleeping Giant, can be seen from the shore of Thunder Bay and from many points of higher ground surrounding the bay and the city, including the adjacent Fort William Indian Reserve. Whenever people, particularly Native youth, familiar with the narrative catch a glimpse of this landmark called The Sleeping Giant they are reminded of the story and that bad things can happen if they do not maintain their traditions. It serves to encourage them to maintain their language, to respect and to learn the traditions of the Elders. But it does so indirectly, consistent with the traditional value of noninterference.

The place name "Thunder Bay" refers both to the bay, the natural deep water harbor created in part by the reclining Sleeping Giant, and to the city on the shore of this harbor, at the head of Lake Superior. The harbor is in actual fact mile one of the famous St. Lawrence Seaway, and today accommodates ocean freighters (salties) from as far away as Europe and Asia. But in pre-contact times it received canoes from around Gitchigumi and many of the great rivers emptying into her. The canoes were invited, called by Animiki Wadjiw, or Thunder Bird Mountain, to participate in intertribal ceremonies. (The Ojibwa term "Animiki" is usually translated simply as "Thunder.") This mountain, which is part of the Fort William Reserve, is the location of their pow wow grounds where traditional intertribal ceremonies are still held to this day. From this plateau near the top of the mountain one has a clear panoramic view of Lake Superior and The Sleeping Giant (of both Gitchigumi and Nanabijou). This is a truly amazing place. Ojibwa youth while participating in traditional ceremonies can look out over the Lake at Nanabijou, a significant rock formation, a manitou, that is a constant reminder of their traditions and their obligation to maintain them. In *Ojibwe Landscapes,* the choir captures some of the excitement of this sacred place as their soaring voices take us up this mountain emotionally, while they sing the words "Animiki Wadjiw" over and over and over, providing background for the narrative. We are also impressed with the narrative itself. Not only does it invoke the Ojibwa narrative tradition, but here, with the help of the choral music, it metaphorically pulls the listener out of the dominant society into the Ojibwa landscape. Most members of the dominant society, most non–Natives, living in the city of Thunder Bay have little or no idea where the name of their city comes from. Most would know the mountain the Ojibwa call Animiki Wadjiw as Mount McKay. The narrative acknowledges this and attempts to rectify the situation. It speaks of "The Mountain Abode of Thunder" and points out that it is "known to the Ojibwe People as Animiki Wadjiw, and to the Europeans as Mt. McKay."

Even before drawing attention to the Ojibwa mountain looming over Thunder Bay, *Ojibwe Landscapes* introduces another traditional creation story, though we maintain that it is, in actual fact, much more than that. "Before Nanabijou fell asleep, there was another giant, Omett. He helped Nanabijou make mountains and lakes." The narrative goes on to tell the legendary love story of Omett and Naiomi, Nanabijou's daughter. Tragically, Omett, in his mountain building, let part of a mountain he was moving fall on Naiomi, killing her. Omett hid her body. Nanabijou searched for his missing daughter and, it is said, sensing her presence sent a thunderbolt into the ground opening a great canyon at the bottom of which he found the body of his daughter. There he buried her, and in punishment turned Omett into stone and "put him on the canyon wall to watch Naiomi's grave forever." As various plaques in the area relating this legend explain, this is how "Ouimett Canyon" and the "Indian Head," a natural rock formation standing against one of its walls, were formed (http://www.canyoncountry-ontario.ca). Ouimett Canyon is a real place less than a one hour drive east of Thunder Bay. We suspect it was named after a French Canadian politician, not an Ojibwa giant called Omett. We also prefer a geological explanation of its origin involving glaciation and erosion. The legend is really a cautionary tale, only metaphorically a creation story. We learn from it to acknowledge our mistakes, to own up to them; otherwise we might find ourselves forced to watch over them forever. We were pleased to see *Ojibwe Landscapes* seems to recognize this. During the narration of the legend the choir sings over and over again "Naiomi, Naioni" as her father searches for her calling out her name. We hear her answer with a feeble "Here am I! I am here!" At the same time the playing of the tympani and the Lake Superior stones provide the sound of Nanabijou striding over the land and releasing his thunderbolt. We hear the choir sing "Omett! what have you done? Omett! what have you done?" This is repeated many times, and the way it is drawn out certainly gives the impression that Omett is being rebuked, while the narration tells us of his eternal punishment. We are left with no doubt that this is primarily a cautionary tale.

The final legend narrated in *Ojibwe Landscapes* tells a very different kind of story. Rather than a cautionary tale about what not to do, it simply relates a story of self sacrifice for the sake of community. If it is offering positive advice, it is doing so in an indirect way following the traditional value of noninterference. Consistent with an Ojibwa philosophy of place, this part of the narration begins (as do most of the others) by locating the place so essential to the story. "Northwest of Animiki Wadjiw, the Kaministiquia River plunges over a cliff on its way to Gitchi-gumi; the waterfall is known among the Ojibwe as Gakaabikaa." It is known to the rest of the world as Kakabeka Falls and is now the principal attraction for a government-run campground: Kakabeka Falls Provincial Park. Known as the Niagara of the North, it is in actual fact the largest waterfall in the Lake Superior watershed with a drop of close to one hundred and thirty feet (http://gowaterfalling.com/waterfalls/kakabeka.shtml). A plaque on the boardwalk overlooking the falls tells the legend of Greenmantle, the daughter of an Ojibwa Chief, who led a Sioux raiding party, canoes and all, over the falls to their death, thus saving her village. This is a story of self-sacrifice, or at least one extolling the virtue of risking all for the sake of community. As the narrative in *Ojibwe Landscapes* puts it: "Some say she perished saving her village, others say that she jumped from her canoe and swam to a rock, while the Sioux followed her canoe over the falls." The choir adds to the emotional impact of this story by singing sounds of fast flowing water, "shiw shiw shiw," and a long, drawn out "Gakaabikaa Gakaabikaa" over and over and over, interspersed with "follow me, follow me, follow me." The projected photographs accompanying the narrative worked particularly well here. One photograph was taken from above the falls looking toward the edge of the precipice. The spray rising above the lip of the falls is a foreboding sign of what lies ahead. The accompanying music here makes us feel like we ourselves are in a canoe caught in the fast moving current just past the point of no return. The next photograph is taken from below looking up at the full height of the water tumbling from the falls over which we feel we are about to plunge. It is a most dramatic passage, the climax of the entire piece, its highest point. We are tempted to say that the height of *Ojibwe Landscapes* reaches the height of the falls themselves.

From this climax the piece cascades toward its conclusion, as the narrative voiceover explains, "The waters of the two cataracts mingle again in the Kaministiqua River, flowing home to the cold waters of Gitchi-gumi and whispering 'Megwetch' to us all as they slip back into the deep." The choir repeatedly echoes this respectful, grateful, expression of enough, that is all, "megwetch, megwetch, megwetch." The music and the river are flowing as one.

Ojibwe Landscapes certainly succeeds in writing music back into the land. It should be an inspiration to philosophers who want to write language back into the land, thus bringing Native and Western philosophy closer together. At the very least it serves as a good start in addressing the incommensurability problem outlined above. As we have seen, Vine Deloria characterizes this problem as the difference between a Native philosophy of place and a Western philosophy of time. A number of philosophers discussing the meaning of music and ceremony have argued that the flow of music somehow captures the meaning of time. For example, philosopher of cognitive science Mark Johnson, the master of metaphor we discussed at length in the previous chapter, argues, "In any musical work ... there is a structure and pattern of temporal flow, pitch contours, and intensity (loudness/softness) that is analogous to felt patterns of the flow of human experience" (Johnson 2007, 238). In this Johnson is following American composer Roger Sessions. He cites Sessions' 1941 essay "The Composer and his Message" to the effect that "the essential medium of music, the basis of its expressive powers and the element that gives it its unique quality among the arts, is *time,* made living for us through its expressive essence, movement" (Johnson 2007, 237). *Ojibwe Landscapes* by bringing together not just place, but Ojibwa places, and the flow of time manifested in music suggests to us how further research in Native philosophy will impact Western philosophy by forcing it to become more transformative in nature. One reason students of Native philosophy need to become familiar with Western philosophy, then, is so that they can help to change Western philosophy. If it is possible to overcome the incommensurability problem, if it is possible to reconcile Native and Western philosophies, we suggest, indeed we predict, it will be by recognizing both as unique forms of transformative philosophy. At any rate, we found *Ojibwe Landscapes* a transformative experience. We believe *Ojibwe Landscapes* is music that will transform the world, as we believe it is already transforming contemporary classical music. We hope that our dis-

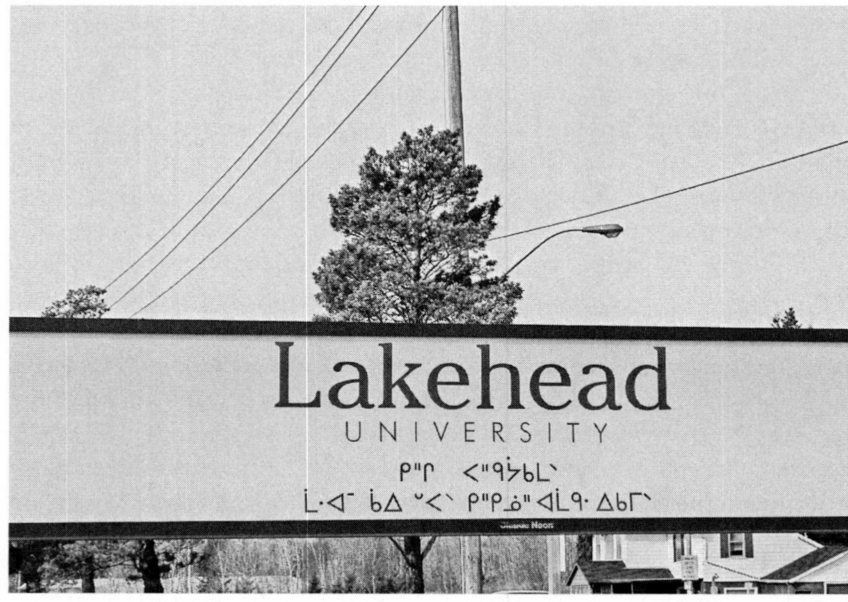

University entrance sign with syllabics. Photograph by J. Douglas Rabb.

cussion of it, in connection with writing language back into the land, will be a reminder to Native youth today that learning a language, particularly one that will help you to become more deeply attached to a community, to a place you call your own, is also a transformative experience. Learning your traditional language, the language of your place, even if you just learn the structure and never become completely fluent, will not only change you, it can also help you to change the world!

Six

Teaching Native American Philosophy through Film and Popular Culture

We argued in chapters four and five that one traditional way of doing Native American philosophy was though narrative, presenting argument with story. It is natural to extend this traditional practice in the 21st century using modern technology such as film, television, and, of course, the Internet, which visionary Marshall McLuhan, back in the 1960s, rightly predicted would revive oral cultures and tribal values on a global scale (Coupland 2009, 16ff., cf. Rosenthal 1968). Also important are novels and graphic novels as well as both traditional and modern music as we saw at the end of the last chapter. In this chapter we discuss examples of film and popular culture which we have found useful in the classroom both to stimulate discussion and to raise sensitive questions indirectly. There are a number of questions which may be too emotionally difficult to discuss, particularly in a cross-cultural class, which, as we will see, can still be addressed if approached metaphorically from related stories in say science fiction or fantasy.

We can also use both film and popular culture to address problems associated with negative stereotypes of Native American Indians. As we discussed in Chapter Four, cognitive science has shown that it makes no sense to demand that everyone just give up their prejudices and be objective and unbiased. That goes completely counter to what we now know about how our brains function. Our brains naturally use stereotypes, or what cognitive scientists call prototypes, to speed up mental processing. We counter negative stereotypes by forcing one stereotype (or prototype) to confront another, thus enlarging the overall perspective by becoming what philosopher of cognitive science Mark Johnson calls "transperspectival," adopting what we have called the polycentric perspective (see Chapter Four). Before illustrating this, using various films and other examples from popular culture, it should be noted that there is no need to appeal to cognitive science in order to deal with stereotypes in this way, though we do think cognitive science does provide further justification for this approach. Nevertheless, D.N. DeVoss and P. R. LeBeau adopt a very similar approach to stereotypes in their *Popular Culture* article "Reading and Composing Indians: Invented Indian Identity through Visual Literacy," though they make no reference to cognitive science at all. In response to the rejection of stereotypes, including negative stereotypes of Native American Indians, DeVoss and LeBeau argue: "Ignoring the rich practices and understandings of students — or dismissing them — erases the potential moments and spaces within which we can make change; ignoring students' preconceived notions negates the fissures within which we can move our understandings of Native Americans into more robust, more appropriate representative spaces" (67). Although negative stereotypes tend to freeze Indians in a sometimes romantic past, leading to the false belief that the only real Indian is a dead Indian, such stereotypes "can be recognized as base knowledge — as an established set of cultural and visual literacies — upon which more dynamic, accurate, contemporary understandings of Native Americans and Native cultures can be formulated" (DeVoss and LeBeau 2010, 55). So, according to this approach, we should not reject stereotypes. We should take them as a form of "base knowledge," explore the origins of such knowledge, and use such stereotypes as a foundation on which to build a more accurate, more complete, understanding of contemporary Native Americans. This is exactly the enterprise that Patrick Russell LeBeau has been embarked upon for, he tells us, the past twenty-three years (DeVoss and LeBeau 2010, 68). During this time he has been teaching and lecturing to audiences "that range from elementary schoolchildren to college age adults" on Native American studies generally, and, more specifically on the history of "Michigan Indians, yesterday and today" (DeVoss and LeBeau 2010, 55). At each presentation, whether he is "introducing a film, giving a lecture, teaching a class, presenting at an elementary school assembly, or conducting a teacher training workshop," LeBeau asks members of his audience right at the beginning of the session "to draw what they think the film/lecture/class/presentation/workshop is about" (68). Of course they know that it has something to do with Native American Indians. LeBeau himself is "an enrolled member of the Cheyenne River Sioux Tribe of South Dakota" on his father's side and "a descendent of the Turtle Mountain Chippewa Tribe of North Dakota" (77) on his mother's side. So his audience is being asked by a contemporary Native American Indian to draw pictures representing what they know about Native American Indians. As LeBeau explains, "Even my Lakota/Plains Chippewa ancestry provides a physiognomic prompt as I stand before them and make my request" (68). Yet most of the pictures drawn were "predictable, stereotypical and frozen in the past" (68). Whether drawn in Michigan or California, by elementary students or adults, including "graduate students, social studies teachers, professors, and community members," most of the drawings could be "reduced to teepees and warriors, with war weapons and feathered headdresses" (68 and 69). Clearly, their pictures do not resemble Patrick LeBeau, a contemporary Native American standing right in front of them. For many in his audience LeBeau may well be the first Native American Indian with whom they have ever come face to face. He raises the question: "Why are the same pictures drawn over and over again by all age groups regardless of gender, age, or educational background? Clearly, the participants came equipped with knowledge of Indians, albeit oversimplified, standardized, and ahistorical" (69). It is not too difficult to see where these stereotypes come from. "Old westerns, dime novels, movies, and myriad other cultural artifacts reflect the Indian as either a war-weary yet majestic chief or a blood-thirsty, untrustworthy brute.... These two representations have watered down to a generic Indian icon prevalent today in a multitude of visual sources, including food wrappers, billboards, and sport utility vehicles" (DeVoss and LeBeau 2010, 49). Of course these stereotypes are frozen in the past. DeVoss and LeBeau note the irony that even "Aunt Jemima and Betty Crocker have both received a new look occasionally over the years to present a more current, updated image" (50). Not so for the American Indian stereotype. "The images of Native Americans circulating in our culture are stale and have not been replaced by more contemporary views of Indian life" (50). Still, the most common stereotypes or prototypes of Native American Indians come from these sources. These are what we have to work with. As DeVoss and LeBeau argue, "The challenge teachers face is not to avoid these ... or to use them without thought ... there must be room for that ... understanding to change and grow as students and teachers develop new knowledge" (65).

Film

One of the ways in which we attempt to develop new knowledge by drawing on old stereotypes is by showing and discussing in class movies like

The Return of a Man Called Horse, Soldier Blue, Where the Spirit Lives, Once Were Warriors, and *BabaKiueria.* It should be noted that transforming old stereotypes is quite consistent with the transformative nature of Native American philosophy, and the notion that thinking employs prototypes, both of which we explained in the previous two chapters. To change or transform a stereotype is also to change the thinking of the person who held that stereotype and thus transform the person as well.

The Return of a Man Called Horse (1976) depicts the evolving relationships of the 1840s between Natives and non–Natives. During this period, the West was wild, the fur trade was in its heyday and settlements were in early stages of development. Although the movie portrays Lord John Morgan (Richard Harris) leading the Yellow Hands Sioux in reclaiming their land from French trappers, the movie also captures first meetings between Native Americans and Europeans. First meetings, as defined by Métis historian Olive Patricia Dickason following fellow historian Urs Bitterli, can be of three basic types: "contacts, collisions and [full blown] relationships" (Dickason 2009, 62). All three are depicted in this drama. We try not to dismiss this movie, or the original *A Man Called Horse,* as just another Hollywood adventure in which the hero (Richard Harris), a white man raised by the Indians, turns out to be a better Indian than the Indians themselves. We are presented with examples of cultural appropriation as we see Lord Morgan seek a vision quest and participate in a sun dance ceremony. We approach *The Return of a Man Called Horse* asking questions like: How does it portray the Indians' attitude toward gold? By what right did Europeans claim title to the land? These questions illustrate long-held misconceptions about the foundations of contemporary relationships between Native Americans and the settler population, namely, that Indians prefer alcohol to gold and that the settlers claim to the land is based on the principle of discovery, as we explained in Chapter Two. Upon Morgan's return to the Yellow Hands, he finds that they have been driven from their traditional lands, and a French fur trading fort has been established there. Indians, hostile to the Sioux, in the employ of the French, after driving the Yellow Hands away, return to the fort and are paid for their services with whiskey rather than gold. In the movie we actually hear a French trader say: "Indians have no use for gold." We also hear the French say that their claim to the land is "by the right of discovery." Relationships portrayed in the movie are not unlike those of today. In the movie we see Indians fighting Indians, Indians fighting white guys, white guys fighting Indians and white guys fighting white guys (the English and the French). Contemporary relationships, though not necessarily as violent as those portrayed in the movie, are still as damaging to Native American communities. For example, as Vine Deloria Jr. has pointed out in *God Is Red*, Indians often work against Indians. "A good deal of the political turmoil on the reservations today is between traditional people and more assimilated people over the use of the land and resources. Traditional people generally want to use land in the same way as their ancestors did while the more assimilated people want to use it as an economic resource" (212).

Soldier Blue (1970) demonstrates that Indians in the old west did have a use for gold. At the beginning of the movie we see the standard stereotype of the warlike savage as the Cheyenne attack an army paymaster wagon en route to Fort Reunion, dismembering and killing all but one of the soldiers guarding the wagon. The Cheyenne are in search of gold to exchange for rifles. There are only two survivors of the attack, Kathy Maribel "Cresta" Lee (Candice Bergen) and a young cavalry private, Honus Gant (Peter Strauss). Miss Lee has more and better survival skills than the naive Private Gant, learned from living peacefully with the Cheyenne. She knows the Cheyenne want the rifles to protect themselves against the "Long Knives." Honus denies the Indians are in any danger from the cavalry. He believes they are there simply to move the Indians to a reservation and open the land for settlement. The movie ends with a graphic depiction of the Sand Creek Massacre of 1864 where Indians, mainly women and children, were massacred by the American cavalry under the command of Colonel John Chivington who ignored both the American flag and the white flag of surrender raised by the Cheyenne. In the movie Col. Iverson (Chivington, in real life) commends his troops in making another part of America "a decent place for people to live." The massacre by Iverson's troops certainly counterbalances the negative stereotype of Native Americans shown at the beginning of the movie and raises the question, Who were the savages?

Another way to make America safe for "civilized settlement" was through government policies of assimilation as we explained in some detail in chapters two and five. The implementation of these policies, directed to kill the Indian but save the child, was through the Indian boarding schools. *Where the Spirit Lives* (1989) is a depiction of what Native children experienced in an Indian residential boarding school. Entering the school at a young age, the children were divested of all of the trappings of their former lives to the extent that their Indian names were replaced by a number and a Christian name. Their Indian clothes were burned, their hair was cut and they were washed down in kerosene. All of this was done by law which mandated the Indian agent to apprehend the children and bring them to the boarding schools. The movie even shows how parents would try to hide their children from the Indian agent. The boarding schools were operated by religious organizations intolerant of Indian ceremonies. We see children punished for attempting to conduct such ceremonies, and for speaking "mumbo jumbo" (their native language). We also see sexual exploitation in the dormitory. The movie brings to life the tragic implications of government polices of assimilation.

Although *Once Were Warriors* (1994) is set in New Zealand, the issues it raises are replicated in Native American communities in North America. The poverty, social welfare, alcoholism, family abuse, sexual abuse, suicide, gangs, and so on, it depicts are all manifest in the life experiences of Native Americans. Also depicted in the movie is the struggle to follow traditional ways while confronted with having to live in the urban ghetto. All of this resonates with Native American viewers.

BabaKiueria (1986) is a much lighter movie. It is a role reversal where a new land is discovered by Australian Aborigines in white uniforms and behaving very much like explorers and colonizers. They plant a flag and ask the white inhabitants, who are having a barbeque on the beach; "What do you call this place?" The locals answer quite honestly that this is the barbeque area, since this is where they are holding the barbeque. The "colonizers" thus christen their new land "BabaKiueria." They proceed to revert the land back to its natural state and assimilate the locals into their customs and traditions. White families are removed from their comfortable suburban homes and relocated to the outback as part of a social experiment. All the while, the white families are saying in compliance, "Oh yes, this is much better." This is an amusing movie but it is also very hard hitting. The movie won the 1987 United Nations Media Peace Prize.

There are hundreds of movies that could be used in a classroom setting. We have discussed only those that we use on a regular basis in our Native American philosophy class. Many useful movies are discussed by a variety of academics, some of whom are Native American, in *Hollywood's Indian: The Portrayal of the Native American in Film* (Rollins and O'Connor, 1999).

Popular Culture

Although important, it is not enough to counter negative stereotypes of Native American Indians by contrasting them with more positive prototypes in a kind of transperspectival exercise. From the standpoint of Native American philosophy, it is also important to understand the origins of the negative stereotype itself. We illustrate this with an example of narrative argument derived from popular culture.

The short-lived television series *Firefly* and its big screen full-length movie spinoff, *Serenity,* both written and directed by Joss Whedon, have, quite rightly, been called futuristic "space Westerns" (Wilcox and Cochran 2008, 1). They are a sort of parody of cowboy and Indian narratives, but they take place in outer space, in the future, far from what is referred to as "Earth-That-Was." Yes, there are space ships. The heroes of the narrative are the crew of a Firefly class ship called "Serenity," hence the titles of the TV series and the movie. Their ship, whose back end glows like a firefly when flying, is named after the battle of Serenity Valley where the Rebels (the browncoats) were finally defeated by the government. This government calls itself "the Alliance." It seems to be an alliance of the two surviving superpowers from Earth-That-Was, China and the USA. Its flag, for example, consists of the single red star from China's flag and the stripes from America's stars and stripes. Everyone speaks English with a smattering of Chinese (Mandarin), usually as expletives. In the part of the story that is of interest to us, the captain of the space ship Serenity takes on as passengers, and eventually as crew, two fugitives from the Alliance, brother and sister Simon and River Tam. It is River who is important for our purposes in exploring the origin of stereotypes. She has been rescued, by her brother, from an Alliance training facility where she seems to have been forced to become a government operative. She certainly sees herself as part of the Alliance, though critical of it. We are shown River as a young girl in primary school explaining to her teacher why the Alliance is unpopular with many on the outer planets (folks on the frontier, the independents). She says, "We meddle ... people don't like to be meddled with. We tell them what to do, what to think ... we're in their homes and in their heads and we haven't the right. We're meddlesome" (*Serenity*). We learn just how meddlesome the Alliance can be, as we see in their operative training facility "a 16-year-old RIVER sitting in a metal chair, needles stuck in her skull ... being adjusted by a technician. A second monitors her brain patterns. The lab is cold, blue steel. Insidiously clean" (Whedon 2005, 43).

The metaphor for the stereotype of the savage Indians in this futuristic cowboy and Indian western are the Reavers. Referring to the sudden arrival of Reaver spaceships at one point, Whedon comments, "Indians ride over the hill and surprise the cavalry" (*Serenity,* DVD commentary). The visual effects supervisor, for the TV series *Firefly,* makes it clear that even their spaceships are supposed to appear threatening: "Our Reaver ship ... was painted with war paint and ... belching dirty smoke, which made it a monster coming to get you" (*Firefly: The Official Companion* 51). Concerning the appearance of a Reaver ship, Whedon himself adds, "Once it was a commercial space liner, now it's a war machine ... ornamented and painted.... Everything about this vessel says 'savage'" (*Firefly: The Official Companion* 43). The Reavers themselves are cannibalistic savages. One of the crew of space ship Serenity describes what would happen if they are ever boarded by Reavers: "If they take the ship, they'll rape us to death, eat our flesh and sew our skins into their clothing and if we're very very lucky, they'll do it in that order" ("Serenity," episode of *Firefly*). In discussing the origins of the Reavers the captain of space ship Serenity speculates that "Reavers ain't men. Or they forgot how to be. Now they're just ... nothing. They got out to the edge of the galaxy, to that place of nothing. And that's what they became" ("Bushwhacked"). A crewmember disagrees, saying, "Of course they are. Too long removed from civilization, perhaps — but men. And I believe there's a power greater than men. A power that heals" ("Bushwhacked"). To this the captain counters: "Reavers might take issue with that philosophy. If they had a philosophy. And if they weren't too busy gnawing on your insides" ("Bushwhacked"). This brief dialogue about the Reavers reminds us of the debates in Europe in the 1500s concerning whether the newly discovered Indians of the Americas were men, beasts or demons. As we noted in Chapter Two, it was not until 1535 that the Pope acknowledged that Indians were men. Given that we are discussing Native American Indian philosophy in this book, we also find it interesting that in the *Firefly* space–Western we see someone doubting that the Reavers even have (or are capable of) a philosophy. The claim that the Native American Indians did not have a philosophy is still used, to this day, as a justification for the European occupancy of North America (cf. Flanagan 58–59). Perhaps that is one reason there has been a reluctance to accept Native American philosophy into the mainstream?

"There can be no doubt that the Reavers represent the 'blood-thirsty savage redskins' in Joss Whedon's futuristic Cowboy-and-Indian narratives, *Firefly* and its movie sequel, *Serenity*" (Rabb and Richardson 2008, 127). Some actually wear fringe! Though Whedon has been criticized by Agnes Curry, in her article "'We Don't Say Indian': On the Paradoxical Construction of the Reavers," for perpetuating negative stereotypes of Native American Indians, we would argue that he is actually doing something much more sophisticated. He is showing us that it is we ourselves, members of the dominant society, who are responsible for this negative stereotype and its perpetuation.

River leads the crew of Serenity to a remote planet which the Alliance seems to have done everything in its power to keep secret: removed from navigation charts, all mention in histories, and so forth. The reason they want it kept secret seems to be that it was involved in a terraforming experiment that went terribly wrong. Many of the planets and moons in this new world far away from Earth-That-Was have been terraformed. "Through atmosphere processing plants, terraforming technologies, gravity regulation and the introduction of every known form of Earthlife, each planet became its own ... Earth" (Whedon 2005, 12). But on this one planet, as the crew of Serenity learn, the Alliance had experimented with the atmospheric conditions being created. The crew learn this from playing a holographic recorder they discover aboard a crashed Alliance research ship: "It's the Pax, the G-32 Paxilon Hydrochlorate that we added to the air processors. It ... was supposed to calm the population, weed out aggression ... it worked. The people here stopped fighting. And then they stopped everything else ... breeding ... talking ... eating.... There's thirty million people here and they all just let themselves die" (*Serenity*). No wonder the Alliance wanted to keep the existence of this planet a secret. As a brief aside, it is amusing to note that the name of the drug that caused the problem was Paxilon Hydrochlorate, since Paxil is the name of a widely used antidepressant today. The recording goes on to explain how the Paxilon Hydrochlorate had the opposite effect on 0.1 percent of the population: "Their aggressor response increased ... beyond madness. They've become ... they've killed most of us ... not just killed, they've done ... things" (*Serenity*). The recording continues, showing a Reaver attack on the scientist trying desperately to finish her holographic report: "She screams continuously as the Reaver tops her, biting at her and tearing at her clothes, at her skin" (Whedon 2005, 129). Although the horrible revelation hits them all at the same time, one of the crew members manages to say it aloud: "Reavers ... they made them" (*Serenity*). The revelation seems to hit River the hardest. The realization overwhelms her: "River falls to her knees vomiting" (Whedon 2005, 130). As argued in more detail elsewhere, "We suggest that this reaction is due partly to River's being raised under the Alliance. She does not have the luxury of.... '*They* made them' which distances ... somewhat from the horrible realization. Just as the young River told her teacher what is wrong with the Alliance is that 'We meddle.... We're meddlesome,' so, though she probably could never articulate it, River has now come to realize that '*We* made them.' Her reaction is due ... to cultural guilt" (Rabb and Richardson 2008, 135). Given that the Reavers are obviously a metaphor for the negative stereotype of Native Americans, "the blood-thirsty savage redskin," viewers of this movie, particularly those of European and British descent, don't just come to realize intellectually but actually feel on a visceral level the "we made them." We discussed the issue of Eurocentric preconceptions being imposed on the Indigenous peoples of the Americas in some detail in both chapters two and four above. However, it is one thing to accept that back in the 1600s uneducated sailors might expect to find cloven-footed devils in the New World and impose their Eurocentric preconceptions on the Native American population; it is quite another to come to the realization that we might well still be doing so (for example when we tell jokes disparaging Native people). That is why we felt it necessary to discuss in some detail, at the end of Chapter Four, Callicott's misguided arguments in favor of a "ferocious and horrific" pre-contact America. We believe that the metaphorical treatment of these issues in popular culture will have more success in countering negative stereotypes than intellectual arguments alone. This explains, in part, why we favor a narrative form of rationality, which does not exclude emotion.

Novels, Short Stories, and Graphic Novels

There is an ever growing number of novels and short stories written by Native American authors. They do provide a rich resource of narrative through which to research Native American philosophy, particularly as it manifests itself in contemporary Native societies both on the rez and in an urban setting. As we argued in Chapter Four, from a Native perspective, narrative itself should be thought of as an indirect form of philosophical argument, a form of imaginative rationality, which includes, rather than ignores, emotion.

We conclude this chapter with a brief look at the graphic novel. Graphic novels tend to be longer and more substantial than comic books, but this is not always the case, as some are released in serial form, to be gathered together later and sold (again) this time as a single volume. Actually the hardcover graphic novel biography of Métis leader Louis Riel, close to three hundred pages in length, complete with footnotes, maps and extensive bibliography, calls itself *Louis Riel: A Comic-Strip Biography* (Brown 2003).

We usually think of a comic strip as a few panels in a newspaper. The terms comic book, comic strip and graphic novel are not clearly defined. Many think *Louis Riel: A Comic-Strip Biography* is the best graphic novel ever published. It is certainly worth a look, whatever it is. Since 2006 it has been available in paperback. (Does that make it a comic book rather than a graphic novel?) Louis Riel and his Métis Nation are not well understood in the United States. Cree-Métis philosopher Lorraine Mayer, for example, discovered this when she moved to the University of Oregon for her Ph.D. "In the United States, I quickly learned that one is either Indian or non–Indian. The very word 'Métis' was incomprehensible. I found myself having to repeatedly define the term Métis and explaining in great detail the significance of Métis people in Canada. After that, people would simply dismiss my explanation and call me Native American" (Mayer 2010, 98).

There are of course many comics which portray Native American Indians, far too many for us to comment on here in any detail. We actually prefer them to regular novels and short stories because, though they keep the important narrative storytelling format, they tell the story in pictures as well as words. This mitigates somewhat the novel's all-too-linear form of writing using the phonetic alphabet, which, as we argued in Chapter Five, has possibly led us away from a more traditional, healthier, relationship with the land. The graphic novel may be one way to help us write language back into the land. After all, Native artists have been telling stories through pictures for thousands of years.

A representative number of comics with Native American content is discussed, from an Indigenous perspective, by Michael Sheyahshe in his *Native Americans in Comic Books: A Critical Study* (2008). Sheyahshe is a member of the Caddo Nation of Oklahoma. Although he discusses the treatment of Native American characters in comic books "as an Indigenous reader," he quite rightly insists: "While I can attempt to give a serious and unbiased opinion from a Native American standpoint, I do not speak for all Native people on this issue, nor would I want to do so" (Sheyahshe 2008, 12). We see this as further confirmation of our claim that the Native American perspective is indeed polycentric or transperspectival. Sheyahshe tell us specifically what he *is* attempting to do in his study: "I relate to the reader what I see in comic books as a Native reader, and I offer insight into a Native worldview in this discussion of cultural misrepresentation in American comic books. It is my hope that this analysis serves not only that purpose but also offers a blueprint for future comic books to rid themselves of the shackles of misrepresentation" (Sheyahshe 2008, 11).

One of the oldest misrepresentations he discusses is what is called "the Mohican Syndrome," a literary device that goes back to the 1820s and the *Leatherstocking Tales* of James Fenimore Cooper. There a white man raised by the Mohican Natives becomes "a better 'Indian' than the real ones" (Sheyahshe 2008, 14). To illustrate the Mohican Syndrome, which is used extensively in comic books, particularly in the 1950s and 60s, Sheyahshe actually cites the movie *A Man Called Horse,* which we referenced above (Sheyahshe 2008, 13). In many comic books "with the Mohican Syndrome, a white man becomes Indian in every way that counts ... these individuals are not only transformed into the best representations of that Indigenous culture, but they also become heroes" (Sheyahshe 2008, 14). In these early comics, it seems, you don't need to have "super powers" to save the day. It is enough just to pretend to be "Indian." Another common stereotype Sheyahshe discusses is the Indian sidekick, like Tonto in *The Lone Ranger.* Tonto wears stereotypical fringe and like many Indians portrayed in comic books seems to belong to "some large generic Plains tribe." As Sheyahshe goes on to observe, "This fact does nothing to convey a sense of the great diversity that exists in Indigenous cultures and therefore serves as a very negative stereotype" (Sheyahshe 2008, 44). Although Sheyahshe is careful to be fair to the various comic books he discusses, noting for example which do not have Indians speaking in Tontoese ("the usual 'ughs' and ... 'get-um up'"), and which do not have Indians frozen in the past (in the old West), still we would have to conclude we do not learn very much about the diversity of Native culture from mainstream comics (Sheyahshe 2008, 15).

Comics and Community

There are, however a number of more recent tribal comics, which Sheyahshe finds hold some hope for the future. In fact he sees his entire study as in effect tracing how "Native American comic book characters progressed through the ages from generic enemy to impotent sidekick to central hero" (Sheyahshe 2008, 10). The comic books with genuine Indigenous heroes and positive role models come from smaller independent publishers, often with tribal affiliation. They produce small runs of what Sheyahshe calls "indie comics" (152). He notes that "it is interesting that smaller titles such as these often depict our culture with more respect and humanity than those from the larger publishers" (Sheyahshe 2008, 152). These titles show some promise of depicting Native culture and Native philosophy with more accuracy and in greater depth. They include *The Raven* by Algonquin author Jay Odjick, *Darkness Calls* produced by and for the Healthy Aboriginal Network dealing with suicide prevention, both from Canada, as well as *A Hero's Voice* and *Dreams of Looking Up,* from the Educational Comic Book Series of the Mille Lacs Band of Ojibwe, the *Chickasaw Adventures* series, from the Chickasaw Nation, and *Peace Party* from Blue Corn Comics. Sheyahshe is most impressed with these titles. He says of *Chickasaw Adventures,* "This is truly something to get excited about: a tribal nation producing their own comic book? Stupendous ... it adds to the importance of Native people telling their own stories" (Sheyahshe 2008, 145). Though he mentions it, he is not critical of the fact that the actual production of the series is contracted out to a professional creative team. He notes that this "only serves to support the importance of this project ... not to mention, it adds to the overall *professional* quality of the books themselves" (Sheyahshe 2008, 145). Besides, "the Chickasaw Nation provided not only the initial project vision but also the cultural oversight to this series" (Sheyahshe 2008, 145). *Peace Party* is written by a non–Native, Rob Schmidt, but several Native American people are on the board of directors of *Peace Party.* The central characters in the comic are Native American. Though it takes place in modern times "their tribal nation (Hopi) is also featured, thus demonstrating that Indigenous people are not extinct and did not die out with the passage of the Old West" (Sheyahshe 2008, 136). Though the main characters wear ordinary modern clothing (shirts and jeans), "when they transform into their metahuman alter egos, their ... costumes more closely resemble traditional Hopi and Pueblo culture than they do the typical Plains Indian version of buckskin and headdresses" (Sheyahshe 2008, 133).

In the publication of these comics Native Americans are included in the creative process, and ten percent of the profits of *Peace Party* go to such non-profit organizations as the Hopi Foundation, the American Indian College Fund, and the First Nations Development Institute. "One of the most important aspects of this comic book is its attention to creating and representing complex Indigenous characters with a spark of humanity ... that make them interesting and believable characters" (Sheyahshe 2008, 136).

It is important to note that though Sheyahshe is very impressed by these "indie comics" in general, he is not uncritical of them. For example, though he heaps praise on *Darkness Calls,* the comic produced in Canada by the Healthy Aboriginal Network, for avoiding most stereotypes and all Tontoese (not even the elders talk like Tonto), he does have one major criticism: "the appearance of feathers and a breastplate in the Hero's costume.

While modern accoutrements — armored boots, a suped-up motorcycle, and even a samurai sword — upgrade this costume, the feathers and breastplate seem to be a step backwards" (Sheyahshe 2008, 151). He cites the writer and artist, Steven Keewatin Sanderson, from a 2007 panel discussion on Native Americans in the comics to the effect "that his main purpose was to present a character that an Aboriginal youth might mentally conjure when hearing a traditional story" (Sheyahshe 2008, 151). But Sheyahshe is obviously not happy that the Aboriginal youth conjures an Indigenous hero with feathers. Now we have to admit that Sheyahshe is writing his *Native Americans in Comic Books* two years before the publication in 2010 of DeVoss and LeBeau's article "Reading and Composing Indians: Invented Indian Identity through Visual Literacy," which we discussed at the beginning of this chapter. DeVoss and LeBeau, it will be remembered, argued that we should not be too critical of the stereotypes that the youth have of Native Americans, but rather we should use them as a kind of base knowledge on which to build more accurate images of contemporary Native American Indians. DeVoss and LeBeau actually describe a classic cartoon in which two young people are talking. One is saying to the other, "But you don't look Indian," while the thought bubble (the one with the dotted lines) above his head depicts someone in feathers and buckskin, the classic stereotype. We should expect Native youth growing up in contemporary culture to pick up the stereotypes inherent in contemporary popular culture. To Sheyahshe's credit he does admit: "Perhaps because of the influence of stereotypic imagery in popular media, even Indigenous kids (who may, at times have more direct interaction with Native culture) might have their imagination tainted with the notion of obligatory feathers. Having grown up around the same time as Sanderson (a youth during the 1980s) and seen similar comic book Natives, I can understand how his portrayal might have come about" (Sheyahshe 2008, 151).

We have one minor critique of Sheyahshe and his high praise of "indie comics." He rightly calls for more community-based comics in which Native American people can find their own voice. For example, in his discussion of the Mille Lacs Band of Ojibwe Educational Comic Book Series, Sheyahshe argues, "Every tribal nation should produce similar comic books to celebrate our culture and educate readers on its importance" (Sheyahshe 2008, 133). In a similar way he also argues, "*Chickasaw Adventures* is entertaining and it provides readers with ample insight to the culture itself. Not many books are able to do this. More tribal nations should take on similar projects and produce their own comic books" (Sheyahshe 2008, 145). In the concluding chapter to his book, *Native Americans in Comic Books: A Critical Study,*

Sheyahshe argues that an important solution to the problem of "misrepresentation and stereotyping in comics and other popular media" is "to place control of popular media in the hands of the very people being victimized by it. Put simply, it is time for Indigenous people to begin authorship of media that portray us, notably in becoming authors and creators of our own comic books" (Sheyahshe 2008, 192). While, as we said above, we agree in principle with this, we would argue that it is important, particularly from the standpoint of Native American philosophy, that each community find its voice through community-based research using appropriate philosophical methods. Only through such research will the voice of the community have the depth of understanding necessary to properly reflect community values and worldviews. In fact, we see this as so vitally important that we devote the entire next chapter, our concluding chapter, to community-based research and education.

SEVEN

Native Control of Native Education Today

Restoring the Hermeneutic Circle

In this concluding chapter, drawing on arguments from all the previous chapters, we use the contemporary theory of philosophical hermeneutics, as a recently acknowledged method of qualitative research, to explain the mechanism of cultural transfer both within Aboriginal cultures and between the dominant society and Native American cultures. This, we contend, explains what was and still is wrong with government policies of assimilation. Native children at residential schools internalized prejudices against their own people and hence against themselves long before they were old enough to develop any critical capacity. Yet, as hermeneutics shows, prejudice as "pre-judgment" or "pre-understanding" is that which makes the understanding, development and interpretation of cultures possible. Both the culture and those pre-judgments are continually modified as new generations attempt to understand their place in the world. This process is a classic instance of the hermeneutic circle. Hermeneutics recognizes that to interpret a culture is to transform that culture. When a culture is written about from the outside with alien pre-understandings, the transformations may well threaten to destroy that culture, particularly if it is a minority, dominated or occupied one. But when people within a culture write about their own culture with pre-judgments derived from that very culture, the resulting transformations are healthy and breathe life into the culture keeping it current and alive. To keep their traditions current and alive, Native American peoples must be allowed to assess their own traditions from their own perspectives. They must decide for themselves which of their traditions continue to be enabling, and which may no longer be helpful. We conclude that the only solution to the crisis in education facing Native American communities today is for those communities to take charge of educating their own people. The solution to this crisis in education must begin with the adults. They in turn can communicate Indigenous values to the younger members of their community, thus, finally, completing the hermeneutic circle, which was so violently broken by misguided government policies of assimilation and the Indian residential school experiences.

Community-Based Research and Education

Throughout our study of Native American philosophy, we have argued that more research needs to be done, particularly at the community level, by community members. As Métis historian Howard Adams, has argued, "Indigenous institutions should be staffed by Native scientists who grow up in Aboriginal societies and, therefore, identify themselves with the future well-being of Aboriginal nations" (Adams 1999, 26). Adams, who has had experience teaching at colleges and universities in both Canada and the United States, is only one of a number of Aboriginal academics who have spent their careers encouraging Native students to complete a university education only to find that the university system in the dominant society is in fact doing Native people more harm than good (McPherson and Rabb 2001). Marie Battiste and James (Sa'ke'j) Youngblood Henderson of the University of Saskatchewan, in their book *Protecting Indigenous Knowledge and Heritage: A Global Challenge*, have argued that "Canadian educational systems view Indigenous heritage, identity and thought as inferior to Eurocentric heritage, identity and thought" (Battiste and Henderson 2000, 88–89). And as James Brown and Patricia Sant explain in their collection *Indigeneity: Construction and Re/Presentation*, "Indigenous Peoples continuing to live in the nation states which colonized them still experience the consequences of past and continuing racism" (Brown and Sant 1999, 3).

We are not defending race-based education. Nor are we making the usual rights-based arguments appealing either to treaty rights or to the fact that Aboriginal people have never relinquished their inherent right to educate their own children, though we suggest that there is merit in those arguments. However, in this concluding chapter we support our position on purely philosophic grounds, not because of any weakness in the other arguments, but because these considerations have rarely been explored in any depth. We maintain that these philosophical arguments present new considerations which we believe to be definitive. We contend that community-based education must begin with the adults researching their own identity through inquiries into Native American philosophy.

Hermeneutics: The Interpretation of Interpretation

Our first philosophical argument draws on recent developments in the theory of hermeneutics. Hermeneutics, as a theory, is in essence the interpretation of interpretation. Lawrence Neuman, in his standard text *Social Research Methods: Quantitative and Qualitative Approaches,* recognizes hermeneutics as "a qualitative method of research" and explains that the term "hermeneutics" "comes from a god in Greek mythology, Hermes, who had the job of communicating the desires of the gods to mortals" (Neuman 2000, 70–71). According to Neuman, the purpose of hermeneutics is to make the obscure plain. In fact, until the last half of the twentieth century, hermeneutics had a poor reputation in the academic world. Following its Classical root meaning it was associated primarily with Biblical hermeneutics, interpreting the word of God. As such it was quite rightly dismissed as a form of exegetical thinking in which one could read one's own beliefs and prejudices into the Bible and get them back imbued with the authority of the word of God, with the authority of Biblical truth.

Starting with the work of the German philosopher Martin Heidegger and some of his followers, particularly Hans Georg Gadamer, by the mid-twentieth century hermeneutics began to acquire a new respectability as a theory of philosophical and cultural interpretation. As Timothy Crusius notes in *A Teacher's Introduction to Philosophical Hermeneutics,* "In *Being and Time* (1962) Heidegger ... provided the impetus for Gadamer's extensive development of philosophical hermeneutics in *Truth and Method* " (Crusius 1991, 4). Accepting that it is impossible to avoid bringing one's prejudices or "pre-judgments" to the text to be interpreted, the point of philosophical hermeneutics is to permit the text to confront those subjective prejudices and, in a sense, speak for itself. As Neuman puts it, although the "reader brings his or her subjective experience to a text ... the researcher / reader tries to absorb or get inside the viewpoint it presents ... through a detailed study of the text, contemplating its many messages and seeking the connections among its parts" (Neuman 2000, 70–71). Interpretation thus turns out to be a kind of dialogue or conversation with a living text.

The concept of "text" must be interpreted very broadly. It can be anything from a written document, or a work of art, to an entire culture. The important insight here is that the text, e.g., the culture being interpreted, is a participant in the conversation, not an artifact to be analyzed. It should not be treated as an object of scientific investigation. Like any living being, it can be expected to contribute to the conversation. This may help us to understand why the sacred stories of the Ojibwa, for example, were always regarded, along with the mythological characters that inhabit them, as "living entities who have existed from time immemorial" (Hallowell 1960, 26ff, cf. Copway 1850, 97, Overholt and Callicott 1982, 26). It is important to show respect by, for example, telling such stories only at appropriate times. This, incidentally, may partly explain why their "recitation is seasonally restricted" (Overholt and Callicott 1982, 26). The fact that it treats text as a living entity rather than a scientific object is the reason why we use philosophical hermeneutics to explore Native American philosophy.

Prejudice and Objectivity

The hermeneutic turn in post-modern philosophy has questioned the very possibility of scientific objectivity by revealing an unacknowledged prejudice pervading the modern scientific world. It is a prejudice against prejudice itself. "We have been taught that prejudice can only be a barrier to truth, that we should want to shed our prejudice and be objective. Truth is the opposite of prejudice" (Crusius 1991, 34). Researchers trained at mainstream universities are taught that "science is value free, unbiased, and objective.... The scientific community is free of prejudice ... [w]ith complete value freedom and objectivity, science reveals the one and only, unified, unambiguous truth" (Neuman 2000, 116–117). For example, the widely used Canadian text *Portrait of Humankind: An Introduction to Human Biology and Prehistoric Cultures* suggests that in order to avoid the pitfalls of ethnocentrism "anthropologists insist that the customs and traditions of the world's cultures must be studied in an objective way" (Driben and Herstein 1994, 27). There is a real sense in which we cannot and should not "shed our prejudice" because prejudice as "pre-judgment" or "pre-understanding" is that which makes interpretation possible. We make sense of our world in terms of our expectations which are either confirmed or modified by further experience. All seeing is a seeing as. "If we do not see as, we do not see at all; to understand is to exist already in pre-understandings.... We could have no experience at all without them" (Crusius 1991, 34). Our pre-understandings or pre-judgments are continually modified in dialogue with the text or whatever it is we are attempting to interpret (e.g., the culture). We continue returning to the text with our modified pre-understandings gaining deeper insights, but also having our pre-understandings modified even further. This is what is meant by dialoguing with a text. As Crusius notes, "Dialogue moves in two directions: 'back' towards our pre-understandings, for nothing exposes them better for us than dialogue with someone whose prejudices do not merely reinforce our own — in such moments of grace, we in fact first become aware of our biases as biases — and 'forward' toward achieving a common understanding, toward agreement, or at least toward recognition of exactly what we disagree about and why" (Crusius 1991, 38–39). Crusius argues that when treated as a scientific object of study, the culture (or text being interpreted) loses what he calls its "transforming power." As Crusius says, "It becomes something for us to operate on, something never allowed to operate on us" (Crusius 1991, 39).

The Hermeneutic Circle and Transformative Philosophy

When the text is allowed to operate on us, exposing and changing our pre-judgments, we begin the cyclical process referred to as the hermeneutic circle. When we return again and again to the text with our modified pre-understandings, it reveals more of itself, challenging, if we allow it, those very pre-understandings, thus beginning the circle anew with further transformations of our biases and hence ourselves. This circle continues, transforming both interpreter and interpretation until what Gadamer calls a "fusion of horizons" is achieved. Although this is a "struggle toward consensus," it is important to note that it also includes a healthy respect for difference. "Our horizons do not fuse in the sense of complete identity: if I become the other, I lose the other's friendly opposition, which prevents me from becoming too hopelessly myself. Rather, our horizons fuse in the sense of a mutual enlargement of horizons which still remain different" (Crusius 1991, 40). This transformation of both interpreter and interpretation ties in rather nicely with the transformative nature of Native American philosophy which we explored in Chapter Three and Chapter Five.

Although we used Crusius' text a number of times in graduate and undergraduate courses offered at a mainstream university, it was not until we discussed philosophical hermeneutics with a class made up entirely of Native American students in an on-reserve setting that we began to understand the far-reaching implications of hermeneutics for community-based research and education. There we began to see the kind of pre-understandings which Native students in their home communities bring to their interpretation of their own traditions.

Native students are able to listen openly for the voices of their communities precisely because their pre-understandings, their prejudices, have been shaped by those very voices early in their childhood. For them, the hermeneutic circle has already begun. It has been working since childhood. This is what is meant by a living tradition. "For where does any prejudice come from? Clearly only from the collective revelation of the past, from books, from tales told over and over, works of art, social and disciplinary practices" (Crusius 1991, 34). The widespread assumption that Native American traditions somehow represent a dying culture is itself a product of the prejudices not just of dominant society in general but also more specifically of the scientific community which, as we have already noted, perpetuates the largely unacknowledged prejudice against prejudice itself. "The prejudice against prejudice is also a prejudice against tradition, a tendency to equate authority with falsehood, as if anything that manages to survive from the past has to be the source of error, ignorance and superstition" (Crusius 1991, 34). Although some traditions may well be founded on ignorance or superstition, other teachings and traditions are in actual fact enabling. As Crusius argues, "The choice is not all or nothing; it is much harder than that. We must detect the right prejudices for our place and time, the ones that allow our truths to emerge with the least distortion, distinguish somehow between traditions worth preserving and those no longer helpful, and offer our allegiance to authorities that actually merit it" (Crusius 1991, 34).

Since the time of the early missionaries to the Americas, Native American people have been told that their traditions are heathen, and are not worth preserving. They were told that they should adopt the traditions of the colonizers. This, as hermeneutics reveals, was merely "substituting one kind of indoctrination for another, one kind of unquestioned authority for another"(Crusius 1991, 82). To keep their traditions healthy and alive, Native people must assess their own traditions from their own perspectives. They must decide for themselves which authorities continue to merit their allegiance, which traditions continue to be enabling, and which may no longer be helpful. This is the only way traditions can support a healthy culture. It may well involve respectfully questioning the wisdom of the elders. Vine Deloria Jr. argues that "elders of the 1960s might well have known some of the old beliefs and ceremonies, but more likely they would have remembered the boarding school days of the 1920s.... An elder today, age 75, would probably remember the Great Depression of the 1930s and the revival ceremonies in the 1950s but would know little else of any importance" (Deloria 2004, 4). For Native people to understand their own traditions requires much more than just accepting, at face value, the wisdom of the elders. We argue in Chapter Five there is more to the wisdom of the elders than Deloria is willing to admit, but the only way to confirm this is for members of each particular community to research Native philosophy within their own community using proper research methods.

Writing as Interpretation

Imagine a group of Native students writing about the community in which they were raised. Then imagine groups of Native students all across North America doing the same thing. Imagine further all these students reading each other's work and engaging in comparative conversations about their different communities. Just think about the rich diversity of pre-understandings and pre-judgments which would be brought to these writings and comparative discussions. One reason we have been citing Timothy Crusius in our exposition of hermeneutics is that he is one of the few teachers of rhetoric, of writing, to draw extensively on the contemporary theory of hermeneutics as indispensable to the teaching of writing. Here he follows James Kinneavy's "The Process of Writing: A Philosophical Basis in Hermeneutics" in recognizing that writing is itself a form of interpretation, a hermeneutical exercise.

Native students engaged in community-based research are writing about their own cultures within hermeneutic circles in which, as Kinneavy points out, "both object and forestructure [pre-understanding] may require radical alterations, even transformations" (Kinneavy 7, Crusius 79). As the Native students think about what they are writing, they cannot help but transform, sometimes radically change, both themselves and their communities. Hermeneutics recognizes that to interpret, to write or learn about a culture, is to transform that culture.

When Native students write about their own cultures they are not only transforming those cultures, they are also transforming themselves, for they are given the opportunity to discover and transform their own pre-judgments. As Crusius notes, "We cannot even know our own history, the complex conventions we have internalized; for the most part we can only live it/them, for we are it/them" (Crusius 79). Native students in learning more about themselves by writing about their own culture are keeping that culture alive by actually making the culture conscious of itself. In other words, they are, quite literally, the culture becoming conscious of itself. This in turn allows it to grow and change while remaining true to itself. For the most part, Native cultures in North America have been deprived of this normal healthy development for a variety of reasons, but in particular, community-based education has not been a part of these cultures since the imposition of religious residential schools and government policies of assimilation.

Hermeneutics exposes the real damage done to Native American children and their cultures by the residential school experience. "The whole dimension of pre-understanding that Heidegger calls 'forhaving'—our thrownness into a welter of preexisting social practices and habits ... are deeply internalized long before any capacity for criticism develops" (Crusius 71). If, as hermeneutics explains, we become the complex forstructures we live but cannot know, what is it that former residents of Indian residential schools have become? What must they live every day of their lives? What pre-understandings, pre-judgments, prejudices, did they "deeply internalize" long before they were old enough to develop any critical capacity which we now know does not develop until the late teens or early twenties? Paulo Freire in *Pedagogy of the Oppressed* speaks of the "oppressor within" (Freire 1997, 45, 76). That is certainly part of it. The helpless Native children at residential schools internalized prejudices against their own people and hence against themselves. Though their own children today do not have to endure the residential school experience, many have nevertheless acquired these same prejudices from their parents, sometimes while they are being raped by them. It is little wonder that so many have exhibited self-destructive behavior. They have either tried to silence the oppressor within with drugs and alcohol, gas and glue; or the oppressor within has dominated, resulting in dysfunctional families and communities with the highest suicide rates in the world. In spite of government apologies, these children are all helpless victims of government policies of assimilation rooted in the efforts of Christian missionaries to convert the Indians. It is not our purpose to assign blame. Our purpose is to show how community-based research and education can address this problem, because it is a problem which, in the final analysis, can only be addressed by education. It is, however, a problem which can also be exacerbated by the wrong kind of education. As noted above, Battiste and Henderson have argued the dominant society's "educational systems view Indigenous heritage, identity and thought as inferior to Eurocentric heritage, identity and thought" (88–89). We contend that Battiste and Henderson are correct and that such educational systems only reinforce the oppressor within, further perpetuating the problem. The kind of education provided by institutions run by and for members of the dominant society reinforces the uncritically internalized prejudices long developed in and by the residential school experience. That is precisely why we argue that "universities today are inadvertently completing the job of assimilation begun by the residential schools" (McPherson and Rabb 2001, 57).

Indian Control of Indian Education: Applying Native American Philosophy

We are forced to conclude that the only solution to the crisis in education facing Native communities today is for those communities to take charge of educating their own people. By this we do not mean merely hiring members of the dominant society to run classrooms for children in Native communities. The solution to this crisis in education must begin with the adults. They must be given the opportunity to achieve an education grounded in their own Indigenous values, which will at the same time prepare them and their communities to deal with the rest of the world in the twenty-first century, and to participate in the global economy on an equal footing.

We are not advocating for the establishment of more tribal colleges or universities accredited by the dominant society using criteria relevant only to the dominant society. We acknowledge the good work done by tribal colleges and universities (*http://www.aihec.org/colleges/*). Instead we contend it is essential that community-based research and educational institutions be immune from any kind of political interference. To ensure this we strongly recommend that such institutions be private community-based corporations owned and operated by those who have the most at stake in them, namely members of the student body.

Educational institutions run by and for members of the dominant society are neither equipped nor inclined to provide this kind of educational opportunity for Native people. These institutions have other priorities. That is as it should be. They are, after all, founded on Euro-western values. What we do object to are universities which proclaim that they are "dedicated to working with Aboriginal peoples in furthering their educational aspirations," while at the same time they are cutting back on what little Aboriginal programming they actually provide. This makes it seem to us quite obvious that such cash-strapped universities are more interested in the dollars that accompany Aboriginal students than they are in the educational aspirations of these students, much less of their communities. We even know of at least one university which was actually caught misallocating Aboriginal funding (Creber and Zaludek 1996, cf. McPherson and Rabb 1998–1999). But the even greater crime here is committed by those universities representing themselves to Aboriginal students as something other than foreign institutions. Of course there is nothing wrong with going to another country for an education. Many Canadian and American students do exactly that. They go abroad. But they know they are attending a foreign university in a foreign country and can adjust their expectations accordingly. Further, they do, in fact, have a choice. Aboriginal students do not have this choice. If they recognize the need to continue their education at the post-secondary level, they must attend, what is to them in their own country, a foreign college or university, where they are unlikely to learn anything about their own identity or their community values. At best they might learn about what some outsider has written about some other Native community (cf. Battiste and Henderson 2000, 88–89; Deloria and Wildcat 2001; McPherson and Rabb 2001, 75).

Native American communities, not the government, must develop their own post-secondary institutions to engage in community-based research aimed at articulating clearly and precisely the Indigenous values and Native American philosophy operant in the cultural interactions to be found within those communities. In her groundbreaking book *Decolonizing Methodologies: Research and Indigenous Peoples,* Linda Tuhiwai Smith argues: "As Indigenous peoples we have our own research needs and priorities. Our questions are important" (Smith 2000, 198). Linda Tuhiwai Smith places high importance on research which she regards as a tool to be used by Indigenous peoples to address their important questions. We have found, in our years of research, that philosophical hermeneutics provides the methodology best used by those fortunate few Indigenous scholars who have the ability to listen for, and articulate, the voice of their own communities. As we have noted above, and have documented elsewhere, "there are today a growing number of Indigenous scholars equipped to engage in critical dialogue with Elders and others in the community" (McPherson and Rabb 2001, 76).

The benefits of community-based educational programs go far beyond just providing well educated leaders, policy analysts, teachers, and community workers trained in culturally congruent social work practice, health care and business administration, and so on, from within the community. Besides increased employment, including spin-off opportunities to house, feed and entertain a growing body of adult students, community-based educational institutes would provide their communities with increased confidence and security on which to base a faith in the future. Such security and confidence in the future are extremely important. For example, medical studies have established a link between anxiety about the future, hopelessness, and hypoglycemia, diabetes (Diamond 1990, 124). We suggest that community-based research and education may well address a root cause of such widespread problems as diabetes and suicide in Native American communities. People who are confident of their identity, secure in their future and proud of their heritage are not prone to suicide. We are convinced that Native American philosophy developed through community-based research and education has the potential to revolutionize Native communities throughout Canada and the United States. We certainly hope that this study in Native American philosophy, with our emphasis on the transformative nature of the discipline, will help to encourage and support such quiet revolutions throughout Turtle Island from sea to sea to northern sea.

May the gizzard of the ruffed grouse now hang aloft.

Notes

Chapter One

1. For an account of the distinctive use of an accommodations sense of reason in Canadian philosophy, see Leslie Armour and Elizabeth Trott, *The Faces of Reason: An Essay on Philosophy and Culture in English Canada, 1850–1950* and J. Douglas Rabb, *Religion and Science in Early Canada.*

2. Since we first introduced the polycentric perspective in this context, the concept has been picked up by a number of Native American philosophers and scholars in explaining the Native value of respect for difference and others' values. We discuss this more fully in Chapter 4.

Chapter Two

1. The Jefferson Encyclopedia is a good on line source for Jefferson's early life and education http://wiki.monticello.org/mediawiki/index.php/Jefferson%27s_Formal_Education.

2. The Jefferson Encyclopedia http://wiki.monticello.org/mediawiki/index.php/John_Locke_%28Portrait%29.

3. For photographs and original architectural drawings of the University of Virginia, see The Jefferson Encyclopedia http://wiki.monticello.org/mediawiki/index.php/Category:Architecture.

4. Jefferson believed that if American Indians were made to adopt European-style agriculture and live in European-style towns and villages, then they would quickly "progress" from "savagery" to "civilization" and eventually be equal, in his mind, to white men. The Jefferson Encyclopedia http://wiki.monticello.org/mediawiki/index.php/American_Indians.

5. In Upper Canada (Ontario) anglophones became the majority with the influx of United Empire Loyalists during and after the American War of Independence.

6. There are many sources for Indian treaties. Rather than give page or web references each time we cite a treaty we simply give the name or number of the treaty in the main text. Reliable web references include http://www.ainc-inac.gc.ca/al/hts/index-eng.asp, a government of Canada site, "Indian and Northern Affairs Canada," containing the full text of all treaties plus commentaries, photographs, maps and so forth. For most American treaties, see Kappler's *Indian Affairs: Laws and Treaties,* available online at http://digital.library.okstate.edu/kappler/index.htm, and for earlier American treaties; visit http://earlytreaties.unl.edu/index.html. For the treaties and commentaries on them by one of Canada's most prominent negotiators for the crown, see Alexander Morris, ed., *The Treaties of Canada*

with the Indians of Manitoba and the North West Territories Including the Negotiations on Which They Were Based.

Chapter Three

1. For an account of Bucke as psychiatrist, see S. E. D. Shortt, *Victorian Lunacy: Richard M. Bucke and the Practice of Late Nineteenth-Century Psychiatry.* For a critical account of Bucke as philosopher, see Leslie Armour and Elizabeth Trott, *The Faces of Reason: An Essay on Philosophy and Culture in English Canada, 1850–1950.*

Chapter Four

1. Kant was in fact on the *Index Librorum Prohibitorum* until the middle of the 20th century. Publications on the *Index* were those prohibited by the Roman Catholic Church. We actually studied with one professor of philosophy, who, being a good Catholic, regularly applied for and received permission to read Kant with his class. His students had to promise to destroy the books on the completion of the course. Though not using Kant's concept of heteronomy, the Church, ironically enough, seems to share his justification of moral authority.

2. The full quotation is "Neurons that fire together wire together; neurons that don't synch, don't link" (Pinker 2002, 92). Reportedly, Pinker was the first to use this famous expression (Holland 2009, 129). For our discussion of second-generation cognitive science including classical and radial categories, metaphor and narrative see also "Medical Ethics, Clinical Judgment, and Cognitive Science" (Rabb and Richardson 2008, 419–422) and "Myth, Metaphor, Morality and Monsters: The Espenson Factor and Cognitive Science in Joss Whedon's Narrative Love Ethic" (Rabb and Richardson 2009).

Chapter Five

1. Actually, we like to point to the syllabic signage as another instance of the "facade of friendliness" greeting Native students at mainstream universities. The majority of programs are, after all, as assimilationist as ever. Besides, including syllabics on the signs makes it permissible to use special funding earmarked for Native education to defray the costs of such campus enhancement projects. As we have argued elsewhere, such campus enhancement projects do nothing to ameliorate the inherently assimilationist tendencies built into the system (McPherson and Rabb 2008).

2. It is sobering to realize that we are not dealing with a hypothetical case here.

3. The phonetic writing of the Ojibwa "Gitchi Manitou" in the Roman alphabet might be compared to the same word in Cree we cited above in the section on syllabics, "Kisemanito." Are they the same word?

Bibliography

Abram, David. 1996. *The Spell of the Sensuous: Perception and Language in a More-Than-Human World.* New York: Vintage.

Adams, Howard. 1999. *Tortured People: The Politics of Colonization.* Penticton, BC: Theytus Books.

Albanese, Catherine L. 1990. *Nature Religion in America: From the Algonkian Indians to the New Age.* Chicago: University of Chicago Press.

A'Llario, Karen. 1999. *Craft Ritual and World View: A Study in Ojibwa Ontology.* M.A. Thesis, Lakehead University, Thunder Bay, ON.

American Philosophical Association Newsletters on American Indians in Philosophy. http://www.apaonline.org/publications/newsletters/americanindians.aspx.

Anderton, Alice J. 2007. "Heart of the Matter." *Cultural Survival Quarterly* 31. 2, 18–23.

Aristotle. 1962. *The Politics.* Trans. T. A. Sinclair. Baltimore: Penguin Books.

Ashcraft, Richard. 1986. *Revolutionary Politics and Locke's "Two Treatises of Government."* Princeton: Princeton University Press.

BabaKiueria. 1986. Dir. Don Featherstone. Australia.

Banks, J. T. 2002. "The Story Inside." *Stories Matter: The Role of Narrative in Medical Ethics.* Ed. R. Charon and M. Montello. New York: Routledge, 218–226.

Basso, Keith H. 1996. *Wisdom Sits in Places: Landscape and Language Among the Western Apache.* Albuquerque: University of New Mexico Press.

Battiste, Marie, and James (Sa'ke'j) Youngblood Henderson. 2000. *Protecting Indigenous Knowledge and Heritage: A Global Challenge.* Saskatoon: Purich.

Berger, Thomas R. 1977. *Northern Frontier, Northern Homeland: The Report of the Mackenzie Valley Pipeline Inquiry.* Vol. 1. Ottawa: Ministry of Supply and Services Canada.

_____. *A Long and Terrible Shadow: White Values, Native Rights in the Americas 1492–1992.* Vancouver: Douglas and McIntyre.

Berkhofer, Robert F., Jr. 1978. *The White Man's Indian: Images of the American Indian From Columbus to the Present.* New York: Alfred A. Knopf.

Bishop, Charles A. 1970. "The Emergence of Hunting Territories among the Northern Ojibwa." *Ethnology* 9, 1–5.

Black, Henry Campbell. 1979. *Black's Law Dictionary.* St. Paul: West.

Brant, Clare. 1990. "Native Ethics and Rules of Behaviour." *Canadian Journal of Psychiatry* 35. 6 (August), 535–539.

Brown, Chester. 2003. *Louis Riel: A Comic-Strip Biography.* Montreal: Drawn and Quarterly.

Brown, James N., and Patricia M. Sant, eds. 1999. *Indigeneity: Constructions and Re/Presentation.* Commack, NY: Nova Science.

Brown, Theodore L. 2008. *Making Truth: Metaphor in Science.* Urbana: University of Illinois Press.

Brundige, Lorraine. 1997a. "Continuity of Native Values: Cree and Ojibwa." M.A. Thesis, Lakehead University, Thunder Bay, ON.

_____. 1997b. "'Ungrateful Indian': Continuity of Native Values." *Ayaangwaamizin: The International Journal of Indigenous Philosophy* 1. 1, 45–54.

Brundige, Lorraine F., and J. Douglas Rabb. 1997. "Phonicating Mother Earth: A Critique of David Abram's The Spell of the Sensuous." *Ayaangwaamizin: The International Journal of Indigenous Philosophy* 1. 2, 78–88.

Bucke, Richard Maurice. 1977. *Cosmic Consciousness: A Study in the Evolution of the Human Mind.* Secaucus, NJ: Citadel Press.

Burns, George E. 1996. "A Critical Pedagogy of Native Control of Native Education: Toward a Praxis of First Nation/Provincial Boards Tuition Negotiations and Tuition Schooling." Paper prepared for presentation at the Aboriginal Peoples' Conference, Lakehead University, Thunder Bay, ON. October 1996.

"Bushwhacked." 2003. *Firefly: The Complete Series.* Writ. and dir. Tim Minear, creat. Joss Whedon. DVD. 20th Century–Fox.

Cairns, Alan C. 2000. *Citizens Plus: Aboriginal Peoples and the Canadian State.* Vancouver: University of British Columbia Press.

Callicott, J. Baird. 1989. *In Defense of the Land Ethic: Essays in Environmental Philosophy.* Albany: State University of New York Press.

_____. 1994. *Earth's Insights: A Survey of Ecological Ethics from the Mediterranean Basin to the Australian Outback.* Berkeley: University of California Press.

_____. 2000. "Many Indigenous Worlds or *the* Indigenous World? A Reply to My 'Indigenous' Critics." *Environmental Ethics* 22. 3, 291–310.

Carlyle, Thomas. 1901. "On History." *Complete Works.* Ed. H. D. Traill. Vol. 27. London: Chapman and Hall.

Citizenship and Immigration Canada. 2004. http://www.cic.gc.ca/english/applications/guides/5445E.html#wp288920.

Clapp, James Gordon. 1967. "John Locke." *The Encyclopedia of Philosophy.* Vol. 4. London: Macmillan, 487–503.

Coe, Michael D. 1992. *Breaking the Maya Code.* New York: Thames and Hudson.

Copway, George. 1850. *The Traditional History and Characteristic Sketches of the Ojibway Nation.* London: Charles Gilpin.

Cordova, V. F. 1996. "Doing Native American Philosophy." *From Our Eyes: Learning from Indigenous Peoples.* Ed. Sylvia O'Meara et al. Toronto: Garamond Press, 13–18.

_____. 1997. "Eco-Indian: A Response to J. Baird Callicott." *Ayaangwaamizin: The International Journal of Indigenous Philosophy.* 1. 1, 31–44.

_____. 1998. "The European Concept of Usen: An American Aboriginal Text." *Native American Religious Identity: Unforgotten Gods.* Ed. Jace Weaver. Maryknoll, NY: Orbis Books, 26–32.

_____. 2007. *How It Is: The Native American Philosophy of V. F. Cordova.* Eds. K. D. Moore, K. Peters, T. Jojola and A. Lacy. Tucson: Arizona University Press.

Coupland, Douglas. 2009. *Marshall McLuhan.* Toronto: Penguin Books.

Cowley, Fraser. 1968. *A Critique of British Empiricism.* London: Macmillan.

Crane, Mary Thomas. 2001. *Shakespeare's Brain: Reading with Cognitive Theory.* Princeton: Princeton University Press.

Craven, Margaret. 1984. *I Heard the Owl Call My Name.* Toronto: Totem Books.

Creber, Jackie, and Paul Zaludek. 1996. *Review of Funding Allocated to Lakehead University—Aboriginal Education and Training Strategy, Final Report.* Toronto: Ministry of Education and Training Project.

Cronon, William. 1983. *Changes in the Land: Indians, Colonists and the Ecology of New England.* New York: Hill and Wang.

Crusius, Timothy W. 1991. *A Teacher's Introduction to Philosophical Hermeneutics*. Urbana: National Council of Teachers of English.

Curry, Agnes. 2008. "'We Don't Say Indian': On the Paradoxical Construction of the Reavers." *Slayage: The On Line International Journal of Buffy Studies* 7.2. http://slayageonline.com.

Darnell, Regna. 1999. "Rethinking the Concepts of Band and Tribe, Community and Nation: An Accordion Model of Nomadic Native American Social Organization." *Papers of the Twenty-ninth Algonquian Conference*. Ed. David H. Pentland. Winnipeg: University of Manitoba Press.

Debates of the House of Commons of the Dominion of Canada. 1876. Ottawa: Maclean Roger & Co.

Deloria, Vine, Jr. 1994. *God Is Red: A Native View of Religion*. Golden, CO: Fulcrum Publishing.

_____. 2004. "Philosophy and the Tribal Peoples." *American Indian Thought: Philosophical Essays*. Ed. Anne Waters. Oxford: Blackwell, 3–11.

_____, and Daniel Wildcat. 2001. *Power and Place: Indian Education in America*. Golden, CO: Fulcrum.

Devoss, Danielle Nicole, and Patrick Russell Lebeau. 2010. "Reading and Composing Indians: Invented Indian Identity through Visual Literacy." *The Journal of Popular Culture*, 43. 1, 45–77.

Diamond, John. 1990. *Life Energy: Using the Meridians to Unlock the Hidden Power of Your Emotions*. St. Paul: Paragon House.

Dickason, Olive Patricia. 2009. *Canada's First Nations: A History of Founding Peoples from Earliest Times*. Oxford: OxfordUniversity Press.

Doxtator, Deborah. 1998. *Fluffs and Feathers: An Exhibition on the Symbols of Indianness. A Resource Guide*. Brantford, ON: Woodland Indian Cultural Education Centre.

_____. 2001. "Inclusive and Exclusive Perceptions of Difference: Native and Euro-Based Concepts of Time, History, and Change." *Decentring the Renaissance: Canada and Europe in Multidisciplinary Perspective 1500–1700*. Eds. Germaine Warkentin and Carolyn Podruchny. Toronto: University of Toronto Press, 33–47.

Driben, Paul, and Donald J. Auger. 1989. *The Generation of Power and Fear: The Little Jackfish River Hydroelectric Project and the Whitesands Indian Band*. Thunder Bay, ON: Lakehead University Centre for Northern Studies, Research Report, No. 3.

Driben, Paul and Harvey Herstein. 1994. *Portrait of Humankind: An Introduction to Human Biology and Prehistoric Cultures*. Scarborough, ON: Prentice-Hall.

Dumont, James. 1979. "Journey To Daylight-land: Through Ojibwa Eyes." *Laurentian University Review* 8. 2.

Elbow, Peter. 1988. "Embracing Contraries in the Teaching Process." *The Writing Teacher's Sourcebook*. 2d ed. Ed. Garry Tate, et al. New York: Oxford University Press, 219–231.

Fesmire, Steven. 2003. *John Dewey and Moral Imagination: Pragmatism in Ethics*. Bloomington: Indiana University Press.

Firefly: The Official Companion. 2006. Vol. I. London: Titan.

Flanagan, Tom. 2000. *First Nations? Second Thoughts*. Montreal: McGill-Queens University Press.

Fleming, Stephanie. 2001. "Native university opens at Couchiching." *Fort Frances Times*, Dec. 12.

_____. 2002. "Native university opens to undergrads." *Fort Frances Times*, Feb. 6.

Freire, Paulo. 1997. *Pedagogy of the Oppressed*. Trans. Myra Bergman Ramos. New York: Continuum.

Fogelson, Raymond D. 1996. "Sequoyah (c. 1770–1843): Inventor of the Cherokee Syllabary." *Encyclopedia of North American Indians*. Ed. F. E. Hoxie. Boston and New York: Houghton Mifflin, 580–582.

Fulton, E. Margaret. 1979. "The Status of Women in Canada." *Between Friends/Entre Amis*. Oxford, OH: Miami University, 26–42.

Gadamer, Hans-Georg. 1989. *Truth and Method.* Trans. G. Barden, et al. New York: Crossroads.

Geyshick, Ron, and Judith Doyle. 1989. *Te Bwe Win (Truth).* Toronto: Impulse Editions, Summerhill Press.

Gil, Joseph. 1998. *Metamorphosis of the Body.* Trans. S. Muecke. Minneapolis: Minnesota University Press.

Grant, George M. 2000. *Ocean to Ocean.* Toronto: Prospero Facsim. Reprint. 1925. Toronto: The Radisson Society of Canada Limited. (Original edition published 1873, Toronto: J. Campbell.)

Guthrie, Daniel. 1971. "Primitive Man's Relationship to Nature." *Bioscience* 21. 13, 721–723.

Haig-Brown, Celia. 1988. *Resistance and Renewal: Surviving the Indian Residential School.* Vancouver: Tillacum Library.

Hallowell, Irving. 1960. "Ojibwa Ontology, Behavior, and World View." *Culture and History.* Ed. S. Diamond. New York: Columbia University Press, 19–52.

Hart, Michael Anthony. 1996. "Sharing Circles: Utilizing Traditional Practice Methods for Teaching, Helping, and Supporting." *From Our Eyes: Learning from Indigenous Peoples.* Ed. Sylvia O'Meara, et al. Toronto: Garamond, 59–72.

Heck, Suzanne. 1996. "Fox/Mesquakie." *Encyclopedia of North American Indians.* Ed F. E. Hoxie. Boston and New York: Houghton Mifflin, 206–207.

Heidegger, Martin. 1962. *Being and Time.* Trans. J. Macquarrie and E. Robinson. New York: Harper and Row.

Hester, Lee, Dennis McPherson, Annie Booth, and Jim Cheney. 2000. "Indigenous Worlds and Callicott's Land Ethic." *Environmental Ethics* 22. 3, 273–290.

_____, _____, _____, and _____. 2002. "Callicott's Last Stand." *Land Value and Community: Callicott and Environmental Philosophy.* Eds. Wayne Ouderkirk and Jim Hill. Albany: State University of New York Press, 253–278.

Hickerson, Harold. 1965. "The Virginia Deer and Intertribal Buffer Zones in the Upper Mississippi Valley." *Man's Culture and Animals.* Eds. A. Leeds and A. P. Vayda. Washington: American Association for the Advancement of Science.

Hinsley, Curtis M. 1996. "Jones, William (Megasiawa; Black Eagle)." *Encyclopedia of North American Indians.* Ed. F. E. Hoxie. Boston and New York: Houghton Mifflin, 308–309.

Hogg, Peter W. 1985. *Constitutional Law of Canada.* Toronto: Carswell.

Holland, Norman N. 2009. *Literature and the Brain.* Gainesville: PsyArt Foundation.

Honderich, Ted, ed. 1995. *The Oxford Companion to Philosophy.* Oxford: Oxford University Press.

Hoxie, Frederick E. 1996. *Encyclopedia of North American Indians.* New York: Houghton Mifflin.

Hubelit, W. Brian. 2008. *Ojibwe Landscapes.* Cornwall, ON: Musical Composition.

Hultkrantz, Åke. 1987. *Native Religions of North America.* New York: Harper & Row.

Ignatieff, Michael. 1998. *Isaiah Berlin: A Life.* New York: Metropolitan Books.

_____. 2000. *The Rights Revolution.* Toronto: House of Anansi Press.

Indian Affairs. 1902. *Annual Report Department of Indian Affairs.* Ottawa: Government of Canada.

Issac, Thomas. 1993. *Pre–1868 Legislation Concerning Indians: A Selected & Indexed Collection.* Saskatoon: Native Law Centre, University of Saskatchewan.

Jabes, Edmond. 1974. *Elya.* Berkeley: Tree Books.

Jenish, D'Arcy. 1999. *Indian Fall: The Last Great Days of the Plains Cree and the Blackfoot Confederacy.* Toronto: Viking.

Johansen, Bruce E. 1995. "Dating the Iroquois Confederacy." *Akwasasne Notes* 3. 4, 62–63.

Johnson, Mark. 1993. *Moral Imagination: Implications of Cognitive Science for Ethics.* Chicago: Chicago University Press.

_____. 2007. *The Meaning of the Body: Aesthetics of Human Understanding.* Chicago: Chicago University Press.

Kant, Immanuel. 1964a. *Groundwork of the Metaphysic of Morals.* Trans. H. J. Paton. New York: Harper & Row.

_____. 1964b. *The Doctrine of Virtue: Part II of the Metaphysic of Morals.* Trans. Mary J. Gregor. New York: Harper & Row.

Kinneavy, James. 1987. "The Process of Writing: A Philosophical basis in Hermeneutics." *Journal of Advanced Composition* 7, 1–9.

Kinsley, David. 1995. *Ecology and Religion: Ecological Spirituality in Cross-Cultural Perspective.* Englewood Cliffs, NJ: Prentice Hall.

Kramer, Heinrich, and James Sprenger. 1971. *The Malleus Maleficarum of Heinrich Kramer and James Sprenger.* Trans. Montague Summers. New York: Dover.

Kumar, Satish, and Freddie Whitefield, eds. 2007. *Visionaries: The 20th Century's 100 Most Inspirational Leaders.* White River Junction, VT: Chelsea Green Press.

Lakoff, George. 1993. "The Contemporary Theory of Metaphor." *Metaphor and Thought,* 2d ed. Ed. A. Ortony. Cambridge: Cambridge University Press, 202–251.

_____, and Mark Johnson. 1980. *Metaphors We Live By.* Chicago: University of Chicago Press.

_____, and Mark Johnson. 1999. *Philosophy in the Flesh: The Embodied Mind and its Challenge to Western Thought.* New York: Basic Books.

Lame Deer, John (Fire), and Richard Erdoes. 1972. *Lame Deer: Seeker of Visions.* New York: Washington Square Press.

Leopold, Aldo. 1949. *A Sand County Almanac.* New York: Oxford University Press.

Lewis, Norman. 1988. *The Missionaries: God Against the Indians.* London: Martin Secker & Warburg.

Locke, John. 1976. *An Essay Concerning Human Understanding.* Ed. and intro. A. D. Woozley. London: William Collins Sons.

Lodge, Rupert C. 1937. "The Comparative Method in Philosophy." *Manitoba Essays Written in Commemoration of the Sixtieth Anniversary of The University of Manitoba.* Ed. R.C. Lodge. Toronto: Macmillan.

_____. 1940. "Synthesis or Comparison?" *Journal of Philosophy* 35.

_____. 1951. *Applied Philosophy.* London: Routledge and Kegan Paul.

Lutz, Ellen L. 2007a. "Saving Americas Endangered Languages." *Cultural Survival Quarterly* 31. 2, 3.

_____. 2007b. "A Language Out of Time." *Cultural Survival Quarterly* 31. 2, 6–7.

Manatowa-Bailey, Jacob. 2007. "On the Brink: An Overview of the Disappearance of America's First Languages: How it Happened and What We Need to do About It." *Cultural Survival Quarterly* 31. 2, Summer, 12–17.

Martin, Calvin. 1978. *Keepers of the Game: Indian-Animal Relationships and the Fur Trade.* Berkeley: University of California Press.

_____. 1987. *The American Indian and the Problem of History.* New York: Oxford University Press.

_____. 1992. *In the Spirit of the Earth: Rethinking History and Time.* Baltimore: Johns Hopkins University Press.

Mayer, Lorraine. 2007. *Cries from a Métis Heart.* Winnipeg: Pemmican Press.

_____. 2010. "Negotiating a Different Terrain: Geographical and Educational Cross-Border Difficulties." *Across Cultures/Across Borders: Canadian Aboriginal and Native American Literatures.* Eds. Paul DePasquale, Renate Eigenbrod and Emma LaRocque. Peterborough, ON: Broadview Press.

_____, and Sandra Tomsons. Forthcoming. *Philosophy and Aboriginal Rights: Critical Dialogues.* Oxford: Oxford University Press.

McPherson, Dennis H. 1997. *Transfer of Jurisdiction for Education: A Paradox in Regard to the Constitutional Entrenchment of Indian Rights to Education and the Existing Treaty No. 3 Rights to Education.* LL.M. Thesis, University of Ottawa. http://www.collectionscanada.gc.ca/obj/s4/f2/dsk2/ftp04/mq26348.pdf.

_____, Connie H. Nelson, and J. Douglas Rabb. 2004. "Applied Research Ethics with Aboriginal Peoples: A Canadian Dilemma." *National Centre for Ethics in Human Research NCEHR Communiqué CNÉRH*. 12. 2, 6–12.

McPherson, D. H. and J. D. Rabb. 1993. *Indian from the Inside: A Study in Ethno-Metaphysics.* Thunder Bay, ON: Lakehead University Centre for Northern Studies.

_____, and _____. 1996. "Age Old New Age Metaphysics: First Nation Philosophies." *Indigenous Learning: Proceedings from the First Biennial Aboriginal Peoples Conference, Oct. 14–16, 1994, Lakehead University.* Thunder Bay, ON: Aboriginal Resource and Research Centre, 151–154.

_____, and _____. 1997. "Some Thoughts on Articulating a Native Philosophy." *Ayaangwaamizin: The International Journal of Indigenous Philosophy* 1. 1, 11–21.

_____, and _____. 1998–1999. "Walking the Talk: An Application of Anishnabe Philosophy or A Tearful Trail toward Culturally Congruent Education." *Ayaangwaamizin: The International Journal of Indigenous Philosophy*. 2 1, 89–99.

_____, and _____. 1999. "Transformative Philosophy and Indigenous Thought: A Comparison of Lakota and Ojibwa World Views." *Proceedings of the 29th Algonquian Conference.* Winnipeg: University of Manitoba Press, 202–210.

_____, and _____. 2001. "Indigeneity in Canada: Spirituality, the Sacred and Survival." *International Journal of Canadian Studies* 23, 57–79.

_____, and _____. 2003. "Restoring the Interpretive Circle: Community-Based Research and Education." *International Journal of Canadian Studies, dedicated issue: Health and Well-Being in Canada* 28, 133–161.

_____, and _____. 2008. "The Native Philosophy Project: An Update." *American Philosophical Association Newsletter on American Indians in Philosophy* 7. 2.

Meyer, Leroy, and Tony Ramirez. 1996. "Wakinyan Hotan, The Thunder Beings Call Out: The Inscrutability of Lakota/Dakota Metaphysics." *From our Eyes: Learning from Indigenous Peoples.* Toronto: Garamond Press.

Miller, Robert J. 2008. *Native America, Discovered and Conquered: Thomas Jefferson, Lewis & Clark, and Manifest Destiny.* Lincoln: University of Nebraska Press.

Mohawk, John C. 1999. *Utopian Legacies: A History of Conquest and Oppression in the Western World.* Santa Fe: Clear Light.

Moody, Raymond A. 1976. *Life After Life.* New York: HarperOne.

_____. 1978. *Reflections on Life After Life.* New York: Bantam Books.

Morris, Alexander, ed. 2000. *The Treaties of Canada with the Indians of Manitoba and the North West Territories Including the Negotiations on Which They Were Based.* Toronto: Prospero Facsim. Reprint. (Original edition published 1880, Toronto: Willing and Williamson).

Morris, David B. 2002. "Narrative Ethics and Pain: Thinking with Stories." *Stories Matter: The Role of Narrative in Medical Ethics.* Ed. R. Charon and M. Montello. New York: Routledge, 196–218.

Morris, Phyllis Sutton. 1976. *Sartre's Concept of a Person: An Analytic Approach.* Amherst: University of Massachusetts Press.

Morse, Bradford W. 1985. *Aboriginal Peoples and the Law: Indian, Métis and Inuit Rights in Canada.* Ottawa: Carleton University Press.

Muecke, Stephen. 1999. "History and the Sacred." *Indigeneity: Constructions and Re/Presentation.* Eds. James N. Brown and Patricia M. Sant. Commack, NY: Nova Science.

Native Literacy and Life Skills Curriculum Guidelines. 1989. Victoria, BC: Ministry of Advanced Education and Job Training, and Ministry Responsible for Science and Technology.

Nawagesic, Leslie. 2001. "Yuma State: A Philosophical Study of the Indian Residential School Experience." M. A. Thesis, Lakehead University, Thunder Bay, ON.

Neihardt, J. G. 1979. *Black Elk Speaks.* London: University of Nebraska Press.

Neu, Dean, and Richard Therrien. 2003. *Accounting for Genocide: Canada's Bureaucratic Assault on Aboriginal People.* Winnipeg: Fernwood.

Neuman, W. Lawrence. 2000. *Social Research Methods: Quantitative and Qualitative Approaches.* Boston: Allyn and Bacon.

Ningewance, Patricia M., et al. n.d. *Anishinaabemodaa.* Winnipeg: Manitoba Association for Native Languages.

Once Were Warriors. 1994. Movie. Dir. by Lee Tamahori. Eastman Motion Picture Films.

Ouderkirk, Wayne, and Jim Hill. Eds. 2002. *Land, Value, Community: Callicott and Environmental Philosophy.* Albany: State University of New York Press.

Overholt, Thomas W., and J. Baird Callicott. 1982. *Clothed-in-Fur and Other Tales: An Introduction to an Ojibwa World View.* Lanham, MD: University Press of America.

Paterson, Pete, and Lesley Kelly. 2006. *The Little Chicken Book: or All You Ever Wanted to Know About Chickens But Never Really Thought to Ask.* Caledon, ON: Blue Barn.

Peacock, Thomas, and Marlene Wisuri. 2002. *Ojibwe: Waasa Inaabidaa, We Look in All Directions.* Foreword by Winona LaDuke. Afton, MN: Afton Historical Society Press.

Pinker, Steven. 2002. *The Blank Slate: The Modern Denial of Human Nature.* New York: Viking.

Pomedli, Michael. 1985. "The Concept of <<Soul>> in the *Jesuit Relations*: Were There Any Philosophers Among the North American Indians?" *Laval théologique et philosophique* 41.1.

_____. 1991. *Ethnophilosophical and Ethnolinguistic Perspectives on the Huron Indian Soul.* Lewiston, NY: Edwin Mellen Press.

Prado, C. G.1983. "Rorty's Pragmatism." *Dialogue* 22. 3.

Pratt, Scott L. 2002. *Native Pragmatism: Rethinking the Roots of American Philosophy.* Bloomington: Indiana University Press.

_____. 2006. "Persons in Place: The Agent Ontology of Vine Deloria Jr." *APA Newsletter on American Indians in Philosophy* 6. 1. http://www.apaonline.org/documents/publications/v06n1_AmericanIndians.pdf.

Rabb, J. Douglas. 1985. *John Locke on Reflection: A Phenomenology Lost.* Washington, DC: University Press of America, Institute for Advanced Research in Phenomenology.

_____. 1988. "A Critical Review of Richard Ashcraft. *Revolutionary Politics and Locke's Two Treatises of Government.* Princeton U. P. 1986." *The Queen's Quarterly* 95. 2, 487–489.

_____. 1995. "Prologues to Native Philosophy." *European Review of Native American Studies* 9. 1, 23–25.

_____. 2000. "The Master of Life and the Person of Evolution: Indigenous Influence on Canadian Philosophy." *Ayaangwaamizin: The International Journal of Indigenous Philosophy* 2. 2, 125–142.

_____. 2002. "The Vegetarian Fox and Indigenous Philosophy: Speciesism, Racism, and Sexism." *Environmental Ethics* 24. 2, 275–294.

Rabb, J. Douglas, and J. Michael Richardson. 2009. "Myth, Metaphor, Morality and Monsters: The Espenson Factor and Cognitive Science in Joss Whedon's Narrative Love Ethic." *Slayage: The Online International Journal of Buffy Studies* 28. http://slayageonline.com.

Rabb, J. D., and J. M. Richardson. 2008a. "Reavers and Redskins: Creating the Frontier Savage." *Investigating* Firefly *and* Serenity. Eds. Rhonda Wilcox and Tanya Cochrane. London: I. B. Tauris, 127–138.

Rabb, J. Douglas, and J. Michael Richardson. 2008b. "Medical Ethics, Clinical Judgment, and Cognitive Science." *Theoretical Medicine and Bioethics.* 29 419–422.

Radin, Paul. 1914. "Religion of the North American Indians." *Journal of American Folklore* 27, 349–350.

Reference re Bill 30, an Act to amend *The Education Act* (Ont.), [1987] 1 S.C.R., 1173.

Return of a Man Called Horse. 1976. Dir. by Irvin Kershner. Fox DVD.

Richardson, Boyce. 1993. *People of the Terra Nullius.* Vancouver: Douglas and McIntyre.

Richardson, J. M., and J. D. Rabb. 2007. *The Existential Joss Whedon: Evil and Human Freedom in* Buffy the Vampire Slayer, Angel, Firefly, *and* Serenity. Jefferson, NC: McFarland.

Rogers, E. S. 1962. *The Round Lake Ojibwa.* Toronto: Royal Ontario Museum, University of Toronto, Art and Archaeology Division, Occasional Paper 5.
Rollins, Peter C., and John E. O'Connor. 1999. *Hollywood's Indian: The Portrayal of the Native American in Film.* Lexington: University Press of Kentucky.
Rorty, Richard. 1979. *Philosophy and the Mirror of Nature.* Princeton, NJ: Princeton University Press.
_____. 1982. *The Consequences of Pragmatism.* Minneapolis: University of Minnesota Press.
_____. 1991. "Science as Solidarity." *Objectivism, Relativism, and Truth: Philosophical Papers.* Cambridge: Cambridge University Press.
Rosch, Eleanor. 1973. "Natural Categories." *Cognitive Psychology.* 4, 326–350.
_____. 1977. "Human Categorization." *Studies in Cross-cultural Psychology.* Ed. Neil Warren. London: Academic Press, I, 1–49.
Rosch, Eleanor, and B.B. Lloyd, eds. 1978. *Cognition and Categorization.* Hillsdale, NJ: Lawrence Erlbaum.
Rosenberg, John. 1985. *Carlyle and the Burden of History.* Cambridge, MA: Harvard University Press.
Rosenberg, Philip. 1974. *The Seventh Hero.* Cambridge, MA: Harvard University Press.
Rosenthal, Raymond, ed. 1968. *McLuhan: Pro and Con.* New York: Funk & Wagnalls.
The Royal Proclamation. http://www.solon.org/Constitutions/Canada/English/PreConfederation/rp_1763.html.
Sartre, Jean-Paul. 1971. *Being and Nothingness: An Essay on Phenomenological Ontology.* Trans. Hazel E. Barnes. New York: Washington Square Press.
Saul, John Ralston. 2008. *A Fair Country: Telling Truths About Canada.* Toronto: Viking.
Schmalz, Peter S. 1991. *The Ojibwa of Southern Ontario.* Toronto: University of Toronto Press.
Scott, James C. 1998. *Seeing Like a State: How Certain Schemes to Improve the Human Condition Have Failed.* New Haven: Yale University Press.
"Serenity." *Firefly: The Complete Series.* Writ. and dir. Joss Whedon. DVD. 20th Century–Fox. 2003.
Serenity. 2005. Writ. and dir. Joss Whedon. Universal Studios.
Sheyahshe, Michael A. 2008. *Native Americans in Comic Books: A Critical Study.* Jefferson, NC: McFarland.
Skelton, Joan. 2007. *The Survivor of the Edmond Fitzgerald.* Manotick, ON: Penumbra Press. A play based on this book was presented at Magnus Theatre in Thunder Bay, ON, in 2007.
Smith, Linda Tuhiwai. 1999. *Decolonizing Methodologies: Research and Indigenous Peoples.* London: Zed.
Soldier Blue. 1970. Dir. by Ralph Nelson. Avco Embassy Pictures.
Somerville, Margaret. 2006. *The Ethical Imagination: Journeys of the Human Spirit.* Toronto: House of Anansi.
Stevenson, J. T. 1992. "Aboriginal Land Rights in Northern Canada." *Contemporary Moral Issues.* Ed. Wesley Cragg. Toronto: McGraw-Hill Ryerson.
Sturm, Fred Gillette. 1996. "Review of *Indian from the Inside.*" *Transactions of the Charles S. Peirce Society: A Quarterly Journal in American Philosophy* 32. 1, 137–142.
Taber, John. 1983. *Transformative Philosophy: A Study of Sankara, Fichte, and Heidegger.* Honolulu: University of Hawaii Press.
Taussig, Michael. 1987. *Shamanism, Colonialism and the Wild Man: A Study in Terror and Healing.* Chicago: Chicago University Press.
Tedlock, Dennis, and Barbara Tedlock, eds. 1978. *Teachings from the American Earth: Indian Religion and Philosophy.* New York: Liveright.
Thwaites, Reuben Gold, ed. 1959. *The Jesuit Relations and Allied Documents: Travels and Explorations of the Jesuit Missionaries in New France 1610–1791.* 73 vols. New York: Pageant Books.
Tooker, Elisabeth. 1996. "Hewitt, J. N. B. Tuscarora Ethnologist and Linguist." *Encyclopedia*

of North American Indians. Ed. F. E. Hoxie. Boston and New York: Houghton Mifflin, 244–245.
Venne, Sharon Helen. 1981. *Indian Acts and Amendments 1868–1975: An Indexed Collection*. Saskatoon: University of Saskatchewan Native Law Centre.
Waddams, S. M. 1984. *The Law of Contracts*. Toronto: Canada Law.
Warren, William W. 1984. *History of the Ojibway People*. St. Paul: Minnesota Historical Society Press.
Waters, Anne, ed. 2004. *American Indian Thought: Philosophical Essays*. Oxford: Blackwell.
Waters, Frank. 1963. *Book of the Hopi*. New York: Ballantine Books.
Watson, John. 1988. "The Relation of Philosophy to Science." *Religion and Science in Early Canada*. Ed. J. D. Rabb. Kingston: Ronald P. Frye.
Weaver, Jace. 1997. *That the People Might Live: Native American Literature and Native American Community*. New York: Oxford University Press.
_____. 1998. *Native American Religious Identity: Unforgotten Gods*. New York: Orbis Books.
_____. 2010. *Notes from a Miner's Canary: Essays on the State of Native America*. Albuquerque: University of New Mexico Press.
Whedon, Joss. 2005. *Serenity: The Official Visual Companion*. London: Titan Books.
Where the Spirit Lives. 1989. Dir. by Bruce Pittman. CBC, Amazing Spirit Productions.
Widdowson, Frances, and Albert Howard. 2008. *Disrobing the Aboriginal Industry: The Deception Behind Indigenous Cultural Preservation*. Montreal: McGill-Queen's University Press.
Wilcox, Rhonda, and Tanya Cochran, eds. 2008. *Investigating* Firefly *and* Serenity. London: I. B. Tauris.
Williams, Robert A., Jr. 1990. *The American Indian in Western Legal Thought: The Discourses of Conquest*. Oxford: Oxford University Press.
_____. 1997. *Linking Arms Together: American Indian Treaty Vision of Law and Peace, 1600–1800*. New York: Oxford University Press.
Wilson, Amelia. 2002. *The Devil*. London: Barron's Educational Series.
Wilson, J. Donald, Robert M. Stamp, and Louis-Philippe Audet. 1970. *Canadian: Education: A History*. Scarbrough: Prentice-Hall.
Wilson, Shawn. 2008. *Research Is Ceremony: Indigenous Research Methods*. Winnipeg: Fernwood.
Winter, Steven L. 2001. *A Clearing in the Forest: Law, Life, and Mind*. Chicago: Chicago University Press.
Wright, H. G. 2007. *Means, Ends and Medical Care*. Philosophy and Medicine Series, ed. H. Tristram Engelhardt, Jr. Volume 92. Dordrecht, Netherlands: Springer.
Woodward, Jack. 1989. *Native Law*. Toronto: Carswell.
Wub-e-ke-niew. 1995. *We Have the Right to Exist*. New York: Black Thistle Press.

Index